World View

The Harvard Business Review Book Series

World View

Global Strategies for the New Economy

Edited with an Introduction by
Jeffrey E. Garten

A Harvard Business Review Book

The *Harvard Business Review* articles in this collection are available as
individual reprints. Discounts apply to quantity purchases. For information
and ordering contact Customer Service, Harvard Business School Publishing,
Boston, MA 02163. Telephone: (617) 783–7500, 8 a.m. to 6 p.m. Eastern
Time, Monday through Friday. Fax: (617) 783–7555, 24 hours a day.

Library of Congress Cataloging-in-Publication Data

World view : global strategies for the new economy / edited with an
    introduction by Jeffrey E. Garten.
        p. cm. — (The Harvard business review book series)
    Includes index.
    ISBN 1-57851-185-2 (alk. paper)
    1. International business enterprises—Management. 2. Strategic planning.
3. Technological innovations—Economic aspects. 4. International economic
integration. 5. Competition, International. I. Garten, Jeffrey E., 1946– .
II. Series.
HD62.4.W67 2000
658.4'012—dc21   99-33734
                                                                      CIP

The paper used in this publication meets the requirements of the American
National Standard for Permanence of Paper for Publications and Documents
in Libraries and Archives Z39.48–1992.

Contents

Part III   Corporate Strategies

Part IV Leadership

Introduction

Jeffrey E. Garten

Earlier this year, AT&T and British Telecom were teaming up to buy a joint stake in Japan Telecom for roughly $1 billion. Interviewed by the *Wall Street Journal*, AT&T President John Zeglis explained what was on his mind: "You are only going to have two kinds of companies in the future: those companies that go global, and those companies that go bankrupt." Allowing for some hyperbole, he has a point. Today, every major company must at least be conscious of the opportunities and threats posed by a global economy. Otherwise, CEOs could miss opportunities to expand their operations to profitable new markets, or even find their business suffering if they fail to outfox or at least learn from foreign competition. But being ready to operate in the global arena entails planning and executing corporate strategies in revolutionary ways. It means rethinking every aspect of your company, its industry, your competitors, and your approach to everything from finance to operations to marketing to human resources.

This book will help business leaders do just that.

New Features in the World Economy

The emergence of a global marketplace is not a new development. The very first era of globalization can be traced back to the Renaissance when the explosion of scientific and technological discovery, combined with the invention of modern banking, began to link

European countries to one another, and also to Asia and to the Americas. Globalization became particularly intense from 1870–1914, when international finance and trade flourished. However, this trend toward globalization ceased with the onset of World War I. A global economy did not begin to rebuild until the early 1950s, when it was propelled by a gradual dismantling of controls on capital flows, successive rounds of trade negotiations, and the growth of multinational companies.

Today, several features make the global structure for business very different from previous eras. In the past, most international interactions took place among the U.S., Europe, Japan, and a few "third world" countries, but now well over 130 countries are involved. Previous varieties of globalization were based heavily on international investment in stocks and bonds, and on trade stimulated by tariff reductions. Today, however, massive flows of direct foreign investment in plants and equipment, as well as waves of cross-border mergers, are the hallmark of global economic interdependence. The structure of modern trade is different, too. Not only has it been spurred on by lower tariffs, but the gradual dismantling of nontariff barriers—such as laws that compel governments to purchase goods and services only from a firm's country of origin—has opened new markets. The volume of trade has also changed, expanding dramatically due to more intra-industry commerce. America once exported cars to Europe and received clothing in exchange. Now there is vigorous two-way trade in both products.

In the past, institutions like the International Monetary Fund and the World Trade Organization did not exist as pillars of a worldwide economic system. In fact, there were few rules and standards for global business. Today, however, financial officials are creating common capital adequacy standards for global banking. A powerful movement is afoot to get agreement from governments on common conventions for accounting. Efforts to forge global rules for the protection of intellectual property rights, protection of the environment, and protection of privacy on the Internet are all in full swing. As a result of the Asian financial crisis of 1996–1999, there is also more focus on international norms and standards for information disclosure on the part of governments and companies, and on common principles for corporate governance.

Unlike past eras of globalization, we are now witnessing the emergence of a form of global capitalism that is based on the shared thinking among government and business leaders that the global economy should move in the direction of Anglo-Saxon capitalism. This doesn't mean that national political preferences or economic cultures will disappear, but that over the next decade we are likely to see most publicly listed corporations focusing on returns to shareholders and better corporate governance. We may also witness more stringent antitrust rules, the emergence of more professional regulators who are independent of prevailing political leaders, and central bank management that is independent of the prevailing government.

What most distinguishes our era of globalization from its predecessors are spectacular advances in technology—technology of all kinds. New production technologies have changed the global workplace forever. They have enabled energy companies like Exxon to find more oil and recover it at lower costs. They've given pharmaceutical companies like Merck the opportunity to develop more medicines, and automobile companies like Toyota the ability to shorten product development cycles. Technology has made it possible for retail companies like Wal-Mart to manage global inventories as precisely as they manage the inventory in any one store. Indeed, the revolution in information technology, symbolized by the Internet, has spawned the ability to transmit voice, images, and data across borders at astounding speed, in ever-larger volumes, and at lower and lower costs. Internet technology, in particular, has allowed companies to leap across borders without moving their operations. It has given them the ability not just to reach consumers in Boston and Brisbane simultaneously, but to interact with them, understand what they want, and customize products to their preferences. It has permitted companies to reduce overhead, increase productivity, and bypass traditional distribution systems. It has, quite simply, changed the business world as we have known it.

Indeed, as a new century dawns, globalization has become one of the key frameworks—if not *the* key one—for every aspect of corporate strategy. It has raised questions not just about how to penetrate new markets, but what the definitions of those markets are. It has raised profound issues regarding how a company should be organized and led. Globalization has become a critical element in a company's approach to career development, organizational culture, the selection of a board of directors, and the setting of standards for social responsibility.

Globalization Equals Continual Restructuring

Both governments and companies are responding to current global-ization with massive restructuring. In the last decade, the United States has moved from an economy with huge competition problems and ever-increasing fiscal deficits to one that is the envy of the world. A nine-year trend of overall business expansion, the longest in this country's history, has been characterized by the emergence of super-competitive firms, low inflation, negligible unemployment, and bud-gets in surplus. The transformation in Europe has been just as dra-matic, with the widening and deepening of the European Union, and the creation of a common currency, the euro. After being an economic superpower in the mid-to-late 1980s, Japan has spent most of this past decade in stagnation. But enormous upheavals in Japan's economic structure are taking place, from wholesale restructuring of its financial system, to a breaking down of the century-old close interrelationships among Japan's leading corporations, to the end of lifetime employ-ment. With its economic reforms, China has managed a more far-reaching internal restructuring in the last decade than any other country in this century in a comparable length of time. But other emerging markets such as Mexico, Brazil, Argentina, South Korea, Taiwan, Singapore, and Thailand have been active, too, with extensive efforts to move toward market-oriented economies and expand their global linkages.

Restructuring on the corporate scene to meet the challenges of glob-alization has been no less pervasive. In fact, virtually every major cor-poration in the world is in a constant state of restructuring these days. Some, like Proctor & Gamble, Sony, and Microsoft, have decided to implement sweeping reorganizations to better respond to customer needs around the world. Others, like SwissAir, Delta, and Lufthansa, have created multinational alliances to reach customers around the globe. Some, like Daimler-Benz and Chrysler, have decided to actually merge in order to achieve a larger scale and serve customers world-wide. Still others have decided to demerge and focus more on the most successful businesses, in the way that AT&T spun off Lucent, or Dupont spun off Conoco. No one strategy fits all companies, of course, but no major company should be without a strategy that looks for new markets in the world economy, defends itself against brutal inter-national competition, makes effective use of the latest technologies, and tries to envision where the world is headed.

And this much is also clear: Globalization has just begun. The transition from a series of national economies doing business with one another to an integrated global economy is in its infancy. According to estimates made by McKinsey and DRI, almost 20% of the world's output is produced and consumed in world markets, whereas by 2030, it will be closer to 80%.[1] As the global marketplace expands, companies will have access to more customers and more talent. But they will also face a variety of new risks relating to financial volatility, unprecedented corporate competition, and individual market failures. As a result, we can expect to see continued radical restructuring of both countries and corporations for many decades to come as both seek to accommodate themselves to new forces, and even get ahead of them. Bottom line: There will be no respite from the challenges of dealing with new opportunities and new threats to survival. When Intel's Chairman Andrew Grove said, "Only the paranoid survive," he wasn't exaggerating, and he wasn't wrong.

Common Themes

The articles in this book have been selected to help corporate leaders think through global strategies at a time when there are few guideposts to navigating the mind-boggling changes that are occurring. They encompass many angles of the global game—from thinking about where to locate your business to making the most of your existing location, or from managing intellectual property rights to reengineering your global supply chain.

Despite the variety of subjects, several themes emerge clearly. First, these articles show that operating in a global market requires CEOs to rethink everything about their strategies—even what strategy means in an environment that is changing so fast and is so brutally competitive. Every asset that a company has—its overseas plants, its people, its R&D, its culture—will have to be reevaluated in light of the many challenges of operating across borders.

Second, the best strategies require organizations that are set up for gathering massive amounts of information and processing it effectively. Learning about your changing environment, learning *about* your competition, learning *from* your competition, transferring ideas throughout your organization—almost every article touches on these concepts.

Third, companies that succeed on a global scale are constant innovators. They learn and implement simultaneously. No time for big reports or staff studies. Just do it. Indeed, in the new global economy there is a premium on moving fast. Although leaders need to process enormous amounts of information, they must be comfortable moving ahead with much less information than they would ideally like to have. The ground below a CEO is shifting too quickly to hesitate.

Fourth, great global companies create a culture conducive to extensive internal and external collaboration. Inside the company, sharing information and intuition, and building effective cross-cultural teams, are critical to success. This requires a careful blend of rigor and flexibility in the structure of an organization. Outside the company, corporate networking—such as broad or highly focused strategic alliances—is critical for understanding the market and positioning the company to serve it. The world has grown too complex for one company to acquire all the resources it needs on its own.

Fifth, virtually all the authors agree that change is bringing unprecedented opportunity to capture markets and enhance shareholder value.

Here is a snapshot of what's ahead.

Articles in This Book

The articles begin with a series on emerging markets, the most dynamic and challenging arena of the new global economy.

In "The End of Corporate Imperialism," C.K. Prahalad and Kenneth Lieberthal argue for a radical change in the mind-set of western and Japanese companies doing business in big emerging markets. In the 1980s, they say, most companies assumed that countries like India, China, or Brazil were new markets for their old products. But now a revolution in thinking is required to succeed in these markets. Successful companies will provide new kinds of products, tailored to the new market, and develop new ways of marketing and distributing them. They will be attuned to the need for new patterns of decision making, new requirements for who to hire and who to promote, new relationships between headquarters and its foreign subsidiaries. In tomorrow's global economy, the authors say, successful multinationals will not only transform big emerging markets but will be transformed by them.

Much thinking about corporate strategy these days embraces the notion that companies work best when they are highly focused on "core competencies"—when they stick to their knitting. But in "Why Focused Strategies May Be Wrong for Emerging Markets," Tarun Khanna and Krishna Palepu argue that indigenous diversified conglomerates in emerging markets often make sense because they are in an environment where they must supply for themselves much of the infrastructure that western firms take for granted in their home countries. For example, Korean *chaebols* or the large family groups in India help their companies obtain financing, build credible brands, weather business cycles, or create a market for skilled labor. As the institutional setting in emerging markets becomes more sophisticated, diversification may prove less advantageous—but that's a long way off.

How can emerging market companies effectively compete with corporate Goliaths from the developed world? In "Competing with Giants: Survival Strategies for Local Companies in Emerging Markets," Niraj Dawar and Tony Frost outline several possibilities and explain how each can be executed. A company can defend its turf by restructuring in order to focus on specific areas of business where the multinationals are weak. Using special assets, such as knowledge of low-end markets or cultural preferences, it can expand its operations into other countries where it would have a comparative advantage based on unique products and targeted marketing. It can enter into a cooperative arrangement with a multinational. It can be bought out. Or it can decide to compete head-on with a foreign multinational, often through niche markets.

CEOs operating in emerging markets need to evaluate the totality of risks—economic, commercial, and political. In my own article, "Troubles Ahead in Emerging Markets," I warn executives that the *combination* of economic and political liberalization—worthy as each may be—is potentially explosive because it is precisely when economies are undergoing restructuring that strong political management is critical. In emerging economies like Mexico, China, Korea, South Africa, and Indonesia, dramatic political changes are occurring concurrently with the opening of economies. This puts enormous strain on already weak regulatory systems and on the ability of governments to handle rising popular expectations that change will be immediately beneficial. Companies need to hedge against these risks through improving their information-gathering systems, giving more attention to how they select and train executives, and staying closer to companies and officials in emerging markets in order to anticipate the inevitable ups and downs.

The next two articles turn to the new Europe and to Asia. "Managing in the Euro Zone" offers five perspectives from European executives on what the euro will mean for European companies. The underlying theme is that the euro should be a catalyst for broad change in how European executives think about all aspects of strategy and organization. For example, because a common currency will add great momentum to the establishment of a single market in Europe, it will be possible for companies to adopt centralized accounting and administrative systems for the first time, as well as coordinate marketing and production for all European operations. Yet the new Euro Zone also raises tricky questions about the proper balance between centralized and decentralized decision making. And ironically, it will require extreme sensitivity to local cultures in situations such as dealing with European consumers who suspect that, as local prices are translated into a new currency, they might not get the same value they once did.

"Asia's New Competitive Game" by Peter J. Williamson looks at regional strategy from the perspective of multinational companies. Focusing on the competition from indigenous Asian firms, he identifies several rules of this brutally competitive environment: Move quickly and be first. Control the bottlenecks in the chain. Seek dominance in at least one industry. Integrate vertically to the extent possible. Know what the host government goals are and align strategies with them. Organize your company like a network of personal computers—not only will you be able to share knowledge and information better, you will also be in step with the local competition. Williamson also discusses the new forms that joint ventures between foreign firms and large Asian companies are going to have to take.

We then turn to views on strategies related to specific challenges faced by companies: managing information technology, building corporate alliances, expanding research and development, establishing foreign factories, handling expatriates, and figuring out how to make the most out of geography.

In "The Right Mind-set for Managing Information Technology," M. Bensaou and Michael Earl draw management principles from Japanese information technology strategies. They explore how Japanese companies often subordinate IT to other business goals—for example, determining what is necessary to compete, improving performance, or strengthening the internal organization. The authors believe that American executives often let IT drive strategy rather than the other way around. They contrast this attitude with the cheaper, more pragmatic, and effective approach that they have observed in Japan, where executives are less mesmerized by the newest technology and focus instead on strategies such as small but continuous improvements in IT, rotating general executives through IT departments, and designing IT systems to fit the individual needs of a company rather than buying systems off the shelf.

Operating on a global scale often entails alliances with other companies. In "Group Versus Group: How Alliance Networks Compete," Benjamin Gomes-Casseres goes beyond the standard model of a two-company linkup and explains what is behind the establishment of networks of companies like Swissair, Delta, and Singapore Airlines. Many of these alliances bring significant benefits, such as greater size and combined market share, but they also carry managerial and operational costs, such as strategic gridlock and unwanted dependence on other companies. The author provides an important framework for evaluating how alliances evolve, the experience of different kinds of alliances, and the pros and cons of building new ones. He also offers advice on how to weigh the benefits of alliances against the drawbacks.

Companies were establishing plants abroad long before the modern global economy came into being. But in "Making the Most Out of Foreign Factories," Kasra Ferdows says that superior manufacturers can gain competitive advantage if they go beyond the limited roles that foreign facilities have traditionally played. He advocates overseas plants as part of a strategy for getting closer to foreign customers and suppliers, attracting skilled employees, gathering market information, and creating specialized knowledge and experience that can be transferred to the company's other factories around the world, including in the home country. Ferdows analyzes the different strategic roles that foreign factories can play, from offshore outpost to lead factory in a global system. And he explains how a CEO can determine which is the most appropriate role and upgrade from one status to another.

Globalizing research and development is an increasingly important dimension of companies' strategies today, and it promises to become even more critical as companies' comparative advantage centers on the knowledge embedded in their people. Indeed, in "Building Effective R&D Capabilities Abroad," Walter Kuemmerle describes why the old centralized approach to R&D will become a liability and why firms should shift instead to global R&D networks. He describes how this shift can take place, starting with establishing a Technology Steering Committee, and then categorizing possible overseas sites, establishing a new facility abroad, determining optimal size, supervising the start-up period, and integrating overseas R&D into an overall global network. As with manufacturing factories, R&D sites can tap into local knowledge and talent and function as a company's local antennae.

All global companies spend a lot of time and money on expatriate employees. Some 80% send professionals abroad, and, on average, expats cost two to three times the equivalent position at home. Yet the experience has been less than successful or satisfying for most expats and their employers. In "The Right Way to Manage Expats," J. Stewart Black and Hal B. Gregersen contend that the companies with the most effective system for managing expats focus on global leadership development, seek out people with cross-cultural abilities, and end expatriate assignments with a deliberate repatriation process that deals with both the tensions of physical relocation to home base and the psychological problems of reintegration. The article explains the criteria for picking the right people and suggests ways to manage their careers both abroad and back at home.

The next two articles deal with geography. Michael E. Porter's "Clusters and the New Economics of Competition" is an analysis of how companies can gain competitive advantage in the world marketplace. Porter challenges the conventional wisdom that the location of a firm doesn't matter because the globalization of capital and trade, and advances in transportation and communication, have rendered geography irrelevant. On the contrary, says Porter. Location does matter. And what *really* matters is not what specific country you are in but that you are in a cluster of firms in a similar industry—a Silicon Valley for entrepreneurial start-ups, a Wall Street for finance, a Hollywood for entertainment. Where clusters of like firms exist, Porter explains, you find the most effective infrastructures for what those companies need, including transportation, accounting services, and exchange of specialized knowledge and skills. There is more peer pressure, and better comparative benchmarking. Most importantly, the environment for continuous innovation—the single biggest imperative for global firms—is greatly heightened because you are cheek-to-jowl with your most fearsome competitors.

It is not only corporate strategy that is affected by globalization. Regions, states, and cities also need to rethink their own strategies for linking themselves to world-class companies. For in the emerging information economy, those cities that fail to make global connections could lose jobs and vitality and become the new underclass. How to connect with such companies is the subject of Rosabeth Moss Kanter's article, "Thriving Locally in the Global Economy." A community can follow one of three strategies, she says. It can seek to attract foreign investment by holding itself out as a location for brainpower, creativity, and innovation—as Boston has done. It can build competence in production and infrastructure with a highly skilled blue-collar workforce—as South Carolina's Greenville and Spartanburg have done. Or it can offer access to foreign cultures and markets—the model being Miami. It is not enough for community leaders to have a vision, however. They must be able to unite their community around a *strategy* in order to make it happen.

Finally, we get an inside look at the thinking of three great global CEOs. In "Fast, Global, and Entrepreneurial: Supply Chain Management, Hong Kong Style," Joan Magretta interviews Victor Fung, chairman of the retail arm of Li & Fung, Hong Kong's largest trading company. Fung explains his notion of borderless manufacturing and the importance of customizing sales and procurement throughout Asia and beyond. In "Growth Through Global Sustainability," Magretta talks to Robert B. Shapiro, CEO of Monsanto, who explains how environmental sustainability can be a critical ingredient in a company's global strategy, supporting the creation of new products and new services. And in "Unleashing the Power of Learning," Steven E. Prokesch interviews John Browne, CEO of BP/Amoco, on the importance of establishing within an organization a culture for continuous learning, and on how Browne builds, leverages, and diffuses knowledge throughout his company.

Conclusion

As CEOs enter a new century, globalization will affect every aspect of their thinking. By pulling together some of the most important writing on global strategies, this book provides valuable insights for business leaders seeking to succeed in this new and uncertain era. The ground is shifting, the corporate models are changing, the rules are up for grabs. Paul Allaire, chairman of Xerox, said, "We are in a brawl with no rules." He is right. Bottom line: There has never been more opportunity for creativity, and the risks have never been higher.

Notes

1. Lowell Bryan, Jane Fraser, Jeremy Oppenheim, and Wilhelm Rall, *Race for the World: Strategies to Build a Great Global Firm* (Boston: Harvard Business School Press, 1999), p. 3.

PART

I

Emerging Markets

1
The End of Corporate Imperialism

C.K. Prahalad and Kenneth Lieberthal

As they search for growth, multinational corporations will have to compete in the big emerging markets of China, India, Indonesia, and Brazil. The operative word is *emerging*. A vast consumer base of hundreds of millions of people is developing rapidly. Despite the uncertainty and the difficulty of doing business in markets that remain opaque to outsiders, Western MNCs will have no choice but to enter them. (See Table 1-1 "Market Size: Emerging Markets versus the United States.")

During the first wave of market entry in the 1980s, MNCs operated with what might be termed an imperialist mind-set. They assumed that the big emerging markets were new markets for their old products. They foresaw a bonanza in incremental sales for their existing products or the chance to squeeze profits out of their sunset technologies. Further, the corporate center was seen as the sole locus of product and process innovation. Many multinationals did not consciously look at emerging markets as sources of technical and managerial talent for their global operations. As a result of this imperialist mind-set, multinationals have achieved only limited success in those markets.

Many corporations, however, are beginning to see that the opportunity that big emerging markets represent will demand a new way of thinking. Success will require more than simply developing greater cultural sensitivity. The more we understand the nature of these markets, the more we believe that multinationals will have to rethink and reconfigure every element of their business models.

Table 1-1   Market Size: Emerging Markets Versus the United States

Product	China	India	Brazil	United States
Televisions (million units)	13.6	5.2	7.8	23.0
Detergent (kilograms per person)	2.5	2.7	7.3	14.4
(million tons)	3.5	2.3	1.1	3.9
Shampoo (in billions of dollars)	1.0	0.8	1.0	1.5
Pharmaceuticals (in billions of dollars)	5.0	2.8	8.0	60.6
Automotive (million units)	1.6	0.7	2.1	15.5
Power (megawatt capacity)	236,542	81,736	59,950	810,964

So while it is still common today to question how corporations like General Motors and McDonald's will change life in the big emerging markets, Western executives would be smart to turn the question around. Success in the emerging markets will require innovation and resource shifts on such a scale that life within the multinationals themselves will inevitably be transformed. In short, as MNCs achieve success in those markets, they will also bring corporate imperialism to an end.

We would not like to give the impression that we think markets such as China, India, Brazil, and Indonesia will enjoy clear sailing. As Indonesia is showing, these markets face major obstacles to continued high growth; political disruptions, for example, can slow down and even reverse trends toward more open markets. But given the long-term growth prospects, MNCs will have to compete in those markets. Having studied in depth the evolution of India and China over the past 20 years, and having worked extensively with MNCs competing in these and other countries, we believe that there are five basic questions that MNCs must answer to compete in the big emerging markets:

- Who is the emerging middle-class market in these countries, and what kind of business model will effectively serve their needs?
- What are the key characteristics of the distribution networks in these markets, and how are the networks evolving?

- What mix of local and global leadership is required to foster business opportunities?
- Should the MNC adopt a consistent strategy for all its business units within one country?
- Will local partners accelerate the multinational's ability to learn about the market?

What Is the Business Model for the Emerging Middle Class?

What is big and emerging in countries like China and India is a new consumer base consisting of hundreds of millions of people. Starved of choice for over 40 years, the rising middle class is hungry for consumer goods and a better quality of life and is ready to spend. The emerging markets have entered a new era of product availability and choice. In India alone, there are 50 brands of toothpaste available today and more than 250 brands of shoes.

Consumers are experimenting and changing their choice of products rapidly. Indians, for example, will buy any product once, but brand switching is common. One survey found that Indian consumers tried on average 6.2 brands of the same packaged-goods product in one year, compared with 2.0 for American consumers. But does this growth of consumer demand add up to a wealth of opportunity for the MNCs?

The answer is yes . . . but. Consider the constitution of the middle class itself. When managers in the West hear about the emerging middle class of India or China, they tend to think in terms of the middle class in Europe or the United States. This is one sign of an imperialist mind-set—the assumption that everyone must be just like "us." True, consumers in the emerging markets today are much more affluent than they were before their countries liberalized trade, but they are not affluent by Western standards. This is usually the first big miscalculation that MNCs make.

When these markets are analyzed, moreover, they turn out to have a structure very unlike that of the West. Income levels that characterize the Western middle class would represent a tiny upper class of consumers in any of the emerging markets. Today the active consumer market in the big emerging markets has a three-tiered pyramid structure. (See Exhibit 1-1 "The Market Pyramid in China, India, and Brazil.")

Exhibit 1-1   The Market Pyramid in China, India, and Brazil

Purchasing power parity in U.S. dollars		Population in millions		
		China	India	Brazil
tier 1	greater than $20,000	2	7	9
tier 2	$10,000 to $20,000	60	63	15
tier 3	$5,000 to $10,000	330	125	27
	less than $5,000	800	700	105

Consider India. At the top of the pyramid, in tier one, is a relatively small number of consumers who are responsive to international brands and have the income to afford them. Next comes tier two, a much larger group of people who are less attracted to international brands. Finally, at the bottom of the pyramid of consumers is tier three—a massive group that is loyal to local customs, habits, and often to local brands. Below that is another huge group made up of people who are unlikely to become active consumers anytime soon.

MNCs have tended to bring their existing products and marketing strategies to the emerging markets without properly accounting for these market pyramids. They end up, therefore, becoming high-end niche players. That's what happened to Revlon, for example, when it introduced its Western beauty products to China in 1976 and to India in 1994. Only the top tier valued and could afford the cachet of Revlon's brand. And consider Ford's recent foray into India with its Escort, which Ford priced at more than $21,000. In India, anything over $20,000 falls into the luxury segment. The most popular car, the Maruti-Suzuki, sells for $10,000 or less. Fiat learned to serve that tier of the market in Brazil, designing a new model called the Palio specifically for Brazilians. Fiat is now poised to transfer that success from Brazil to India.

While it is seductive for companies like Ford to think of big emerging markets as new outlets for old products, a mind-set focused on incremental volume misses the real opportunity. To date, MNCs like Ford and Revlon have either ignored tier two of the pyramid or conceded it to local competitors. But if Ford wants to be more than a small, high-end player, it will have to design a robust and roomy $9,000 car to compete with Fiat's Palio or with a locally produced car.

Tailoring products to the big emerging markets is not a trivial task. Minor cultural adaptations or marginal cost reductions will not do the job. Instead, to overcome an implicit imperialism, companies must undergo a fundamental rethinking of every element of their business model.

RETHINKING THE PRICE-PERFORMANCE EQUATION. Consumers in big emerging markets are getting a fast education in global standards, but they often are unwilling to pay global prices. In India, an executive in a multinational food-processing company told us the story of a man in Delhi who went to McDonald's for a hamburger. He didn't like the food or the prices, but he liked the ambience. Then he went to Nirula's, a successful Delhi food chain. He liked the food and the prices there, but he complained to the manager because Nirula's did not have the same pleasant atmosphere as McDonald's. The moral of the story? Price-performance expectations are changing, often to the consternation of both the multinationals and the locals. McDonald's has been forced to adapt its menu to local tastes by adding vegetable burgers. Local chains like Nirula's have been pushed to meet global standards for cleanliness and ambience.

Consumers in the big emerging markets are far more focused than their Western counterparts on the price-performance equation. That focus tends to give low-cost local competitors the edge in hotly contested markets. MNCs can, however, learn to turn this price sensitivity to their advantage. Philips Electronics, for example, introduced a combination video-CD player in China in 1994. Although there is virtually no market for this product in Europe or the United States, the Chinese quickly embraced it as a great two-for-one bargain. More than 15 million units have been sold in China, and the product seems likely to catch on in Indonesia and India. Consumers in those countries see the player as good value for the money.

RETHINKING BRAND MANAGEMENT. Armed with powerful, established brands, multinationals are likely to overestimate the extent of Westernization in the emerging markets and the value of using a consistent approach to brand management around the world.

In India, Coca-Cola overvalued the pull of its brand among the tier-two consumers. Coke based its advertising strategy on its worldwide image and then watched the advantage slip to Pepsi, which had adopted a campaign that was oriented toward the Indian market. As one of Coke's senior executives recently put it in the *Wall Street Journal*, "We're so successful in international business that we applied a tried and true formula . . . and it was the wrong formula to apply in India."

It took Coke more than two years to get the message, but it is now repositioning itself by using local heroes, such as popular cricket players, in its advertising. Perhaps more important, it is heavily promoting a popular Indian brand of cola—Thums Up—which Coke bought from a local bottler in 1993, only to scorn it for several years as a poor substitute for the Real Thing.

RETHINKING THE COSTS OF MARKET BUILDING. For many MNCs, entering an emerging market means introducing a new product or service category. But Kellogg, for example, found that introducing breakfast cereals to India was a slow process because it meant creating new eating habits. Once the company had persuaded Indians to eat cereal, at great expense, local competitors were able to ride on Kellogg's coattails by introducing breakfast cereals with local flavors. As a result, Kellogg may discover in the long run that they paid too high a price for too small a market. Sampling, celebrity endorsements, and other forms of consumer education are expensive: regional tastes vary and language barriers can create difficulties. India, for example, has 13 major languages and pronounced cultural differences across regions.

Multinationals would do well to rethink the costs of building markets. Changing developed habits is difficult and expensive. Providing consumers with a new product that requires no reeducation can be much easier. For example, consider the rapid adoption of pagers in China. Because telephones are not widely available there, pagers have helped fill the void as a means of one-way communication.

RETHINKING PRODUCT DESIGN. Even when consumers in emerging markets appear to want the same products as are sold elsewhere, some redesign is often necessary to reflect differences in use, distribution, or selling. Because the Chinese use pagers to send entire messages—which is not how they were intended to be used—Motorola developed pagers capable of displaying more lines of information. The result: Motorola encountered the enviable problem of having to scramble to keep up with exploding demand for its product.

In the mid-1980s, a leading MNC in telecommunications began exporting its electronic switching systems to China for use in the phone system. The switching systems had been designed for the company's home market, where there were many customers but substantial periods when the phones were not in use. In China, on the other hand, there were very few phones, but they were in almost constant use. The switching system, which worked flawlessly in the West, simply couldn't handle the load in China. Ultimately, the company had to redesign its software.

Distribution can also have a huge impact on product design. A Western maker of frozen desserts, for example, had to reformulate one of its products not because of differences in consumers' tastes, but because the refrigerators in most retail outlets in India weren't cold enough to store the product properly. The product had been designed for storage at minus 15 degrees centigrade, but the typical retailer's refrigerator operates at minus 4 degrees. Moreover, power interruptions frequently shut down the refrigerators.

RETHINKING PACKAGING. Whether the problem is dust, heat, or bumpy roads, the distribution infrastructure in emerging markets places special strains on packaging. One glass manufacturer, for example, was stunned at the breakage it sustained as a result of poor roads and trucks in India.

And consumers in tiers two and three are likely to have packaging preferences that are different from consumers in the West. Single-serve packets, or sachets, are enormously popular in India. They allow consumers to buy only what they need, experiment with new products, and conserve cash at the same time. Products as varied as detergents, shampoos, pickles, cough syrup, and oil are sold in sachets in India, and it is estimated that they make up 20% to 30% of the total sold in their categories. Sachets are spreading as a marketing device for such items as shampoos in China as well.

RETHINKING CAPITAL EFFICIENCY. The common wisdom is that the infrastructure problems in emerging markets—inefficient distribution systems, poor banking facilities, and inadequate logistics—will require companies to use more capital than in Western markets, not less. But that is the wrong mind-set. Hindustan Lever, a subsidiary of Unilever in India, saw a low-cost Indian detergent maker, Nirma, become the largest branded detergent maker in the world over a seven-year period by courting the tier-two and tier-three markets. Realizing that it could not compete by making marginal changes, Hindustan Lever rethought every aspect of its business, including production, distribution, marketing, and capital efficiency.

Today Hindustan Lever operates a $2 billion business with effectively zero working capital. Consider just one of the practices that makes this possible. The company keeps a supply of signed checks from its dealers. When it ships an order, it simply writes in the correct amount for the order. This practice is not uncommon in India. The Indian agribusiness company, Rallis, uses it with its 20,000 dealers in rural India. But this way of doing things is unheard of in Unilever's home countries, the United Kingdom and the Netherlands.

Hindustan Lever also manages to operate with minimal fixed capital. It does so in part through an active program of supplier management; the company works with local entrepreneurs who own and manage plants whose capacity is dedicated to Hindustan Lever's products. Other MNCs will find that there is less need for vertical integration in emerging markets than they might think. Quality suppliers can be located and developed. Their lower overhead structure can help the MNCs gain a competitive cost position. Supply chain management is an important tool for changing the capital efficiency of a multinational's operations.

Rather than concede the market, Hindustan Lever radically changed itself and is today successfully competing against Nirma with a low-cost detergent called Wheel. The lesson learned in India has not been lost on Unilever. It is unlikely to concede tier-two and tier-three markets in China, Indonesia, or Brazil without a fight.

How Does the Distribution System Work?

One of the greatest regrets of multinational executives, especially those we spoke with in China, was that they had not invested more in distribution before launching their products. Access to distribution is often critical to success in emerging markets, and it cannot be taken for granted. There is no substitute for a detailed understanding of the unique characteristics of a market's distribution system and how that system is likely to evolve.

Consider the differences between China and India. Distribution in China is primarily local and provincial. Under the former planned economy, most distribution networks were confined to political units, such as counties, cities, or provinces. Even at present, there is no real national distribution network for most products. Many MNCs have gained access to provincial networks by creating joint ventures. But these JVs are now impediments to the creation of the badly needed national network. Chinese JV partners protect their turf. This gap between the MNCs' need for a national, cost-effective distribution system and the more locally oriented goals of their partners is creating serious tensions. We expect that many JVs formed originally to allow multinationals market and distribution access will be restructured because of this very issue during the next five to seven years.

In India, on the other hand, individual entrepreneurs have already put together a national distribution system in a wide variety of businesses. Established companies such as Colgate-Palmolive and Godrej in personal care, Hindustan Lever in packaged goods, Tatas in trucks, Bajaj in scooters—the list is long—control their own distribution systems. Those systems take the form of long-standing arrangements with networks of small-scale distributors throughout the country, and the banking network is part of those relationships. Many of the established packaged-goods companies reach more than 3 million retail outlets—using trains, trucks, bullock-drawn carts, camels, and bicycles. And many companies claim to service each one of those outlets once a week.

Any MNC that wants to establish its own distribution system in India inevitably runs up against significant obstacles and costs. Ford, for example, is trying to establish a new, high-quality dealer network to sell cars in India. To obtain a dealership, each prospective dealer is expected to invest a large amount of his own money and must undergo special training. In the long haul, Ford's approach may prove to be a major source of advantage to the company, but the cost in cash and managerial attention of building the dealers' network will be substantial.

Ironically, the lack of a national distribution system in China may be an advantage. MNCs with patience and ingenuity can more easily build distribution systems to suit their needs, and doing so might confer competitive advantages. As one manager we talked to put it, "The trick to sustained, long-term profitability in China lies not in technology or in savvy advertising or even in low pricing, but rather in building a modern distribution system." Conceivably, China may see consolidation of the retail market earlier than India.

The Chinese and Indian cases signal the need for MNCs to develop a market-specific distribution strategy. In India, MNCs will have to determine who controls national distribution in order to distinguish likely partners from probable competitors. In China, multinationals seeking national distribution of their products must consider the motivations of potential partners before entering relationships that may frustrate their intentions.

Will Local or Expatriate Leadership Be More Effective?

Leadership of a multinational's venture in an emerging market requires a complex blend of local sensitivity and global knowledge. Getting the balance right is critical but never easy. MNCs frequently lack the cultural understanding to get the mix of expatriate and local leaders right.

Expatriates from the MNCs' host country play multiple roles. They transfer technology and management practices. They ensure that local employees understand and practice the corporate culture. In the early stages of market development, expatriates are the conduits for information flow between the multinational's corporate office and the local operation. But while headquarters staff usually recognizes the importance of sending information to the local operation, they tend to be less aware that information must also be received from the other direction. Expatriates provide credibility at headquarters when they convey information, especially information concerning the adaptations the corporation must make in order to be successful in the emerging market. Given these important roles, the large number of expatriates in China—170,000 by one count—is understandable.

Every multinational operation we observed in China had several expatriates in management positions. In India, by contrast, we rarely saw expatriate managers, and the few that we did see were usually of Indian origin. That's because among the big emerging markets, India is unique in that it has developed, over time, a cadre of engineers and managers. The Indian institutes of technology and institutes of management turn out graduates with a high degree of technical competence.

Perhaps more important from the perspective of a multinational, Indian managers speak English fluently and seem adept at learning a new corporate culture. At the same time, they have a much better appreciation of local nuances and a deeper commitment to the Indian market than any expatriate could have.

Those seeming advantages may be offset, however, by two disadvantages. First, a management team of native-born managers may not have the same "share of voice" at corporate headquarters that expatriate managers have. Yet maintaining a strong voice is essential, given the difficulty most managers at corporate headquarters have in understanding the dynamics and peculiar requirements of operating in emerging markets. Second, the "soft technology" that is central to Western competitive advantage—the bundle of elements that creates a dynamic, cost-effective, market-sensitive organization—is hard to develop when the management team consists of people who have worked only briefly, if at all, in such an organization.

Several multinationals have sent expatriates of Chinese or Indian origin from their U.S. or European base back to their Chinese or Indian operations in order to convey the company's soft technology in a culturally sensitive way. But that strategy has not, in general, been successful. As one manager we spoke to noted, "Indians from the United States who are sent back as expatriates are frozen in time. They remember the India they left 20 years ago. They are totally out of sync. But they do not have the humility to accept that they have to learn." We heard the same sentiment echoed in China, both for Chinese-Americans and, less frequently, for Chinese who had obtained a higher education in the United States and then returned as a part of a multinational management team.

Using American or West European expatriates during the early years of market entry can make sense, but this approach has its own set of problems. Cultural and language difficulties in countries like China and India typically limit expats' interaction with the locals as well as their effectiveness. In addition, the need to understand how to deal with the local political system, especially in China, makes long-term assignments desirable. It often takes an expatriate manager two years to get fully up to speed. From the company's perspective, it makes sense to keep that manager in place for another three years to take full advantage of what he or she has learned. But few Western expatriates are willing to stay in China that long; many feel that a long assignment keeps them out of the loop and may impose a high career cost. Multinationals, therefore, need to think about how to attract and retain high-quality expatriate talent, how to maintain expats' links to the parent company, and how to use and pass along expats' competencies once they move on to another post.

Is It Necessary to "Present One Face"?

Beyond the normal organizational questions that would exist wherever a company does business, there is a question of special importance in emerging markets: Do local political considerations require the multinational to adopt a uniform strategy for each of its business units operating in the country, or can it permit each unit to act on its own?

As with the issue of distribution, the contrasts between China and India make clear why there is no one right answer to this question. In China, massive governmental interference in the economy makes a uniform country strategy necessary. The Chinese government tends to view the activities of individual business units as part of a single company's effort, and therefore concessions made by any one unit—such as an agreement to achieve a certain level of local sourcing—may well become requirements for the others. An MNC in China must be able to articulate a set of principles that conforms to China's announced priorities, and it should coordinate the activities of its various business units so that they resonate with those priorities.

Given the way most multinationals operate, "presenting one face" to China is very difficult. Business units have their own P&L responsibilities and are reluctant to lose their autonomy. Reporting lines can become overly complex. Although we observed many organizational approaches, not a single MNC we looked at is completely satisfied with its approach to this difficult issue.

Is it any wonder? Consider the life of one MNC executive we visited in China. As the head of his company's China effort, he has to coordinate with the company's regional headquarters in Japan, report to international headquarters in Europe, and maintain close contact with corporate headquarters in North America. He also has to meet with members of the Chinese government, with the MNC's business-unit executives in China, and with the leaders of the business units' Chinese partners. Simply maintaining all of these contacts is extraordinarily taxing and time consuming.

There is somewhat less need to present one face to India. Since 1991, the Indian government has scaled back its efforts to shape what MNCs do in the country. Business units may therefore act more independently than would be appropriate in China. The strategy for India can be developed on a business-by-business basis. Nonetheless, the market is large and complex. National regulations are onerous, and state-level governments are still so different from one another that MNCs are well advised to develop knowledge that they can share with all their business units in India.

Do Partners Foster Valuable Learning?

In the first wave of market entry, multinationals used joint ventures extensively as a way not only to navigate through bureaucratic processes but also to learn about new markets. With few exceptions, however, JVs in emerging markets have been problematic. In some cases, executives of the multinationals mistakenly thought the JVs would do their strategic thinking for them. In most cases, tensions in JV relationships have diverted management attention away from learning about the market.

One consistent problem is that companies enter joint ventures with very different expectations. One Chinese manager described the situation in terms of an old saying: We are sleeping in the same bed, with different dreams. The local partner sees the MNC as a source of technology and investment, and the multinational sees the partner as a means to participate in the domestic market.

When they come to an emerging market, multinationals usually are still building their manufacturing and marketing infrastructures, and they don't expect immediate returns. Local partners, however, often want to see short-term profit. This disparity of aims leads to enormous strain in the relationship. The costs associated with expatriate managers also become a bone of contention. Who controls what can be yet another source of trouble—especially when the domestic partner has experience in the business. And when new investment is needed to grow the business, local partners often are unable to bring in the matching funds, yet they resent the dilution of their holding and the ensuing loss of control.

MNCs are finally learning that their local partners often do not have adequate market knowledge. The experience of most local partners predates the emergence of real consumer markets, and their business practices can be archaic. But as markets evolve toward greater transparency, as MNCs develop senior managers who understand how "the system" works, and as the availability of local talent increases, multinationals have less to gain by using intermediaries as a vehicle for learning.

The MNCs' need for local partners clearly is diminishing. In 1997, a consulting firm surveyed 67 companies invested in China and found that the percentage of their projects that became wholly foreign-owned enterprises grew steadily from 18% in 1992 to 37% in 1996. A *passive* partner that can provide a local face may still be important in some industries, but this is a very different matter from the JV.

Success Will Transform the Multinationals

As executives look for growth in the big emerging markets, they tend quite naturally to focus on the size of the opportunity and the challenges that lie ahead. Few, however, stop to think about how success will transform their companies. But consider the magnitude of the changes we have been describing and the sheer size of the markets in question. Success in the big emerging markets will surely change the shape of the modern multinational as we know it today.

For years, executives have assumed they could export their current business models around the globe. That assumption has to change. Citicorp, for example, aims to serve a billion banking customers by 2010. There is no way Citicorp, given its current cost structure, can profitably serve someone in Beijing or Delhi whose net wealth is less than $5,000. But if Citicorp creates a new business model—rethinking every element of its cost structure—it will be able to serve not only average Chinese people but also inner-city residents in New York. In short, companies must realize that the innovation required to serve the large tier-two and tier-three segments in emerging markets has the potential to make them more competitive in their traditional markets—and therefore in *all* markets.

Over time, the imperialist assumption that innovation comes from the center will gradually fade away and die. Increasingly, as multinationals develop products better adapted to the emerging markets, they are finding that those markets are becoming an important source of innovation. Telecommunications companies, for example, are discovering that people in markets with no old technology to "forget" may accept technological changes faster. MNCs such as Texas Instruments and Motorola are assigning responsibility for software-oriented business development to their Indian operations. China has become such a significant market for video-CD players that the Chinese are likely to be major players in introducing the next round of video-CD standards around the world.

The big emerging markets will also have a significant influence on the product development philosophy of the MNCs. One major multinational recognized to its surprise that the Chinese have found a way of producing high-quality detergents with equipment and processes that cost about one-fifth of what the MNC spends. Stories like that get repeated in a wide variety of businesses, including fine chemicals, cement, textile machinery, trucks, and television sets.

As product development becomes decentralized, collaboration between labs in Bangalore, London, and Dallas, for example, will gradually become the rule, not the exception. New-product introductions will have to take into consideration nontraditional centers of influence. Thus in the CD business at Philips, new-product introductions, which previously occurred almost exclusively in Europe, now also take place in Shanghai and California.

As corporate imperialism draws to a close, multinationals will increasingly look to emerging markets for talent. India is already recognized as a source of technical talent in engineering, sciences, and software, as well as in some aspects of management. All high-tech companies recruit in India not only for the Indian market but also for the global market. China, given its growth and its technical and managerial-training infrastructure, has not yet reached that stage, but it may well reach it in the not-too-distant future.

A major shift in geographical resources will take place within the next five years. Philips is already downsizing in Europe and reportedly employs more Chinese than Dutch workers. Over 40% of the market for Coke, Gillette, Lucent, Boeing, and GE power systems is in Asia. And in the last two years, ABB has shrunk its European head count by more than 40,000 while adding 45,000 people in Asia.

In addition to these changes, an increasing percentage of the investment in plant and equipment and marketing will go to the emerging markets. As those markets grow to account for 30% to 40% of capital invested—and even a larger percentage of market share and profits—they will attract much more attention from top management.

The importance of these markets will inevitably be reflected in the ethnic and national origin of senior management. At present, with a few exceptions such as Citicorp and Unilever, senior management ranks are filled with nationals from the company's home country. By the year 2010, however, the top 200 managers from around the world for any multinational will have a much greater cultural and ethnic mix.

How many of today's multinationals are prepared to accommodate 30% to 40% of their top team of 200 coming from China, India, and Brazil? How will that cultural mix influence decision making, risk taking, and team building? Diversity will put an enormous burden on top-level managers to articulate clearly the values and behaviors expected of senior managers, and it will demand large investments in training and socialization. The need for a single company culture will also become more critical as people from different cultures begin to work together. Providing the right glue to hold companies together will be a big challenge.

That challenge will be intensified by an impending power shift within multinationals. The end of corporate imperialism suggests more than a new relationship between the developed and the emerging economies. It also suggests an end to the era of centralized corporate power—embodied in the attitude that "headquarters knows best"—and a shift to a much more dispersed base of power and influence.

Consider the new patterns of knowledge transfer we are beginning to see. Unilever, for example, is transferring Indian managers with experience in low-cost distribution to China, where they will build a national distribution system and train Chinese managers. And it has transferred Indian managers with knowledge of tier-two markets to Brazil. The phenomenon of using managers from outside the home country to transfer knowledge is relatively new. It will grow over time to the point where the multinational becomes an organization with several centers of expertise and excellence.

Multinationals will be shaped by a wide variety of forces in the coming decades. The big emerging markets will be one of the major forces they come up against. And the effect will be nothing short of dramatic change on both sides. Together, they will challenge each other to change for the better as a truly global twenty-first century economy takes shape. The MNCs will create a higher standard of products, quality, technology, and management practices. Large, opaque markets will gradually become more transparent. The process of transition to market economies will be evolutionary, uneven, and fraught with uncertainties. But the direction is no longer in question.

In order to participate effectively in the big emerging markets, multinationals will increasingly have to reconfigure their resource base, rethink their cost structure, redesign their product development process, and challenge their assumptions about the cultural mix of their top managers. In short, they will have to develop a new mind-set and adopt new business models to achieve global competitiveness in the postimperialist age.

2

Why Focused Strategies May Be Wrong for Emerging Markets

Tarun Khanna and Krishna Palepu

Core competencies and focus are now the mantras of corporate strategists in Western economies. But while managers in the West have dismantled many conglomerates assembled in the 1960s and 1970s, the large, diversified business group remains the dominant form of enterprise throughout most emerging markets. Some groups operate as holding companies with full ownership in many enterprises, others are collections of publicly traded companies, but all have some degree of central control.

As emerging markets open up to global competition, consultants and foreign investors are increasingly pressuring these groups to conform to Western practice by scaling back the scope of their business activities. The conglomerate is the dinosaur of organizational design, they argue, too unwieldy and slow to compete in today's fast-paced markets. Already a number of executives have decided to break up their groups in order to show that they are focusing on only a few core businesses.

There are reasons to worry about this trend. Focus is good advice in New York or London, but something important gets lost in translation when that advice is given to groups in emerging markets. Western companies take for granted a range of institutions that support their business activities, but many of these institutions are absent in other regions of the world. (See "What Is an Emerging Market?") Without effective securities regulation and venture capital firms, for example, focused companies may be unable to raise adequate financing; and without strong educational institutions, they will struggle to hire

Table 2-1   How Institutional Context Drives Strategy

Institutional Dimension	United States	Japan	India
Capital market	equity-focused; monitoring by disclosure rules and the market for corporate control	bank-focused; monitoring by interlocking investments and directors	underdeveloped, illiquid equity markets and nationalized banks; weak monitoring by bureaucrats
Labor market	many business schools and consulting firms offering talent; certified skills enhance mobility	few business schools; training internal to companies; company-specific development of talent	few business schools and little training; management talent scarce
Product market	reliable enforcement of liability laws; efficient dissemination of information; many activist consumers	reliable enforcement of liability laws; efficient dissemination of information; some activist consumers	limited enforcement of liability laws; little dissemination of information; few activist consumers
Government regulation	low; relatively free of corruption	moderate; relatively free of corruption	high; corruption common
Contract enforcement	predictable	predictable	unpredictable
Result	**diversified groups have many disadvantages**	**diversified groups have some advantages**	**diversified groups have many advantages**

skilled employees. Communicating with customers is difficult when the local infrastructure is poor, and unpredictable government behavior can stymie any operation. Although a focused strategy may enable a company to perform a few activities well, companies in emerging markets must take responsibility for a wide range of functions in order to do business effectively.

As a result, companies must adapt their strategies to fit their *institutional context*—a country's product, capital, and labor markets; its regulatory system; and its mechanisms for enforcing contracts. Unlike advanced economies, emerging markets suffer from weak institutions in all or most of these areas. (See Table 2-1 "How Institutional Context Drives Strategy.") It is this difference in institutional context that explains the success of large, diversified corporations in developing economies such as Indonesia and India and their failure in advanced economies such as the United States and the United Kingdom.

In our research, we have found that highly diversified business groups can be particularly well suited to the institutional context in most developing countries. From the *chaebols* of Korea to the *business houses* of India to the *grupos* of Latin America, conglomerates can add value by imitating the functions of several institutions that are present only in advanced economies. Successful groups effectively mediate between their member companies and the rest of the economy.

What is an Emerging Market?

Most analysts define an emerging market according to such characteristics as size, growth rate, or how recently it has opened up to the global economy. In our view, the most important criterion is how well an economy helps buyers and sellers come together. Ideally, every economy would provide a range of institutions in order to facilitate the functioning of markets, but developing countries fall short in a number of ways.

For the purposes of our argument, there are three main sources of market failure:

- **Information Problems.** Buyers—broadly defined not only as consumers in product markets but also as employers in labor markets and investors in financial markets—need reliable information to assess the goods and services that they purchase and the investments that they make. Without adequate information, they are reluctant to do business.

- **Misguided Regulations.** When regulators place political goals over economic efficiency, they can distort the functioning of markets. Many emerging markets, for example, restrict the ability of companies to lay off workers. These rules do add some stability to society—and in some cases, they may even be intended to overcome market failures from other sources. However, the result is that companies are less able to take advantage of opportunities than they are in advanced economies.

- **Inefficient Judicial Systems.** Companies are reluctant to do business without ways of ensuring that their partners will hold up their end of the bargain. Contracts can facilitate cooperation by aligning the incentives of the different parties. Markets therefore depend on judicial systems that are strong enough to enforce contracts in a reliable and predictable way.

In advanced economies, companies can rely on a variety of outside institutions that minimize these sources of market failure. In such a context, companies create value primarily by focusing on a narrow set of activities. At the opposite extreme, stagnant or declining economies usually suffer from near-complete market failure because of the utter absence of basic institutions.

Emerging markets, in the middle of this continuum, offer the prospect of substantial growth because they have developed at least some of the institutions necessary to encourage commerce. But institutional voids are still common enough to cause market failures; as a result, companies in emerging markets often have to perform these basic functions themselves. In our view, that is the crucial distinction between doing business in an emerging market and operating in an advanced economy.

Filling the Institutional Voids

Emerging markets are hardly uniform. Nevertheless, they all fall short to varying degrees in providing the institutions necessary to support basic business operations.

PRODUCT MARKETS

In the case of product markets, buyers and sellers usually suffer from a severe dearth of information for three reasons. First, the communications infrastructure in emerging markets is often underdeveloped. Even as wireless communication spreads throughout the West, vast stretches in countries such as China and India remain without telephones. Power shortages often render the modes of communication that do exist ineffective. The postal service is typically inefficient, slow, or unreliable; and the private sector rarely provides efficient courier services. High rates of illiteracy make it difficult for marketers to communicate effectively with customers.

Second, even when information about products does get around, there are no mechanisms to corroborate the claims made by sellers. Independent consumer-information organizations are rare, and government watchdog agencies are of little use. The few analysts who rate products are generally less sophisticated than their counterparts in advanced economies.

Third, consumers have no redress mechanisms if a product does not deliver on its promise. Law enforcement is often capricious and so slow that few who assign any value to time would resort to it. Unlike in advanced markets, there are few extrajudicial arbitration mechanisms to which one can appeal.

As a result of this lack of information, companies in emerging markets face much higher costs in building credible brands than their counterparts in advanced economies. In turn, established brands wield tremendous power. A conglomerate with a reputation for quality products and services can use its group name to enter new businesses, even if those businesses are completely unrelated to its current lines. Groups also have an advantage when they do try to build up a brand because they can spread the cost of maintaining it across multiple lines of business. Such groups then have a greater incentive not to damage brand quality in any one business because they will pay the price in their other businesses as well.

The Korean chaebols are famous throughout the world for extending their group identity over multiple product categories. Samsung, for example, has used its name for a range of goods from televisions to microwave ovens. Groups in India and Malaysia are beginning to follow suit. The business media in India, for example, abound with advertisements that promote group identity rather than emphasize the products or services of individual companies within a group.

CAPITAL MARKETS

Similar problems occur in capital markets because, without access to information, investors refrain from putting money into unfamiliar ventures. The U.S. capital markets minimize these problems through institutional mechanisms such as reliable financial reporting, a dynamic community of analysts, and an aggressive, independent financial press. Venture capital firms and other intermediaries specialize in investigating and assessing new opportunities. The Securities and Exchange Commission and other watchdog bodies make it difficult for unscrupulous entrepreneurs to mislead unsophisticated investors. As a result, investors have a free flow of largely accurate information about companies. And they can hold corporate managers and directors accountable through the threat of securities litigation, proxy fights, and hostile takeovers. By reducing risks to investors, these institutions make it possible for new enterprises to raise capital on approximately equal terms as big, established companies.

Almost all the institutional mechanisms that make advanced capital markets work so well are either absent or ineffective in emerging markets. Having little information and few safeguards, investors are reluctant to put money into new enterprises. In such a context, diversified groups can point to their track record of returns to investors. As a result, large and well-established companies have superior access to capital markets. This advantage is so pronounced that governments in India and South Korea, for example, have attempted to restrict the amount of credit exposure that banks are permitted to have in large companies.

Conglomerates also can use their internally generated capital to grow existing businesses or to enter new ones. In fact, their superior ability to raise capital makes groups a prime source of capital for new enterprises and gives them a great advantage over small companies seeking funding. Besides acting as venture capitalists, groups also act as lending institutions to existing member enterprises that are otherwise too small to obtain capital from financial institutions. And some Indian groups, especially those in the automobile sector, have set up subsidiaries whose primary purpose is to provide financing to important suppliers and customers.

At the same time, conglomerates are attractive to foreign investors eager to put money into these often fast-growing markets. With so few financial analysts and knowledgeable mutual-fund managers available to guide them, outsiders instead turn to diversified groups and invest in a wide range of industries. Investors trust groups to evaluate new opportunities and to exercise an auditing and supervisory function. The groups thus become the conduit for large amounts of investment in their capital-starved countries.

LABOR MARKETS

Most emerging markets suffer from a scarcity of well-trained people. While the United States has more than 600 business schools training thousands of future managers every year, Thailand has a handful of high-quality business schools that produce far fewer entry-level managers than the economy needs. Vocational training facilities are also scarce in emerging markets.

Groups can create value by developing promising managers, and they can spread the fixed costs of professional development over the businesses in the group. Many of the large groups in India, for example, have internal management-development programs—often with dedicated facilities. These programs typically are geared toward developing the skills of experienced managers; but some groups, such as the Malaysian conglomerate Sime Darby, have instituted training programs for all levels of employees in an attempt to develop their human capital. And some of the Korean chaebols have set up special programs in collaboration with top U.S. business schools in order to train their own people.

Groups also can provide much needed flexibility for labor markets in general. Governments in emerging markets usually make it difficult for companies to adjust their workforces to changing economic conditions. Rigid laws often prevent companies from laying off their employees, and labor unions insist on job security in the absence of government-provided unemployment benefits. To counteract the rigidities of the overall labor market, groups can develop extensive internal labor markets of their own. When one company in a group faces declining prospects, its employees can be transferred to other group companies that are on the rise—even to companies in otherwise undesirable locations. India's Aditya Birla group, for example, has acquired a reputation for building communities around its manufacturing plants in the remotest parts of the country. Because the group provides services such as schools, hospitals, and places of worship, managers and other trained employees are more willing to relocate. The growing companies benefit by receiving a ready source of reliable employees.

Groups are also able to put new talent to good use. By allocating talent to where it is most needed, conglomerates have a head start in beginning new activities. The Wipro Group in India successfully moved beyond computers into financial services by relocating skilled engineers first to computer-leasing services that would make use of their technical know-how and then to a broad range of financial services. In contrast, unaffiliated companies usually have to recruit publicly in order to build their operations—a difficult proposition in countries where labor varies widely in quality and lacks certification from respected educational institutions.

REGULATION

As multinational companies know all too well, governments in most emerging markets operate very differently from those in the West. Not

only does the state intervene much more extensively in business operations, but companies also have a hard time predicting the actions of
regulatory bodies.

Governments in emerging markets are heavily involved in an intri-
cate array of business decisions. Despite the elimination of the old "li-
cense raj," for example, Indian law still requires that companies get
permission for a range of decisions, such as exiting businesses, changing prices on commodities, and importing raw materials. The law es-
tablishes subjective criteria for many of these decisions, so Indian bureaucrats have a great deal of discretion in how they apply the rules.

Diversified groups can add value by acting as intermediaries when
their individual companies or foreign partners need to deal with the
regulatory bureaucracy. Experience and connections give conglomerates an advantage. The larger the company, the easier it is to carry
the cost of maintaining government relationships. Indeed, political
economist Dennis Encarnation found that India's large groups maintain "industrial embassies" in New Delhi to facilitate interaction with
bureaucrats. Several groups in India also are known for their ability
to manage bureaucratic relations at levels all the way down to the vil-
lage council.

India and other countries may be bearing costs for the uncertainty
of their regulatory systems. But as long as government officials have
so much discretion, companies often end up working with them. Intri-
cate relations between business and government actually appear to be
the norm throughout the developing world. The major Malaysian political parties, for example, all have affiliated conglomerates. Until recently, the ties between government and industry in South Korea
have been a centerpiece of that country's economic program. Even today in Indonesia, there are groups whose greatest assets appear to include access to high government officials. Because political leaders are
so eager to work with companies, managers must be prepared to deal
with the government and the bureaucracy.

Bribes and other corrupt practices may be part of working with the
bureaucracy. But that's not the whole story. In many cases, educating
officials is more important than exchanging favors. The Enron Corporation, a large U.S.-based multinational, discovered just that when it
entered the power generation sector in India. Prepared to invest $2.8
billion, the single largest foreign venture in Indian history, the company had to spend four years and about $20 million educating regula-
tors on the ways international power projects are financed and

regulated. Along the way, Enron learned its own lessons about dealing with the Indian bureaucracy and government; the project was almost canceled when Enron's aggressive deal-making style put off newly elected officials in the state where the power plant was to be built. As Enron's executives now acknowledge, experience with Indian politics and bureaucracy might have saved the company a great deal of trouble.

CONTRACT ENFORCEMENT

Despite the extensive involvement of government in emerging markets, these economies lack effective mechanisms to enforce contracts. In advanced economies, companies can work together under arm's-length contractual arrangements because they know the courts will protect them if their partners break their contracts. Confidence in the judicial system makes it easier for everyone to do business. But courts in emerging markets often enforce contracts capriciously or inefficiently; as a result, companies are less likely to be able to resolve disputes through judicial channels.

In such situations, conglomerates can leverage reputations established by honest dealings in the past. Because the misdeeds of one company in a group will damage the prospects of the others, all the group companies have credibility when they promise to honor their agreements with any single partner. They provide a haven where property rights are respected. As a result, suppliers and customers are more willing to work with them.

This credibility pays off the most in relationships with companies seeking to enter emerging markets. Foreign providers of technology or finance need local partners to carry out their strategies, but they worry about being cheated. A reputation for honesty and reliability thus can be a source of enormous competitive advantage. As Alice Amsden and Takashi Hikino have argued, conglomerates in several emerging markets have based much of their success on their ability to access foreign technology. And in India, the largest and most diversified business groups receive a disproportionate share of technology and financial support from advanced economies around the world. The head of RPG Enterprises, India's third largest conglomerate, considers his group's relations with foreign providers—including 16 of the 500 largest U.S. companies—to be among its greatest assets.

Managing the House of Tata

India's largest conglomerate in sales and assets exemplifies how well-run groups can add value in emerging markets. Spanning most sectors of the Indian economy, the Tata companies employ close to 300,000 people and had sales of Rupees 289 billion (U.S. $8.6 billion) in the fiscal year 1995 to 1996. Of the group's 90 companies, more than 40 are publicly traded, and these account for approximately 8% of the total capitalization of the country's publicly traded companies. The companies are all held together by the internationally recognized Tata name and by interlocking investments and directorates.

The Tatas began as a textile mill in 1874, but Indian independence in 1947 brought antimonopoly legislation and high taxes on dividends that encouraged the group to diversify into a variety of unrelated areas. When India began liberalizing its economy in 1991, removing the barriers to growth within any given sector, the group had a stark choice to make. Outside experts advised executives to concentrate on a few strong sectors of economic activity instead of continuing as an extensively diversified entity. But the executives decided to remain in most of their existing businesses.

One reason for staying diversified was the difficulty of exiting businesses because of some remaining legal restrictions in India as well as the Tatas' reputation as a benevolent employer. But the Tatas also believed that they could leverage their size and wide scope to help their constituent companies in a variety of ways. So they decided to diversify even further.

Historically, the Tata companies have always come together to finance the launch of new enterprises. But initially there was no formal structure for doing so. Then in 1982, the group created Tata Industries, a venture capital vehicle funded with a special pool of investment money drawn from the member companies. Since then, Tata Industries has sought to lead the Tata group into information technology, process control, advanced materials, oil-field services, and other areas. It has provided seed money for several successful ventures, including two computer-manufacturing enterprises—one cosponsored by Honeywell and another cosponsored by IBM. Today the Tatas are leading the way in building an information-technology industrial park in cooperation with the state of Karnataka and with money and expertise from a consortium that includes the government of Singapore.

The Tatas were so active in new ventures that by 1995 they needed additional capital. They decided to sell a stake in Tata Industries at a substantial premium to Jardine Matheson, itself a diversified company based in Hong Kong. As a result of the sale, Jardine Matheson ended up owning 20% of the equity in Tata Industries. The sale gave the Tatas (and the Indian economy) $200 million in "patient" capital from a conglomerate that shared their long-term approach to investment. Jardine Matheson, in turn, gained exposure to sectors across the Indian economy without having to supervise individual companies.

Many of the group's new ventures benefited from being able to borrow skilled managers from the Tatas' existing businesses. Since 1956, Tata Administrative Services (TAS)—an in-house training program with a national reputation for excellence—has aimed to create a cadre of general managers. Entry into TAS is extremely selective and primarily restricted to graduates of Indian management institutes. Recruits spend their first year on courses, interactive sessions with Tata executives, and visits to major Tata plants around the country. Mentoring and career direction continue for at least five years, as candidates are exposed to three different line functions in three industries to gain a general management perspective.

Fully half of these trainees remain with the Tatas over the long term, in contrast to some other large Indian groups that have to reinvent themselves every few years because of high turnover. For those who do leave, the exit options are attractive, increasing the appeal of joining the Tatas in the first place. In effect, the group provides both management education and a certification service in a country where both are scarce.

TAS consciously organizes its recruits into cohorts according to the year they entered. As recruits spread out to the different companies within the group, they maintain lasting ties with their cohort group, and these networks improve information flows across the group. The head office, mindful of the resources invested in these graduates, encourages group companies to "sacrifice" a talented employee to another company if it is in the interest of both the managers' career development and the group. Cross-company teams of "stars" are assembled to resolve knotty problems that individual companies are having. The group now plans a new initiative, the Tata Group Mobility Plan, to improve the mobility of all skilled managers, including non-TAS graduates, across group companies—and without any loss of benefits.

The Tatas are a favorite of foreign technology providers that are comfortable entering India only with a reputable party. Tata executives consider their reputation for honesty and integrity to be among their greatest assets, and that reputation has led to joint ventures with Daimler-Benz and AT&T, as well as a number of computer companies. Understanding the value of its reputation, the group is developing an internal code of conduct and other elaborate standards regarding the use of the group name. Special fees from the member companies will pay for an internal auditing function to enforce those standards. To foster an orientation toward quality among its companies, Tata also has set up an internal system of awards akin to the United States' Baldrige awards.

By keeping and extending their diversified holdings, the Tatas have maintained a scale and scope that gives them a host of advantages within India's specific institutional context. And these advantage are mutually reinforcing. The more access Tata or any group has to financial capital, the more business opportunities it can offer to talented employees—which in turn helps the group improve quality and enhance its reputation with consumers. Continued success in existing lines of business has made it all the easier for the Tatas to enter new lines of business. The Tatas today have the largest market shares in many sectors of the Indian economy, from steel to computers to hotels.

The Tatas, in turn, benefit the Indian economy. When management consultants told a Tata executive that diversification into unrelated activities did not create value, he replied, "Don't enunciate a theory that will bring everything to a dead halt. If we don't start these businesses, no one else will either, and society will be worse off."

Ensuring That Diversification Adds Value

Once one understands the institutional context of any given emerging market, it is clear why diversified business groups have the potential to add value. (See Table 2-2 "How Groups Can Add Value.") Nevertheless, groups do not automatically realize that potential. They must be actively managed to capture the advantages offered by scale and scope. Our statistical analysis comparing groups and independent companies in India—and a similar analysis on South Korean companies that Tarun Khanna conducted with Yishay Yafeh—suggests that

Table 2-2 How Groups Can Add Value

Institutional Dimension	Institutions That Groups Imitate
Capital market	venture capital firm, private equity provider, mutual fund, bank, auditor
Labor market	management institute/business school, certification agency, head-hunting firm, relocation service
Product market	certification agency, regulatory authority, extrajudicial arbitration service
Government regulation	lobbyist
Contract enforcement	courts, extrajudicial arbitration service

many groups add little or no value to their operations. The largest and most diversified groups, however, do add a good deal of value—perhaps because only these groups have the scale and scope to perform the kind of functions we have described.

Indeed, many groups have actually diminished the value of their member companies through poor management. Conglomerates in emerging markets, after all, suffer from the same problems that plague those in the West: the more activities a business engages in, the harder it is for the head office to coordinate, control, and invest properly in them. Unless a group is ready to offer concrete benefits to its affiliates, companies are better off independent.

Group executives should ask in a systematic way whether they are adding enough value to overcome the costs of complexity and coordination. They should start by assessing their conglomerate's strengths. A group that enjoys brand name recognition in rural markets might think of leveraging its name in unrelated products targeted to the same markets. Or a group that enjoys preferential access to large amounts of capital might consider ventures that require substantial investment.

Of course, not every group will be able to add value in the same way, and no group can hope to fill every institutional void. Decisions to diversify should be based on the group's strengths, not just on growth prospects. Today a number of groups are rushing willy-nilly into power plants and other infrastructure projects all over Asia, and their total-capacity plans already appear to outstrip the likely demand. But there are a few exceptions, such as India's Satyam Group. This group has tried to leverage its reputation for honest and efficient partnerships with foreign companies in order to win the better contracts.

Once a group identifies its opportunities, its executives need to install systems to ensure consistent execution. For example, they must impose discipline over field managers, who will be tempted to take advantage of ready financing to try to build empires. The most successful groups usually have a strong internal auditing system. Sime Darby, the Malaysian conglomerate, benefits from a tradition of strict financial controls and planning that began under its original British managers. Its recent entry into financial services by acquiring UMBC bank was welcomed by the Southeast Asian stock markets, which saw the conglomerate adding value through its management discipline to a large but underperforming company in a rapidly growing sector.

Another strategic imperative for groups is to manage their corporate identities. Given that much of their success depends on the trust of their customers and partners, diversified groups must enforce standards of reliability and quality. The head of Mahindra & Mahindra, a group operating in automobiles and infrastructure in India, grabs every symbolic opportunity he gets to dramatize the importance of never compromising on the product and after-sales service offered to customers.

When a group's strategy depends on supplying functions that are absent in the institutional context, it is important to move with deliberation. Mimicking institutions that are undeveloped in the economy at large requires time and effort. A group that acts as a venture capital firm, for example, needs to develop a track record for nurturing businesses in order to become a magnet for risk capital. It needs to train and retain individuals who are skilled at identifying deals and who can bring their start-up expertise to bear on a variety of situations; it also needs to have disciplined managers to run its high-risk ventures.

Communicating the Strategy to Investors

Even successful conglomerates still face resistance from Western investors and partners who believe that focus is always best. Although many executives may well be tempted to concentrate their operations in order to win favor with outside analysts, a better solution for well-managed groups is to educate investors about the logic underpinning the group's corporate strategy. (See "What Is the Best Institutional Context?")

What Is the Best Institutional Context?

Even if they admit to the advantages of diversification in emerging markets, some investors or partners may still urge companies to concentrate on a few core activities on the grounds that all markets will eventually develop the West's set of institutions. But their advice assumes that there is one single set of institutions toward which all countries should move. It is unclear, however, whether any one institutional context is obviously superior to others.

Consider the financial system in the United States. That system, based on atomistic shareholders, ensures great liquidity, which generally reduces the cost of funds. Because shareholders can "vote with their feet" if they do not like what management is doing, however, they are less inclined to expend the effort needed to discipline management. As a result, corporate governance may suffer. Similarly, a labor market in which employees freely move from one company to another increases the likelihood that, at any given time, there will be an efficient match between workers' skills and the opportunities to which those skills can be applied. But it reduces the likelihood that workers will invest in anything but the most general skills; as a result, society does not reap the benefits of the long-term, company-specific training of workers.

Japan's institutional context reveals a different resolution to these trade-offs. Japan's capital market is bank centered, not equity centered. Banks monitor managers through equity cross-holdings between companies and board directorships, and the difficulty financial institutions have in unloading their shares encourages them to keep management in line. (Banks, in fact, are at the center of Japan's major *keiretsu*, and these groups offer some of the same advantages of conglomeration that are present in emerging markets.) Japanese managers and workers get their training largely within companies. Managers rarely move around because their expertise is geared toward the specific needs of their company and because they lack credentials from such external institutions as business schools.

Institutional context also takes a long time to evolve. Because different aspects of the institutional environment have often co-evolved into a well-functioning system, changes along any one dimension of an institutional environment can have unanticipated, adverse effects along other dimensions. Economies around the world today are experimenting with moving from one system to another using either "shock therapy" or gradual adjustment—there is much debate about which is the better approach. Deep-seated institutional voids might take decades to be filled. The United States is an extreme example of a country where there are relatively few such voids.

Even if the institutional context of emerging markets evolves to the point that there are no advantages to diversification, executives there should realize that their current opportunities will persist for some time. They are much better served by developing corporate strategies that match their particular contexts instead of blindly applying the management mantra of the day.

Institutional investors are often most worried not about diversification per se but about the lack of openness in internal group operations. Under the current structure of many conglomerates, investment analysts find it difficult to tell which business segments are creating value within a conglomerate. They fear that a group executive will shuffle funds from one company to another. Faced with these concerns, managers of conglomerates should increase the transparency of their operations, communicate this change to investors, and develop a reputation for doing so.

The Indian group Mahindra & Mahindra is doing just that. While it focuses on automobiles and closely related businesses, the group has set up a holding company to invest in a range of other projects. The automobile company has made a onetime, fully documented infusion of capital to start the holding company so that the group will not have to make repeated transfers of funds for ad-hoc line extensions. If and when the holding company's ventures take off and require new capital, the group will take the company public rather than draw on funds from the automobile company.

If groups are not adding value, they should consider focusing. But they should not break up simply because their competitors are focused foreign companies from advanced economies. Western companies have access to advanced technology, cheap financing, and sophisticated managerial know-how. In the absence of institutions providing these and other functions in emerging markets, diversification may be the best way to match up against the competition.

3

Competing with Giants: Survival Strategies for Local Companies in Emerging Markets

Niraj Dawar and Tony Frost

As protectionist barriers crumble in emerging markets around the world, multinational companies are rushing in to find new opportunities for growth. Their arrival is a boon to local consumers, who benefit from the wider choices now available. For local companies, however, the influx often appears to be a death sentence. Accustomed to dominant positions in protected markets, they suddenly face foreign rivals wielding a daunting array of advantages: substantial financial resources, advanced technology, superior products, powerful brands, and seasoned marketing and management skills. Often, the very survival of local companies in emerging markets is at stake.

Strategists at multinational corporations can draw on a rich body of work to advise them on how to enter emerging markets, but managers of local companies in these markets have had little guidance. How can they overcome—and even take advantage of—their differences with competitors from advanced industrial countries? Many of these managers assume they can respond in one of only three ways: by calling on the government to reinstate trade barriers or provide some other form of support, by becoming a subordinate partner to a multinational, or by simply selling out and leaving the industry. We believe there are other options for companies facing stiff foreign competition.

In markets from Latin America to Eastern Europe to Asia, we have studied the strategies and tactics that successful companies have adopted in their battles with powerful multinational competitors. Vist in Russia and Shanghai Jahwa in China, for example, have managed to successfully defend their home turfs against such multinationals as

Compaq and Unilever. Others, including Jollibee Foods in the Philippines and Cemex in Mexico, have built on strength at home and launched international expansion strategies of their own. By studying these examples, managers of other companies from emerging markets can gain insight into their own strategic options.

Aligning Assets with Industry Characteristics

When India opened its automotive sector in the mid-1980s, the country's largest maker of motor scooters, Bajaj Auto, confronted a predicament similar to what many "emerging-market" companies face. Honda, which sold its scooters, motorcycles, and cars worldwide on the strength of its superior technology, quality, and brand appeal, was planning to enter the Indian market. Its remarkable success selling motorcycles in Western markets and in such nearby countries as Thailand and Malaysia was well known. For the independent-minded Bajaj family, a joint venture with Honda was not an option. But faced with Honda's superior resources, what else could the company do?

A closer look at the situation convinced Bajaj's managers that Honda's advantages were not as formidable as they first appeared. The scooter industry was based on mature and relatively stable technology. While Honda would enjoy some advantages in product development, Bajaj would not have to spend heavily to keep up. The makeup of the Indian scooter market, moreover, differed in many ways from Honda's established customer base. Consumers looked for low-cost, durable machines, and they wanted easy access to maintenance facilities in the countryside. Bajaj, which sold cheap, rugged scooters through an extensive distribution system and a ubiquitous service network of roadside-mechanic stalls, fit the Indian market well. Honda, which offered sleekly designed models sold mostly through outlets in major cities, did not.

Instead of forming a partnership with Honda, Bajaj's owners decided to stay independent and fortify their existing competitive assets. The company beefed up its distribution and invested more in research and development. Its strategy has paid off well. Honda, allied with another local producer, did quickly grab 11% of the Indian scooter market, but its share stabilized at just under that level. Bajaj's share, meanwhile, slipped only a few points from its earlier mark of 77%. And in the fall of 1998, Honda announced it was pulling out of its scooter-manufacturing equity joint venture in India.

Bajaj's story points to the two key questions that every manager in emerging markets needs to address: First, how strong are the pressures to globalize in your industry? Second, how internationally transferable are your company's competitive assets? By understanding the basis for competitive advantage in your industry, you can better appreciate the actual strengths of your multinational rivals. And by assessing where your own competitive assets are most effective, you can gain insights into the breadth of business opportunities available to you. Let's take each question in turn.

Despite the heated rhetoric surrounding globalization, industries actually vary a great deal in the pressures they put on companies to sell internationally. At one end of the spectrum are companies in such industries as aircraft engines, memory chips, and telecommunications switches, which face enormous fixed costs for product development, capital equipment, marketing, and distribution. Covering those costs is possible only through sales in multiple markets. A single set of rules governs competition worldwide, and consumers are satisfied with the standardized products and marketing appeals that result.

At the other end of the spectrum are industries in which success turns on meeting the particular demands of local consumers. In beer and retail banking, for example, companies compete on the basis of well-established relationships with their customers. Consumer preferences vary enormously because of differing tastes, perhaps, or incompatible technical standards. Multinationals can't compete simply by selling standardized products at lower cost. Alternatively, high transportation costs in some sectors may discourage a global presence. In all of these industries, companies can still prosper by selling only in their local markets.

Most industries, of course, lie somewhere in the middle of the spectrum. International sales bring some advantages of scale, but adapting to local preferences is also important. By thinking about where their industry falls on the spectrum, managers from emerging markets can begin to get a picture of the strengths and weaknesses of their multinational competitors. But they need to place their industry carefully. As Bajaj found, industries that seem similar may be far apart on the spectrum—pressures to globalize scooters turn out to be much weaker than those to globalize automobiles. Bajaj may go global in the future, as the Indian market evolves, but it has no need to do so now.

Once they understand their industry, managers need to evaluate their company's competitive assets. Like Bajaj, most emerging-market companies have assets that give them a competitive advantage mainly in their home market. They may, for example, have a local distribution network that would take years for a multinational to replicate. They may have long-standing relationships with government officials that are simply unavailable to foreign companies. Or they may have distinctive products that appeal to local tastes, which global companies may be unable to produce cost effectively. Any such asset could form the basis for a successful defense of the home market.

Some competitive assets may also be the basis for expansion into other markets. A company can use its access to low-cost raw materials at home, for example, to undercut the price of goods sold in other countries. Or a company may use its expertise in building efficient factories to establish operations elsewhere. Assets that may seem quite localized, such as experience in serving idiosyncratic or hard-to-reach market segments, may actually travel well. By paying close attention to countries where market conditions are similar to theirs, managers may discover that they have more transferable assets than they realize. The more they have, the greater their chance of success outside the home base.

These two parameters—the strength of globalization pressures in an industry and the degree to which a company's assets are transferable internationally—can guide strategic thinking. If globalization pressures are weak, and a company's own assets are not transferable, then, like Bajaj, the company needs to concentrate on defending its turf against multinational incursion. We call a company employing such a strategy a *defender*. If globalization pressures are weak but the company's assets can be transferred, then the company may be able to extend its success at home to a limited number of other markets. That sort of company is an *extender*.

If globalization pressures are strong, the company will face bigger challenges. If its assets work only at home, then its continued independence will hang on its ability to dodge its new rivals by restructuring around specific links in the value chain where its local assets are still valuable. Such a company, in our terminology, is a *dodger*. If its assets are transferable, though, the company may actually be able to compete head-on with the multinationals at the global level. We call a company in that situation a *contender*.

We can plot these four strategies on a matrix. (See Exhibit 3-1 "Positioning for Emerging-Market Companies.") As with any strategic framework, our matrix is not intended to prescribe a course of action but to help managers think about the broad options available.

Exhibit 3-1   *Positioning for Emerging-Market Companies*

Competitive Assets

	Customized to home market	Transferable abroad
High	**Dodger** focuses on a locally oriented link in the value chain, enters a joint venture, or sells out to a multi-national.	**Contender** focuses on upgrading capabilities and resources to match multi-nationals globally, often by keeping to niche markets.
Low	**Defender** focuses on leveraging local assets in market segments where multi-nationals are weak.	**Extender** focuses on expanding into markets similar to those of the home base, using competencies developed at home.

Pressures to Globalize in the Industry

To gain a clearer view of all four options, let's look at how companies have used them to succeed in a newly competitive environment. We'll start with industries where the globalization pressures are weak, then move to industries where those pressures are strong.

Defending with the Home Field Advantage

For defenders like Bajaj, the key to success is to concentrate on the advantages they enjoy in their home market. In the face of aggressive and well-endowed foreign competitors, they frequently need to fine-tune their products and services to the particular and often unique needs of their customers. Defenders need to resist the temptation to try to reach all customers or to imitate the multinationals. They'll do better by focusing on consumers who appreciate the local touch and ignoring those who favor global brands.

Shanghai Jahwa, China's oldest cosmetics company, has thrived by astutely exploiting its local orientation—especially its familiarity with the distinct tastes of Chinese consumers. Because standards of beauty vary so much across cultures, the pressure to globalize the cosmetics industry is weak. Nevertheless, as in other such industries, a sizable market segment is attracted to global brands. Young people in China, for example, are currently fascinated by all things Western. Instead of trying to fight for this segment, Jahwa concentrates on the large group of consumers who remain loyal to traditional products. The company has developed low-cost, mass-market brands positioned around beliefs about traditional ingredients.

Many Chinese consumers, for instance, believe that human organs such as the heart and liver are internal spirits that determine the health of the body. *Liushen,* or "six spirits," is the name of a traditional remedy for prickly heat and other summer ailments, and it's made from a combination of pearl powder and musk. Drawing on this custom, Jahwa launched a Liushen brand of eau de toilette and packaged it for summer use. The brand rapidly gained 60% of the market and has since been extended to a shower cream also targeted at the Liushen user. Unilever and other multinational companies lack this familiarity with local tastes; they have found their products appeal mainly to fashion-conscious city dwellers.

For those product lines that don't have such an intrinsic appeal to consumers, Jahwa has found that it can compete on price. Here Jahwa has taken advantage of the constraints that multinational companies face in adapting Western-designed products to developing countries. Multinationals typically optimize their operations on a global level by standardizing product characteristics, administrative practices, and even pricing, all of which can hamper their flexibility. Products designed for affluent consumers often aren't profitable at prices low enough to attract many buyers in emerging markets. And even if they are, a multinational might damage its global brand by selling its products cheaply.

As a result, a number of Jahwa's foreign rivals have been stuck in gilded cages at the top of the market, giving Jahwa an advantage in reaching consumers with little discretionary income. Revlon, for example, estimates its target market in China to be just 3% of the country, or 39 million people, whereas Jahwa aims at over half the market. (See "The Importance of Staying Flexible.")

Jahwa has also benefited from the sheer visibility of the multinationals' strategies. Product formulations, brand positioning, and pricing are often well known long before a multinational launches its brands in a foreign market. This transparency affords defenders both the knowledge and the time to preempt a new brand with rival offerings of their own. Jahwa quickly launched its G.LF line of colognes, for example, to protect itself from the entry of a global brand targeted at the upscale urban male segment, which Jahwa had ignored.

The Importance of Staying Flexible

Multinational enterprises bring enormous advantages when they enter emerging markets, but they are also subject to important constraints. In the early 1990s, managers of Johnson & Johnson in the Philippines were looking for new products to boost local sales. They discovered that young Filipino women were using one of their most successful products—Johnson & Johnson baby talcum powder—to freshen their makeup. These users typically carried a small amount of the powder in a knotted handkerchief to use outside the home. To target this latent market, Johnson & Johnson Philippines developed a compact holder for the talcum powder, complete with mirror and powder puff. An advertising campaign was targeted at this segment, and distribution was secured through supermarkets and corner shops.

A few days before the product's launch, however, corporate headquarters in the United States asked that it be canceled. The reason: "We are not in the cosmetics business." Local managers were stunned. They argued that the compact would be a test of their ability to develop products for the local market. Only after the chief marketer in the Philippines flew to headquarters and made a personal plea for the product did the company allow the launch to go ahead.

The product was a great success; sales exceeded projections by more than a factor of ten. Nevertheless, Johnson & Johnson has not introduced the product in other markets. And even in the Philippines, the company has subsumed the product into a broad line of toiletries instead of promoting it separately. Johnson & Johnson preferred to give up sales rather than run the risk of being seen as a cosmetics producer in the company's more-established markets.

Companies based in emerging markets don't have to contend with such constraints arising from established positions in affluent markets. Not only are they closer to their own market, but they are also free to let the market define them. This flexibility is one of a number of advantages that local managers may overlook when they face the prospect of multinationals entering their own market.

> For more on the constraints confronting multinational companies, see
> Chapter 1, "The End of Corporate Imperialism."

Jahwa's strategy has allowed it to weather the initial opening of
China's markets—a period when multinational companies often appear irresistible to consumers and local competitors alike. At first, consumers often flock to foreign brands out of curiosity or out of a blind
belief in their virtues. Procter & Gamble, for example, grabbed over
half the Chinese market for shampoo in just a few years, despite the
substantially higher price of its product. But by focusing on offerings
that reflect local preferences, Jahwa was able to protect some sales and
buy time in which to build up the quality of its products and marketing. Jahwa's managers have good reason to believe that many consumers will eventually shake off their expensive infatuation with foreign brands and go back to Jahwa and other local lines.

Other defenders have been able to blunt the force of foreign competition by beefing up their distribution network. Grupo Industrial
Bimbo, the largest producer of bread and confectionery products in
Mexico, seized on that asset when faced with foreign competition.
Over the years, Bimbo had built up an extensive sales and distribution
force to get its products into *tiendas*, the ubiquitous corner stores
where Mexicans still do most of their shopping. The company employs
14,000 drivers who blanket the country with 420,000 deliveries daily
to 350,000 clients.

At the time that Mexico was opening its markets, Bimbo's managers
were considering a lower-cost approach that would have cut out a
number of these daily runs to tiendas, many of which brought only
about $10 in revenue per delivery. When PepsiCo aggressively en-
tered the Mexican bakery market in 1991, however, those plans were
quickly shelved. The move shocked Bimbo's managers into examining their actual sources of competitive advantage. Far from weighing
down operations with low-margin sales, Bimbo's distribution network
was the key to defending its home turf. The network tapped into
Mexican consumers' preference for freshness and their habit of shopping daily at a nearby store, creating a huge barrier to entry for foreign competitors. Instead of reducing deliveries, Bimbo's managers
increased them—although they did lower costs by sending to the
smaller tiendas trucks with multiple products instead of the single-
product deliveries sent everywhere else. Their defensive strategy paid

off: Bimbo has maintained leading positions in each of its major market segments.

Extending Local Advantages Abroad

In some cases, companies in local industries can go beyond defending their existing markets. With the right transferable assets, these extenders can use their success at home as a platform for expansion elsewhere. A selective policy of international expansion, carefully tied to the company's key assets, can reap added revenue and scale economies, not to mention valuable learning experiences.

Extenders can leverage their assets most effectively by seeking analogous markets—those similar to their home base in terms of consumer preferences, geographic proximity, distribution channels, or government regulations. Expatriate communities, to take a simple case, are likely to be receptive to products developed at home.

Jollibee Foods, a family-owned fast-food company in the Philippines, has extended its reach by focusing on Filipinos in other countries. The company first overcame an onslaught from McDonald's in its home market, partly by upgrading service and delivery standards but also by developing rival menus customized to local tastes. Along with noodle and rice meals made with fish, Jollibee created a hamburger seasoned with garlic and soy sauce—allowing it to capture 75% of the burger market and 56% of the fast-food business in the Philippines. Having learned what it takes to compete with multina tionals, Jollibee had the confidence to go elsewhere. Using its battle-tested recipes, the company has now established dozens of restaurants near large expatriate populations in Hong Kong, the Middle East, and California.

Similarly, managers can look for countries with a common cultural or linguistic heritage. Televisa, Mexico's largest media company, used that approach to become the world's most prolific producer of Spanish-language soap operas. Recognizing that its programs would have considerable value in the many Spanish-speaking markets outside Mexico, the company targeted export markets in Latin America, Spain, the U.S. border states, and Florida. Recently, Televisa has begun its own news broadcasts, teaming up with Rupert Murdoch's News Corporation for distribution to Spanish-language markets worldwide.

The concept of analogous markets can be stretched far indeed. India's Asian Paints controls 40% of the market for house paints in its home base, despite aggressive moves by such major multinationals as ICI, Kansai Paints, and Sherwin Williams. The company has thrived against foreign competitors by developing its local assets, notably an extensive distribution network. Its paint formulations and packaging practices make for an extremely low-cost product—one that, its managers have discovered, holds considerable appeal in other developing countries. After its success exporting to neighbors such as Nepal and Fiji, the company is now pursuing joint ventures abroad.

Asian Paints brings substantial advantages to these countries. Its managers are used to dealing with the kind of marketing environment there—thousands of scattered retailers, illiterate consumers, and customers who want only small quantities of paint that can then be diluted to save money. Multinational rivals, by contrast, have built their operations around the demands of affluent customers looking for a wide choice of colors and finishes. Their expatriate managers are used to air-conditioned offices and bottled water that costs more per liter than most customers are willing to pay for paint. Even after they develop a low-end paint product, the multinationals will still have a long way to go to catch up in emerging markets. Asian Paints already knows how to speak the language of these customers.

Dodging the Onslaught

In industries where pressures to globalize are strong, managers will not be able to simply build on their company's local assets—they'll have to rethink their business model. If their assets are valuable only in their home country, then the best course may be to enter into a joint venture with, or sell out entirely to, a multinational. The Czech carmaker Skoda took that latter step after the collapse of the Soviet Union in 1989. Like many companies in communist countries, Skoda's position as an official producer under the old Soviet regime had allowed the company simultaneously to survive and to stagnate. Only the choice-starved consumers in the former Eastern bloc could appreciate Skoda's cars, and even they recognized how outdated the designs were, how poor the quality was, and how limited the appeal of the brand was compared with Western makes.

When markets opened in Eastern Europe, Skoda's position became untenable. Multinational carmakers arrived with the sort of insurmountable advantages made possible by their global scale: superior models, well-known brands, and financial muscle. The Czech government soon sold the company to Volkswagen, which subsequently restructured Skoda's operations, invested heavily in new products and technology, and positioned it as the value brand in Volkswagen's global line of vehicles.

In many cases, however, there are alternatives to selling out. Consider the Russian personal-computer maker Vist. When Russia liberalized its economy, Vist's managers knew they would win few battles going head to head with the likes of Compaq, IBM, and Hewlett-Packard. Rather than sell out or seek a joint venture, however, they sidestepped oblivion by redefining their core business. They dodged the global threat by focusing on links in the value chain where Vist's assets provided competitive advantage. Instead of viewing the company as a manufacturer of personal computers, they increasingly emphasized the downstream aspects of Vist's existing business—distribution, service, and warranties.

While its multinational rivals concentrated on selling machines to government and corporate markets in Moscow, Vist took advantage of its familiarity with the wider market. It reached into the interior of the country through an extended dealer network and developed exclusive distribution agreements with several key retailers. It also established its own full-service centers in dozens of Russian cities.

That approach was well suited to the Russian computer market, which is still in its early stages. Russians need much more information and reassurance than most Western buyers before they will purchase a computer, and they appreciate a local presence. All of Vist's manuals are in Russian, and the company provides lengthy warranties, unlike rivals, which simply sell extended service contracts. The computers that Vist sells—the product of a low-cost assembly operation using mostly imported components—are unremarkable; nevertheless its downstream assets have made Vist the leading brand in Russia with 20% of the market. And as the Russian computer market advances, Vist's network of service centers will alert the company to changes before its rivals see them.

Just as defenders focus on market segments responsive to their local strengths, dodgers like Vist move to links in the value chain where their local assets still work well. But, as Skoda's experience shows, not all companies can make the jump that dodgers have to make. Vist was able to restructure around distribution and service because it was already active in those areas; Skoda had little room to maneuver because it was devoted almost entirely to one part of the value chain. Skoda also had enormous investments in capital-intensive manufacturing (not to mention a large number of jobs) that the Czech government was understandably reluctant to drop in order to refocus on other parts of the business.

While distribution and service are common recourses for dodgers, there are others. One approach is to supply products that either complement multinationals' offerings or adapt them to local tastes. When Microsoft moved into China, for example, local software companies shifted their focus from developing Windows look-alike operating systems to developing Windows application programs tailored to the Chinese market.

Dodgers can also move to the other end of the value chain. As Mexico has opened its markets, many manufacturing companies have reoriented themselves, becoming local component suppliers to the newly built factories of foreign multinationals.

Dodging may be the most difficult of the four strategies to execute because it requires a company to revamp major aspects of its strategy—and to do so before it's swept under by the tide of foreign competition. But by focusing on carefully selected niches, a dodger can use its local assets to establish a viable position.

Contending on the Global Level

Despite the many advantages of their multinational rivals, companies from emerging markets should not always rule out a strategy of selling at the global level. If their assets are transferable, they may be able to become full-fledged multinationals themselves. The number of these contenders is steadily increasing, and a few, such as Acer of Taiwan and Samsung of Korea, have become household names. The reasons for their success are similar to those of any thriving company that competes in a global industry. However, contenders often have to take into consideration a different set of opportunities and constraints.

Most contenders are in commodity industries where plentiful natural resources or labor give them the low-cost advantage. From

Indonesia, Indah Kiat Pulp & Paper (IKPP), for example, has aggressively moved into export markets by drawing on a ready supply of logs—the product of favorable tropical growing conditions, low harvesting costs, and government-guaranteed timber concessions. In its core paper business, it enjoys production costs that are nearly half those of its North American and Swedish competitors, a huge advantage in export markets.

IKPP's cost advantage is not due entirely to geography. The company has also invested heavily in advanced machinery to make its production more efficient. This is an important lesson for all companies trying to capitalize on lower costs of resources or labor, particularly as multinationals set up their own operations in developing countries. Rather than being content to let resources provide the sole advantage, contenders need to measure themselves against the practices of leading companies in their industry. Many, like IKPP did, will find their quality or productivity levels lacking. Others will have severe deficiencies in service, delivery, or packaging. As a result, the cost advantage they enjoy will often be undermined by deficiencies in other areas. But by moving toward the productivity, quality, and service levels of their competitors from developed countries, local contenders in commodity industries can build a sustainable basis for long-term competitive success.

For would-be contenders that lack access to key resources, finding a distinct and defensible market niche is vital. One increasingly common approach is to join a production consortium, in which a lead company manages a regional or global web of component developers and suppliers. Few emerging-market companies have the market presence, coordination capabilities, or innovative technology they would need to act as the lead organization in a far-flung production network. Most of them will need to concentrate on building scale and expertise along particular pieces of their industry's value chain.

When General Motors decided to outsource the production of radiator caps for its North American vehicles, India's Sundaram Fasteners seized the opportunity to go global. Sundaram bought an entire GM production line, moved it to India, and a year later became the sole supplier of radiator caps to GM's North American division. In addition to the obvious benefits to the bottom line that accrue from the guarantee of selling 5 million radiator caps a year, participation in GM's supply network made it easier for Sundaram to develop its capabilities and learn about emerging technical standards and evolving customer needs. Sundaram was one of the first Indian companies to achieve QS 9000 certification, a quality standard developed by U.S. automakers, which GM requires for all its component suppliers. The skills learned during the certification process also benefited Sundaram's core fastener business, putting it in a position to target the European and Japanese markets. Unlike local suppliers to multinational companies, Sundaram's Indian operations are capable of supplying factories all over the world. (See "How to Stay Independent with Partnerships.")

How to Stay Independent with Partnerships

For companies in many emerging markets, giving up control is the option of last resort. This is especially true for the family-owned businesses that play a leading role in most of these economies. But alliances with multinationals do not always involve a loss of independence. When carried out within well-defined parameters, they can actually help a company preserve its freedom in the face of competitive threats.

Companies using any of the four strategies to counter the entry of multinationals into their markets can benefit from forming alliances, but the nature and objectives of the alliances will differ depending on which strategy they adopt. Alliances can help defenders fortify their positions. Shanghai Jahwa, for example, saw that multinational rivals were offering a broader product line than it could. By forming alliances with the Japanese companies Kanebo and Lion, Jahwa was able to offer to the distribution trade a line of household and personal care products as broad as those of the competition. Jahwa was careful, however, to limit the partnership to a small part of its lineup, which enabled it to maintain financial and managerial control over its products. Dodgers can also benefit by establishing similar sorts of limited partnerships to fill gaps in their capabilities quickly as they move to a different part of the value chain and redefine themselves.

For extenders and contenders, alliances are often essential. They can range from supply chain partnerships, like the one Sundaram Fasteners joined with General Motors, to distribution arrangements with retailers in other countries. Forming manufacturing partnerships to supply private-label goods may be the only way for many companies to crack international markets. Before investing in its own brands and becoming a full-fledged contender, Acer of Taiwan made computers for sale under the Compaq brand; similarly, Kia Motors of Korea manufactured the Ford Fiesta.

Private-label partnerships can be useful even for extenders that have no global ambitions. Balsara, an Indian hygiene-products and cosmetics company best known for its Promise brand of clove toothpaste, is facing stiff domestic competition from Colgate-Palmolive. Balsara's managers are committed to defending their home market, but Colgate's strengths as an international brand are imposing. By winning private-label toothpaste agreements from such nonrivals as Henkel and the Beecham Group, Balsara was able to strike back at its rival's turf in the West. But more important, the partnerships enabled Balsara to upgrade its factories and the quality of its products and packaging—improvements that will help the company protect its market share at home.

Sundaram was able to transfer the knowledge it gained by being part of a production consortium directly to its core business. But finding a viable niche in a global industry usually means an extended process of restructuring. Many companies may have to shed businesses that can't be sustained on the global level. To many managers in emerging markets who are conscious of links between their businesses, that process will be difficult. But shedding businesses, outsourcing components previously made in-house, and investing in new products and processes are the keys to repositioning contenders as focused, global producers. Indeed, the need to get smaller before getting larger is one of the major themes in the corporate restructuring process under way in Eastern Europe.

In Hungary, Raba, for example, used to produce a diverse line of vehicles and components—from engines and axles to complete buses, trucks, and tractors. When markets in Eastern Europe opened, the company faced a collapse in demand. Yet as the automotive industry rapidly consolidated globally, Raba managed to avoid Skoda's fate. It focused on the worldwide market for heavy-duty axles, a segment in which its technology was fairly close to the standards of international competitors. Restructuring has paid off, especially in the United States, where the company has captured 25% of the large market for heavy-duty tractor axles. Axles now account for over two-thirds of Raba's sales, and nearly all of them are exported.

By contrast, the company's remaining operation in the wider engine and vehicle market, where it operates only in Eastern Europe, is facing a severe challenge from such major multinationals as Cummins and DaimlerChrysler. Despite Raba's extensive service network, the globalization pressures in that industry, throughout its value chain, may be too strong to withstand.

Perhaps the greatest challenge for contenders is to overcome deficiencies in skills and financial resources. Especially in high-tech industries, where product life cycles are short, contenders are often put at a disadvantage by their distance from leading-edge suppliers, customers, and competitors. The cost of capital is also much higher for them than it is for their multinational rivals, a direct result of the greater political and economic risk in emerging markets. The most successful contenders—those that have moved beyond competing solely on the basis of cost—have learned to overcome those disadvantages by accessing resources in developed countries.

An extreme example is Korea's Samsung, which moved to the frontier of memory chip technology by establishing a major R&D center in Silicon Valley and then transferring the know-how gained there back to headquarters in Seoul. But even contenders in mature industries can benefit from looking abroad.

Consider Mexico's Cemex, which has transformed itself from a diversified business group into a focused producer of cement—now the third largest in the world. Although Cemex enjoys low production costs at home, it has had to overcome major disadvantages. To lower its cost of capital, Cemex tapped international markets by listing its shares on the New York Stock Exchange. The acquisition of two Spanish cement producers in 1992 put it in the backyard of a major international competitor, France's Lafarge, and also allowed Cemex to shift its financing from short-term Mexican peso debt to longer-term Spanish peseta debt. What's more, its foreign acquisitions greatly reduced the company's dependence on the Mexican cement market, always a concern given the country's history of economic volatility.

In addition, Cemex has aggressively sought to be on the forefront of information technology—a key factor for success in the logistics-intensive cement industry. Its managers have worked closely on systems development with IBM, and the company has invested extensively in employee development programs designed to support its emphasis on logistics, quality, and service. Through its efforts, Cemex has become one of the world's lowest-cost producers of cement, and it has applied the lessons it has learned to boost efficiency in its acquired companies. Instead of being the target of multinationals, Cemex has since bought additional companies of its own. In the eat-or-be-eaten world of global competition, Cemex is positioning itself at the top of the food chain.

Managing Transitions

A recurring theme in these examples is the importance of being flexible in response to market opportunities. This familiar advice is often forgotten by managers from emerging markets, for whom industry boundaries have traditionally been taken as a given, in many cases established by government mandate. Liberalization is now making the structure of many industries much more fluid, and managers exposed to new kinds of competitors need to realize that they can respond by positioning their companies in a variety of ways.

By better understanding the relationship between their company's assets and the particular characteristics of their industry, managers can also anticipate how their strategies may evolve over time. As more and more companies learn to compete in global markets, we are bound to see a growing number of aggressive contenders like Cemex. But few are likely to make the jump soon, in part because globalization pressures in many industries will continue to be weak. We suspect that many of the most successful companies will remain focused on their local markets, strengthening their main sources of competitive advantage. Others will build on a successful defense of their home base and look for opportunities abroad, but they may never make the final step up to global competition. Managers will need to revisit their assumptions and conclusions as the capabilities of their companies develop.

Not only will managers find their strategies likely to evolve over time, but the nature of their industry may change as well. A company in a predominantly local business may prosper because of its superior service and distribution. But a competitor may make a move that changes the industry fundamentally, giving advantages to global players. That is what happened in the insulin business, when the major players raised the ante by developing a superior product—genetically engineered human insulin—at a fixed cost that only companies with global reach could justify. The new manufacturing process drove prices below anything that local producers could sustain.

Just as the structure of some industries favors companies that operate on a large scale, so can the structure of other industries evolve to favor companies operating at a small scale. In India, Arvind Mills took a seemingly global product—blue jeans—and refashioned it to fit the budgets of millions of rural villagers. While Levi Strauss and other multinationals aim for the urban middle class, Arvind has built a new and protected market for itself. (See "A Tale of Two Strategies.")

A Tale of Two Strategies

It's not just individual businesses that need to consider how their competitive assets match the globalization pressures of their industry. Many companies from emerging markets belong to multibusiness organizations. By mapping their business portfolio on the matrix, the heads of diversified companies in emerging markets can see potential trouble spots and areas of opportunity, and make decisions accordingly.

India's Arvind Mills is a good example of a company that pursued opposite strategies in adjusting its different businesses to competitive threats. In the 1980s, Arvind found itself being squeezed by low-cost foreign integrated mills and nimble domestic power-loom operators. Stuck in the middle, Arvind's managers realized that the company would not be viable if India's textile industry became fully liberalized. Central to their company's turnaround was their recognition that, despite similar symptoms, their two main businesses were suffering from different maladies—and required different cures.

Success in the fabric division increasingly depended on economies of scale, and the managers decided that the company could survive only by moving onto the global stage. As contenders, they were careful to concentrate on a niche market that allowed them to catch up with existing producers quickly. That market was denim, a fabric that at the time accounted for only 10% of Arvind's output. The denim fabric itself is essentially a commodity; while fashions in denim do change, those changes are imposed by the apparel makers, not the cloth manufacturers. A few large buyers choose from a fragmented base of cloth suppliers. Once a company pays the high price of entry—expensive, high-output technology—it is in business.

Arvind developed relationships with key buyers, and it applied innovative process engineering to reduce costs below those of most competitors. Arvind's installed capacity in denim is now ten times that of its closest Indian rival, and the company exports over half of its total output. From a standing start 13 years ago, Arvind Mills is today the world's third largest manufacturer of denim and the fastest growing.

Arvind's managers focused on denim for the apparel division as well, but they chose a completely different strategy. Going global in apparel would have been prohibitively expensive—developing a global consumer brand is beyond the resources of most contenders, which is why they almost always specialize in producer goods. Arvind's managers went on the defensive and emphasized the local aspects of the industry's value chain—tailoring and distribution. They built capabilities and local brand appeal to sell jeans specifically in India. Recognizing that major brands like Levi's would have little choice but to target the top end of the market, Arvind saw huge potential in the mass-market segment, which would include many first-time jeans buyers. The question was how to make the price attractive to those consumers.

Arvind's radical solution was to launch a brand—Ruf & Tuf—sold in kit form. The kit consisted of fabric, a metal zipper and rivets, a leather Ruf & Tuf patch, a pattern, and sewing instructions. The company launched the concept in conjunction with a major advertising campaign and an education program intended to reach some 6,000 tailors.

Arvind's insight was to accommodate its product to local buying practices. It was the custom of people to purchase fabric and use local tailors to stitch the final product. The company knew that major multinationals would be powerless to follow that approach since local tailoring undermined a key value proposition of foreign brands—the consistency of the product.

At the same time, Arvind could use its marketing and cost advantages to nullify the smaller local competitors. Within the first year, sales of the new product exceeded expectations by an order of magnitude, as more than 250,000 units shipped every month. Arvind has now carved out a dominant position in the local market.

For more on the prospects for diversified business groups operating in emerging markets, see Chapter 2 "Why Focused Strategies May Be Wrong for Emerging Markets."

In many emerging markets around the world today, we've found a fundamental dynamic. Multinationals are seeking to exploit global scale economies while local enterprises are trying to fragment the market and serve the needs of distinct niches. The former bring an array of powerful resources that can intimidate even the most self-assured local manager. But like David against Goliath, the smaller competitor can rise to the challenge and prevail.

4
Troubles Ahead in Emerging Markets

Jeffrey E. Garten

Throughout the 1990s, financial investors, corporate strategists, and political leaders in the United States, Western Europe, and Japan have been intensifying their focus on emerging markets. Such companies as Morgan Stanley, General Electric, and Johnson & Johnson are placing enormous bets on these markets. The Clinton administration's export-promotion strategy is based on the premise that the most promising markets are not in Europe and Japan but in the so-called big emerging markets. And the U.S. approach is mirrored abroad as presidents and prime ministers from France to Japan make pilgrimages to China, India, Brazil, and elsewhere to hawk their countries' wares.

Emerging markets are indeed the new frontier. But like all frontiers, they present a mix of opportunity and risk. The question now is whether businesses and governments in the industrialized world are sober enough about the problems that lie ahead. I do not believe they are. There is considerable evidence indicating that the tides of capitalism, which rose so powerfully after the collapse of the Soviet Union, are poised to recede. This reversal may signal much more than the usual ebb and flow of political and economic progress in the developing world, and could amount to a fundamental disruption of the generally upward trajectory in so many countries.

What can governments and businesses in the developed world do in the face of such likely turmoil? The industrial-world member-nations of the Organization for Economic Cooperation and Development (OECD) must ask whether they are pushing enough for growth and trade liberalization. Multinational companies, meanwhile, can no longer leave foreign policy to politicians and bureaucrats. They must develop capabilities that will allow them to anticipate and respond to the upcoming disruptions in emerging markets. And they must remain open to opportunities for cooperation between private and public sectors in those markets. Such cooperation can improve the economic environment and mitigate the risks of doing business in developing countries.

The Clash of Capitalism and Democracy

Emerging markets do represent undeniable commercial opportunities. In the last decade, the ten big emerging markets—Mexico, Brazil, Argentina, South Africa, Poland, Turkey, India, South Korea, the ASEAN region (Indonesia, Thailand, Malaysia, Singapore, and Vietnam), and the Chinese Economic Area (China, Hong Kong, and Taiwan)—have opened their markets to foreign investment and trade. The gross domestic product of the big emerging markets has been increasing two to three times faster than that of developed countries. At the same time, emerging markets have made genuine progress in reining in deficits and inflation, as well as in selling off bloated state enterprises to private investors. Of course, the measures taken have been uneven, and there is a long way to go in every case, but it is indisputable that Adam Smith's philosophy has won the day.

It should not be surprising, therefore, that long-term projections for market expansion have been optimistic. In 1995, the ten big emerging markets accounted for about 10% of the world's economic output. The U.S. Department of Commerce believes that percentage may more than double over the next two decades, as those countries boost their share of global imports from 19% to 38%. Private capital has been flowing to emerging markets in unprecedented amounts, rising 19% in 1996 to a new high of $230 billion. Enormous potential exists for further expansion: for example, whereas all emerging markets account for 40% of global production, they still represent only 15% of global stock-market value.

Any optimistic reading of the future, however, is based on a critical assumption: the economic reforms that have been so impressive in the 1990s will continue more or less along a straight line. There are good reasons to doubt that developing countries will continue to liberalize at the pace of the last few years. The threat does not lie in a repetition of the financial shocks that have hit emerging markets (such as the peso crisis that struck Mexico in the mid-1990s). Today governments and financial institutions in the OECD are reasonably well equipped to respond to such events. The worrisome problems are of a different order of magnitude—going well beyond the ups and downs of the business cycle, the usual gyrations in countries undergoing difficult transitions, or the episodic political crises that have always characterized such societies.

Something deeper is at play in the late 1990s, the collision of two forces that have not coexisted before in emerging markets: free-market capitalism and democracy. The philosophy of Adam Smith is giving rise to powerful new pressures that have enriched many, impoverished others, created enormous social changes, and unleashed new political forces. But Thomas Jefferson's part of the equation is not working so well. Democratic structures in many emerging markets are either nonexistent or too weak to ensure the modicum of economic fairness necessary to sustain democratic capitalism. As a result, emerging markets may well lose some of the progress they have made toward regulating markets and creating the rule of law that is essential to any commercial regime.

Moreover, in previous eras of crisis, the companies and governments of the industrialized world essentially wrote off emerging markets and left them to fend for themselves. Now, however, foreign investors, creditors, and governments will not be able to walk away from trouble without damaging themselves. Companies in the industrialized world depend on overseas markets for both economies of scale and increasing profits. The countries in the developed world want the jobs at home that come with expanding exports. And many pension-plan investors are banking on the high returns that can result from investing in the developing world.

Threats to Reform

A number of emerging markets already are under severe pressure. In Mexico, the path to progress has some enormous obstacles along its way. True, the economic reforms of the 1980s and 1990s were impressive, even if the government badly mismanaged its currency devaluation at the end of 1994. Today the country appears to be on the road to recovery from the peso crisis: forecasters estimate growth in the range of 4% to 5% for 1997, and the nation's export economy is flourishing. But the current-account deficit is rising again. Mexico's external debt has grown from 35% of GDP in 1992 to more than 60% in 1996. High interest rates and taxes are strangling the middle class. The banking system borders on insolvency. In the recession of the past two years, 5 million Mexicans have been added to the 22 million citizens (one-fourth of the population) who already live in extreme poverty. And the government estimates that an annual growth rate of 6% is necessary to absorb the 1 million new entrants into the labor force each year—a rate that does not appear to be attainable anytime soon.

Mexico's ability to deal with those daunting problems depends on an effective government. The country has been ruled by the iron fist of the Institutional Revolutionary Party for more than 60 years, but the party has become arthritic and corrupt. It is incapable of acting as a safety valve for the wellspring of popular discontent in Mexico, let alone as a vehicle for implementing critical new policies necessary for a rapidly changing economy. The party is in fact resisting change, having recently overturned President Ernesto Zedillo's far-reaching proposal to open and modernize Mexico's political process.

Nevertheless, political change will come—if not peacefully then violently. Already, crime, kidnapping, assassinations, and guerrilla activity are on the rise, signaling both a mounting level of dissatisfaction and the inability of the public sector to maintain order. But even if a more open and representative government emerges, it will lack the experience and the underlying institutions—such as honest courts—to govern effectively in the short run. Initially, that government may be besieged by the accumulated demands of tens of millions of Mexican citizens who have felt disenfranchised. It also will have its hands full cleaning up the old system—getting a grip on wide-spread criminality and creating a rule of law that all segments of the population can respect.

In light of those pressures, future governments may put off liberalizing the economy and instead concentrate on the immediate welfare of ordinary citizens. A democratic administration could become more nationalistic and more protectionist than the existing oligarchy. It could take many years before Mexico restores its current trajectory, at least in the eyes of foreign companies and governments.

Consider also Indonesia, the largest Muslim nation and the fourth largest country in the world by population. As in Mexico, the political system there may soon be unable to cope with economic and social pressures. By any measure, Jakarta's economic performance has been strong. GDP growth has been on the order of 6% to 7% annually, non-oil exports have been growing, and billions of dollars of foreign investment have poured in. But the country is a powder keg waiting to explode. With the exception of China, no major country is more dominated by autocratic rule than Indonesia. The 75-year-old president Suharto, who has ruled since he came to power in the mid-1960s in a bloody coup, *is* the political system. The only opposition allowed is government-approved parties that support the president. Any challenge is immediately squelched—by military force if necessary.

Enormous pressures are building below the surface. When the aging president leaves the scene, they are likely to explode. It is difficult to envision a scenario that will contain those pressures when there are no existing political institutions to modulate them aside from the apparatus that Suharto now dominates. The military will want to maintain order. The Chinese minority will want to maintain its wealth. Both will be challenged by the Muslims, who constitute the overwhelming majority of the population; by the labor unions, which have been suppressed; and by the students, whose activism has been outlawed.

In a politically repressive society, change usually does not come gradually; it bursts on the scene. Some recent events are telltale signs of Indonesia's possible fate after Suharto. Last August, for example, when government pressure suppressed the voice of the leader of an opposition party, the largest riots of the past two decades ensued, followed by a brutal military crackdown. Afterward, the government began a systematic persecution of other potential "troublemakers," including the leader of the largest independent labor union. He and several labor and student leaders are currently on trial for subversion, a crime punishable by death. In early 1997, a Muslim mob burned a Chinese temple as well as Christian churches. The alleged cause was a complaint by an ethnic Chinese trader that the call to prayer from a mosque near his home was too loud. The incident highlighted the seething ethnic rivalries and resentments that will play out in the open once Suharto departs. It's difficult to see how economic progress won't suffer.

What about countries that have better track records politically? Several of the big emerging markets have practiced democracy for years, but even those nations are struggling with political pressures stemming from economic change. In India, for example, Prime

Minister P.V. Narasimha Rao's measures in the early 1990s to open the economy astounded outside observers. For nearly half a century, India had been a closed economy wedded to socialism, and its sudden embrace of capitalism stimulated high levels of economic growth and trade as well as an influx of capital from abroad. But in the national elections of 1996, the Indian people jettisoned Rao's government. In its place emerged a coalition of 13 parties—an unwieldy assemblage that includes nearly every major and parochial interest group in the country, from communists to religious extremists.

Such a fractured group will struggle to make the hard political decisions that are necessary to continue economic liberalization—including massive reduction of subsidies, new infrastructure development, and labor reform. If India stands still because of political polarization—in fact, if it doesn't move ahead quickly—it faces a dire situation as popular expectations rise. India has a long way to go to overcome a host of problems such as food production that loses 30% each year to spoilage; an energy distribution system that loses 25% to leakage during delivery; crumbling roads, ports, and airports; and a primitive telecommunications sector. India is falling farther behind its Asian rivals in economic reforms, a problem that may jeopardize its ability to attract foreign capital in the future.

Economic pressures also are straining South Korea's politics. No one can deny the progress that this country has made in the past several years on both economic and political fronts, but now it must move out of the ranks of emerging markets to join those that have emerged. It can no longer compete internationally with such countries as China and Brazil, where the costs of doing business are much lower. South Korea must move from a system founded on paternalism and authoritarianism to one based on democratic values, for there is no other way to unlock the initiative of the Korean people and create an economy flexible enough to cope with rapid technological change.

Nowhere are these challenges more evident than in the need to reform labor laws, which derive from an era when Korea was a military dictatorship. The challenge is to balance the ability of employers to control costs with a system of free collective bargaining. With no experience walking this tightrope, the administration of Kim Young Sam has badly mishandled the task. Last December, it passed legislation making it easier to lay off workers and postponing the right of labor to unionize until the year 2000. The laws were passed in a secret closed session with no public hearings and without the involvement of the political opposition. The unsurprising results were the largest strikes in South Korea's history. Today the government and the unions are still trying to work out a viable long-term settlement.

This bruising struggle is likely to make it more difficult to enact future reforms—reforms that are needed now more than ever. The country's GDP growth is slowing, the current-account deficit is soaring, and the Seoul stock market is at its lowest point in several years. Moreover, of all the major emerging markets, South Korea is the most hostile to foreign investment. And in the wake of the prolonged strikes, workers are especially sensitive to the issue of job security— which makes measures to open up the economy politically difficult. Such measures, however, are essential if the South Korean economy is to maintain its competitive position.

Other big markets are showing worrisome signs. In South Africa, President Nelson Mandela has not been able to bring about either prosperity or social justice. In fact, political wrangling within the ruling party has rendered it incapable of action, and critics fear that the nation is headed toward anarchy or permanent third-world status. In Brazil, the populist congress is resisting constitutional changes that would enable such reforms as large-scale privatization. In Argentina, unemployment has reached 17%, a level that is severely straining the ability of the ruling party—itself built around the labor movement—to streamline the economy any further. And in Turkey, economic reform has been all but taken off the table amid the election of the first Islamic government in the country's modern history.

Interpreting the Turmoil

There are several ways to account for the mounting pressures in emerging markets. One explanation is that many of the easier economic-reform measures already have been taken. A country's leaders can reduce tariffs from 300% to 50% more easily than they can reduce them from 50% to 5%; similarly, they can sell off the most viable government companies—such as the hard-currency-earning airlines— more readily than they can the money-losing steel plants. That first set of reforms can be enacted quickly: foreign and local investors respond positively, and foreign governments applaud. But the afterglow doesn't last long. Soon the domestic opposition organizes a counterattack, and those who haven't benefited from liberalization measures throw up roadblocks. Ordinary citizens, having heard about the magic of the marketplace, wonder why they can't get hot water or why the phones don't work. And top-level decision makers get worn out fighting battles over such questions.

In many emerging markets, the list of what still needs to be done is long. Market regulation is highly underdeveloped. Rigid labor laws need to be restructured. Limits on prices for energy and telecommunications discourage foreign investment. Government payrolls need to be pared down; at the same time, however, more skilled and experienced people need to be attracted to the bureaucracy. Expensive social-welfare policies need to be dismantled and rebuilt. The massive amounts of red tape that still interfere with normal business transactions need to be slashed. And legal systems need to be strengthened.

But by far the biggest reason for anxiety about economic reforms is the political dynamics of the reforms themselves. Those who have embraced emerging markets with enthusiasm have failed to consider a number of factors: the political dimension of change, the difficulty of implementing massive transformation in a short period, and the lack of skills and institutions needed to manage democratic capitalism. In moving toward open political and economic systems simultaneously, emerging markets are on uncharted and precarious ground.

As economic liberalization in emerging markets replaces rigid control, a new, more laissez-faire, but more sophisticated, kind of economic and commercial regulation needs to be put in place. Governments need to shrink in size while managing more difficult tasks more effectively—a trick even the leaders in Washington, Bonn, and Tokyo have not yet mastered. In the absence of such a new set of political arrangements, those who held power under the old regime end up in favored positions under the new one and simply increase their dominance and privileges. In addition, the transition from a command to a market economy brings with it a hiatus of order that invites a serious increase in fraud and corruption. Leaders in emerging markets rarely have the skills and experience to make the transition smoothly.

On the political side, democracies are defined by more than just voting; they also require a complex infrastructure. Without the solid foundations of a professional civil service, a strong independent judiciary, and arm's-length regulators, the leaders of new democracies can spend all their time dealing with the pressure groups that emerge from an open economy. They cannot attend to the requirements of everyday management, let alone plan for essential long-term investments, and they are unable to deal with the popular demands critical to their legitimacy. Under those pressures, a new democracy sometimes drifts toward weak administrations and deadlock. At other times, the government moves in the opposite direction—toward the very dictatorial systems it replaced. Then comes a popular backlash, which reduces a government's ability to pursue the economic reforms that once constituted its primary mission.

These observations do not apply to every emerging market. Poland, for example, seems to have made an exemplary transition. In seven years, it has created a mature democracy, achieved the highest growth rate in Europe, and reduced the share of GDP stemming from government-owned activity from 100% to 33%. Warsaw did have special advantages: it once had a very sophisticated economy, it has a highly educated population, and it was greatly helped by sitting on Europe's doorstep. Taking another tack, China has managed to combine rigid political control with gradual economic liberalization—perhaps because its system of political control is so highly developed, and because its very size and economic potential is mesmerizing to foreign investors, who have made China the largest destination for foreign capital among emerging markets.

It would be misleading, too, to say that there are no other scenarios for Mexico, Indonesia, South Korea, and India than those described above. Political change in Mexico may come at a slow but steady pace at the municipal or state level. A more conciliatory military group may replace Suharto. South Korea may apply Asian-style discipline and determination, and persevere on the course of economic reform. India may muddle through. In the end, of course, it is not possible to predict with complete confidence the course of such profound and complex transitions.

Still, it is best now to be sober. The prevailing optimistic view of what will happen in key emerging markets underestimates the impact of variables that cannot be measured: frustration about missing out on the boom times and anxiety about the massive changes wrought by foreign investment and technology. Moreover, those who say that Mexico has always had pervasive poverty or that India has always progressed slowly are underestimating both the current pace of global change, which is new, and the impact of seeing and knowing what a better life is all about, which is now more possible than ever because of modern communications. This much is sure: the risks of setbacks in many big emerging markets are escalating. Over time, democracy and free markets can reinforce each other, but the journey will be precarious. And we are entering its most dangerous phase.

Pressure on the Developed World

A slowing of economic reforms in emerging markets would be a disaster for the industrialized world on several counts.

First, powerful trade and investment ties have made the emerging markets essential to the continued economic expansion of industrialized OECD countries. For example, exports have been responsible for about one-third of U.S. economic growth in the past few years, and already the ten big emerging markets account for a greater proportion of U.S. exports than the European Union and Japan combined. Exports to the big emerging markets have been equally important for both Europe and Japan.

The ability to increase exports to emerging markets is all the more important because those markets will be selling a growing amount to industrialized countries. The enhanced competitiveness of emerging markets stems from the economic reforms they have already undertaken, as well as from low wage rates and increasing productivity. In the United States, for example, the average hourly wage in 1996 was $17.20. In South Korea, it was $7.40; in Taiwan, $5.82; in Brazil, $4.28; in China, 25 cents. And productivity in these markets will be greatly enhanced because of growing access to Western technology and supervision by foreign managers. To avoid unmanageable trade deficits and the flaring up of protectionist sentiments, the West and Japan will need to offset the likely increase of imports with their own exports. And that can happen only if emerging markets grow at a strong pace.

Second, the developed nations are counting on the growth of emerging markets to help finance pensions for their aging populations. The demographics are well known. People in the industrialized world are living longer, and there are fewer workers to support retirees. Public spending on pensions as a percentage of GDP in OECD countries is projected to soar from 8% in 1990 to more than 15% over the next 25 years. The easiest way to raise the financial returns on workers' savings is to look for a good portion of those returns in those areas where growth will be the fastest. In other words, it means looking for those returns largely in emerging markets.

Third, a slowdown in the growth of emerging markets may lead to destructive competition among governments in the developed world. Encouraged by the boom overseas, multinational companies, often backed by the financing and lobbying of their home governments, have already intensified their competition. Free and fair competition is to be welcomed, but the pressure on companies to win big contracts in emerging markets has led to bribery, violations of OECD trade-financing agreements, and escalation of political pressure by home governments on those awarding contracts. There is no sign that such competition will let up anytime soon, because the contracts in question are of the utmost national importance to countries suffering from high levels of unemployment. It is not an exaggeration to say that rivalries in this arena are becoming major wedges between countries that were allies during the Cold War. Left unchecked, these contests could create major international tensions.

There also are larger dimensions to economic failures in the developing world. Borders in a number of emerging markets are contested, and civil wars in others are possible. The economic strains caused by slower growth and a reversal of reforms could exacerbate tensions in any of these hot spots. Setbacks in economic development also would hamper the countries' efforts to invest in environmental protection. And continued growth is the only way to boost the livelihood of hundreds of millions of people who are living in miserable conditions.

What Can Be Done?

There was a time, just a few decades ago, when the industrialized countries thought they could build democracies and capitalist societies by injecting massive amounts of foreign aid, making trade concessions, and providing technical advice. Following great disappointments with programs such as the U.S. government's Alliance for Progress in Latin America, ambitions about directing such transformations have been greatly deflated. In the last decade, OECD governments have either reduced aid or redirected it toward the poorest countries. The emerging markets in the meantime have entered the mainstream of the world economy, linking their fates not to other governments' largesse but to private capital, foreign direct investment, and global trade. In 1990, for example, net financial aid to emerging markets was four times the flow of private capital. By 1996, that ratio was reversed: the flow of private capital was five times that of government aid.

If aid is not the answer, what can governments in the West and Japan do? They will need to manage their economies in a way that keeps the world economy buoyant and conducive to the expansion of trade. That will take some effort. The United States, the European Union, and Japan are all growing at a much slower rate than they have historically, and fiscal contraction is everywhere in vogue. Meanwhile, enthusiasm for trade liberalization seems to be waning; there is little appetite for new rounds of trade negotiations.

As for multinational companies, they should not be mere bystanders to political and economic change abroad. They can take steps to prepare for trouble. For example, they can apply higher discounts on earnings projections and diversify their activities rather than gamble on any one country or region. Managers can engage in serious contingency planning in order to cope with political and economic turmoil in emerging markets. They can improve their efforts to gather information on economic and social trends as well as on upcoming political decisions. In addition, they can work harder at collecting information about which local businesses are in the best position to survive a prolonged transitional period and might therefore make good partners. Executives can sensitize colleagues and board members to conditions in a particular country or region so that new developments do not take them by surprise and cause ill-advised knee-jerk reactions.

Astute human-resource management also can make a difference. For the most part, plenty of capital is available to facilitate entry into the emerging markets. What is often lacking are managers who know how to operate amid uncertainty and instability—managers who appreciate local politics and cultures and can build the relationships that not only enhance today's sales but also act as a safety valve in turbulent times. How to recruit, develop, and train managers who can operate in emerging markets is the key question. Companies should make their best effort to obtain highly adaptable men and women from the local scene. In addition, they should learn as much as possible about the mistakes that other multinational companies have made. Finally, it is essential that companies provide courses to their managers on the history and the political and economic institutions of individual developing countries.

Companies also have an opportunity, sometimes in partnership with Western governments or the World Bank, to assist emerging markets in their quest for progress. From Brazil to Thailand, countries need sophisticated technical assistance. Merrill Lynch, for example, is helping public officials in India devise sensible regulatory policy for stock markets. In China, Aetna and Procter & Gamble are helping local schools and universities train and educate leaders who understand how capitalist economies work. In Malaysia, Motorola and Intel have instituted training programs to enhance the skills of local workers. Companies that establish deep local roots and show, by dint of example rather than empty rhetoric, that their strategies are aligned with the long-term goals of the host country stand the best chance of prospering. At the same time, such companies help keep up-and-coming countries on the track of economic and political progress.

To be sure, no one can predict exactly how economies and regimes will develop. The emergence of so many capitalist economies within a few years is unprecedented and holds great opportunities—as well as equally great risks. In the 1980s, experts failed to see the rise of Japan or that of the Asian tigers. They failed to predict the collapse of Mexico, Brazil, and Argentina in the 1980s or the implosion of the Soviet Union. When it comes to the future of big emerging markets, however, enough warning signals are flashing. The penalty for not recognizing them will be severe.

PART

II

Europe and Asia

5
Managing in the Euro Zone

Introduction by Nicholas G. Carr

On January 1, 1999, 11 European nations—Austria, Belgium, Finland, France, Germany, Ireland, Italy, Luxembourg, the Netherlands, Portugal, and Spain—joined in a monetary union with the euro as their common currency. In one sense, the euro's launch could be considered a formality—just one more step on a long march toward economic convergence. Preparations for the monetary union have, after all, been going on for years, and the old currencies won't actually go out of existence until July 1, 2002. But in another, deeper sense, January 1 represents a moment of profound upheaval—the end of one economic order and the beginning of another. And it represents, as well, a moment of profound uncertainty. No one can say what shape the new order will take.

One thing is clear: the transition to a single currency will force managers to rethink many of their assumptions about doing business in Europe. The patchwork of national currencies has always made it hard for companies to think on the continental level. Shifts in exchange rates have often undermined even the most well-considered pan-European strategy. It was easier—and safer—to manage product and brand positioning, pricing and marketing, manufacturing and sourcing, finance and control at the national level.

With the arrival of the euro, the currency risks disappear. Pan-European thinking becomes not only practicable but essential. A company's efficiency and competitiveness will in many cases turn on its ability to streamline its supply chains, consolidate its production capacity, and create integrated product and marketing plans.

The introduction of the euro, however, does not mean that national perspectives will become unimportant. The monetary union will not be accompanied by cultural or linguistic union; the differences in national markets will remain profound. It does mean that companies will have to seek, as never before, the right balance between the national and the continental view.

To help readers think through the implications of the euro for their own businesses, we present five perspectives from European executives who have been wrestling with the consequences of the single currency. The authors represent a range of industries—from retailing to consumer products to heavy manufacturing—and present a range of opinions. Some of them see the arrival of the euro as a continuation of familiar trends in the business world. Others see the euro's launch as a point of discontinuity, a tear in the fabric of business. In combination, their perspectives help define the problems that the euro creates and bring into focus some possible solutions.

The Catalyst for a New Organization
by Francesco Caio

FRANCESCO CAIO *is the chief executive officer of Merloni Elettrodomestici, a leading European manufacturer of consumer appliances with headquarters in Fabriano, Italy.*

The introduction of the euro marks one more advance in the long and continuing process of integrating Europe's economy. In most industries, including the white-goods industry in which my company competes, much has already changed. Distribution channels have consolidated; a handful of retailers have gained larger shares of the market. Regulatory regimes have become increasingly standardized across the Continent. And the rise of pan-European media and communications has brought people and companies closer together and increased the appeal of international brands.

But while the operating environment has changed dramatically, the way most companies organize and manage themselves remains stuck in the past. Despite attempts to create more integrated organizations, business units still tend to focus on individual countries, managerial practices still follow long-standing national patterns, and cross-border processes remain rare. For European businesses to take the next big leap toward greater productivity and competitiveness, the traditional organizational structure needs to be rethought. European organizations need to become borderless.

It's in this context that the introduction of the euro is such an important event. The adoption of a common currency marks a moment of great disruption and discontinuity in European business and, indeed, in European life. Executives can take advantage of this historic opportunity to make fundamental changes in their companies' organization and culture and, perhaps most important, in their own leadership style. At Merloni, which has business units throughout the Continent, we have been focusing our efforts on spurring these kinds of changes. While we are paying close attention to the many technical issues the euro raises—in such areas as treasury operations and information systems—we are not getting lost in the fine details. We view the introduction of the euro as a platform for broad change.

Consider performance measurement and reporting practices. The establishment of a single currency makes it possible, for the first time, to establish shared, centralized accounting and administrative systems. Local management teams throughout Europe can have real-time access to information not only on their own performance but also on the performance of their sister companies in other countries. What's really powerful, though, is not the information itself but the information's ability to form a common language. Managers can use the performance data, all denominated in the euro, as a basis for exploring variations in performance, sharing best practices in all facets of operations and marketing, and building a unified management team with a shared perspective on corporate strategies and priorities.

Over the past year, we have been instituting technological and organizational changes that will enable us to capitalize fully on a common information base. We have established a centralized performance database, updated monthly, that all corporate and subsidiary executives can tap into in order to analyze sales and costs by product, brand, channel, and so forth. We also now circulate a daily, euro-denominated flash report on sales. And to make sure we put the information to the best use, we have scheduled regular videoconferences and teleconferences to bring corporate and national managers together to discuss the numbers.

The adoption of common accounting procedures throughout the European Monetary Union is enabling us to streamline our organization by centralizing many administrative functions that were previously performed locally. This consolidation not only saves money by reducing duplicated effort, it also frees our subsidiaries to focus their energy on sales and marketing. They can look outward, toward the customer, rather than inward.

The euro's dramatic impact on pricing also provides a catalyst for re-thinking some basic business practices. Because prices throughout the Continent will now be expressed in a single currency, they will become transparent to consumers—a shopper in Spain will easily be able to compare the price of a washing machine in a local store with the price of an identical or similar machine in France or Italy. As a result, coordinating marketing and product strategies across countries will become essential. To start this process, we have launched an effort to create a common, companywide format for marketing plans. This effort in turn requires a common view of the key elements of such plans. To attain this joint perspective, we have created small teams of corporate and subsidiary marketing managers that are visiting all our subsidiaries to develop an understanding of their particular needs and challenges and to prepare the ground for a shared set of marketing priorities.

The establishment of more consistent processes does not mean that national cultural differences are no longer important. In fact, in pursuing a more integrated organization, I have become more attuned than ever to cultural differences. People in different countries will continue to have different values and ways of thinking. They will continue to have conflicting views about the proper relationship between a head office and a subsidiary. And they will continue to speak different languages. These barriers are in one sense obstacles to cross-border cooperation. But in another sense they are the building blocks of a rich, diverse organization.

Pursuing a more integrated organization while respecting national identities requires a new style of management—one that's based on openness and participation. Here again, the disruption created by the euro provides an opportunity to shake up the status quo. At Merloni, we've recently created a multinational management board, consisting of 15 corporate and subsidiary executives, that will be involved in all major operating decisions. The meetings of this group are held in different locations throughout Europe, providing all our senior executives with a much broader view of the company. In the past, major decisions tended to be made by a small group of corporate executives, and the resulting plans would then be presented to the subsidiary managers at the head office. In addition to improving the quality of our decision making, the new management board stands as a potent symbol for all our employees. It shows that we are becoming a less hierarchical, more networked organization that values teamwork, joint problem solving, and the free flow of ideas.

The new stress on participation is not limited to just the top managers. We have launched a companywide human-resources program aimed at identifying our high-potential employees, no matter where they work, and moving them into the jobs that will give them the best growth opportunities, no matter where those jobs are located. Employees' opportunities are no longer limited by the region in which they work; they can move from location to location as their skills and development needs warrant. Merloni as a whole will benefit greatly from this program because it will help ensure that new ideas and perspectives circulate throughout our organization.

The euro makes many things possible. The analogy I like to use is the rapid rise of the Internet. Companies invested vast sums of money in proprietary data networks, and then the Internet came along—for free—and provided a global communication standard that rendered proprietary networks obsolete. Similarly, large European companies have spent a great deal of money on training, organizational restructuring, and change programs in their attempts to break down corporate borders, and now the euro comes along—for free—and lays the foundation for a true European community.

Soothing the Disoriented Consumer
by Jacques-Etienne de T'Serclaes

JACQUES-ETIENNE DE T'SERCLAES *is a partner of Pricewaterhouse-Coopers in Paris, where he is responsible for their global retailing practice. He was formerly the managing director of Euromarché, a French hypermarket chain.*

Over the past two years, the euro has been promoted heavily by the European Commission, by national governments, and by the press. Most of the communications, though, have been aimed squarely at companies and their managers; consumers have been given much less attention and much less information. Yet it is consumers who will determine the extent of the euro's impact. The way shoppers behave when confronted with the new currency will have immediate and lasting repercussions for retailers, manufacturers, and the entire European economy.

Right now, the indicators of consumers' likely behavior are troubling. Previous currency reforms, such as the introduction of the new franc in France in 1960 and the decimalization of the British sterling in 1972, have shown that alterations in existing price and wage levels disorient people, even if the alterations are superficial. When prices and wages are translated from existing national currencies into euros, the changes will be particularly dramatic. A pair of shoes that may have cost 600 francs in Paris will suddenly cost 100 euros. And Italian workers who have gotten used to taking home more than a million lira every month will suddenly find that they're no longer "millionaires."

Such changes will have a strong psychological impact. While the prices of everyday goods will in most cases fall in nominal terms, making consumers feel that products are cheaper, their paychecks will also be nominally lower, making them feel poorer. And because paychecks tend to involve bigger sums than price tags, the seeming diminishment in wages will tend to have the larger psychological effect. At the same time, merchants will need to adjust the converted prices in order to arrive at rational euro prices. A price that translates into, say, 44 euros will probably need to be either rounded up to 49 euros or rounded down to 39 euros. Consumers will know that such adjustments are taking place and will be suspicious that retailers are using rounding to cheat them.

At this point, no one can say for certain how such forces will play out. But disoriented and suspicious consumers are almost always conservative consumers—they put off purchases until they are able to regain their psychological bearings. So it seems a safe bet to say that the immediate impact of the euro's introduction will be a decrease in consumer demand, particularly for big-ticket items.

On the face of it, then, the euro looks like bad news for Europe's retailers. Not only will they have to cope with a confused and suspicious public, they will also incur major up-front costs in implementing the changeover to the new currency. They will have to train their workers to anticipate and answer customers' questions about the new currency. They will have to modify their computer systems and checkout machines. They will have to reprice everything in their stores and, in most cases, maintain two prices for each product—the new euro price and the old national-currency price. Margins in retailing are tight, and all these additional costs will directly threaten the bottom line.

But, as so often happens in business, big challenges also bring big opportunities. Precisely because the euro will create widespread confusion among shoppers, it will also offer a rare chance for retailers to reposition themselves in the marketplace. Consumers will seek out those stores that make it easy for them to cope with the new prices and that make them feel confident that they are not being cheated. Retailers able to gain the trust of shoppers will not only be better able to maintain their sales in the near term, they will also enhance their customer loyalty—and their market share—for the long term.

During the changeover period, successful retailers will likely engage in three characteristic activities. First, they will carefully monitor shoppers' attitudes and behaviors to pinpoint sources of confusion and suspicion. Second, they will invest in ameliorating consumer fears— through explanatory signs, pamphlets, and advertisements, for example, or by hiring additional clerks to answer questions. And finally, they will state—and fulfill—a commitment to delivering fair prices. They may, for example, launch advertising campaigns guaranteeing that they will always round down when converting prices to euros.

Of course, such programs add major costs. Fortunately for retailers, they'll be able to share much of the expense with their suppliers. At present, wholesale prices in Europe for the same item can vary by 20% or more from country to country. The switch to a common currency will lay bare those variations, rendering pricing transparent across the Continent. Retailers will be able to look throughout Europe for the best available prices, giving them considerable leverage over manufacturers and distributors. And, as the pricing pressure grows, manufacturers will have strong incentives to establish pan-European distribution networks in place of the old country-specific networks, creating more efficient pipelines and leading to even lower wholesale prices.

That doesn't mean, though, that retailers should simply squeeze their suppliers. In many cases, product and service innovation will be even more important than price cutting, and such innovation will require close working relationships between retailers and suppliers. Achieving rational and economical euro price points may require, for example, the reconfiguration of products. Beer packages may need to be redesigned to hold one or two fewer bottles, or a new, stripped-down model of a microwave oven may need to be introduced. Similar modifications may be required when regional variations in supply and demand continue to make regional variations in prices necessary. It would not make sense for an Italian pasta maker to offer the same prices in Spain, where pasta sales are relatively low, as it does in its home market, where sales are very high. Retailers and manufacturers will need to work together to create products that can be offered at prices perceived to be fair even if they are not the lowest prices available on the Continent.

In the end, the introduction of the euro promises to reconfigure two of the fundamental relationships in the European economy: the relationship of the consumer to the retailer and the relationship of the retailer to the supplier. As the transition proceeds, the risks to all three parties will be great, but the potential gains will be even greater.

The Coming Competitive Shakeout
by Manfred Gentz

MANFRED GENTZ *is a member of the Board of Management of DaimlerChrysler in Stuttgart, Germany, with responsibility for finance and control. In 1996, he was appointed to lead DaimlerChrysler's euro initiative.*

In October 1997, the future of the euro remained clouded in controversy. No one could say with certainty when the new currency would be introduced, which countries would join in the monetary union, or how a central European bank would be structured. Yet during that month, Daimler-Benz publicly announced that it would adopt the euro as its single corporate currency on January 1, 1999. As of that date, we said, we would use the euro in everything from our financial reporting to our advertising, from our computer systems to our employee communications.

We took a risk in making such a clear and early commitment to the euro, but we felt it was a risk we had to take. We believed then, as we believe today, that the establishment of a monetary union with a common currency would reshape the business landscape in a way that would make European industry more competitive and European people more prosperous. It would also open important new opportunities for DaimlerChrysler to be more flexible and creative in organizing and managing its businesses. The euro, in our view, was a key to growth.

The most immediate and obvious benefit of a single currency is that it dramatically reduces currency exchange costs. In the past, European companies were burdened by having to do business with 14 different currencies. The annual transaction costs for currency exchange in recent years amounted to DM 100 billion. Even if the euro did nothing more than eliminate those costs, it would provide a great boost to Europe's capacity for industrial expansion.

But the euro does much more than cut transaction expenses. By eliminating exchange-rate risks, it removes an obstacle to effective business planning. In the past, fluctuating exchange rates could undermine even the best-thought-out business strategies and quickly erase hard-won productivity gains. German companies were particularly penalized, as the deutsche mark was chronically overvalued. The elimination of currency risk will spur companies to dedicate far more management energy to formulating strategy, at both the corporate and business-unit level, which promises to lead to a new wave of business creativity and innovation throughout the Continent.

Finally, the euro will be a much more stable currency than the national currencies it replaces. The European Monetary Union will rival the United States in size and economic strength, making the euro attractive as a potential new reserve currency for the world economy. The greater stability and power of the European currency will make it easier for European companies to compete successfully in North America, Asia, and all other parts of the globe.

By committing to the euro in 1997, we sent a message to our employees, to our customers, and to European politicians and policy-makers that the adoption of a common currency was essential to the growth of our own company and of the entire European economy. We also sent a signal to our suppliers that, in order to continue to do business with us successfully after January 1, 1999, they, too, would need to begin the changeover to the euro.

While we have tried to be a leader in the push for a single currency, we have not been blind to the fact that the benefits of the euro will be accompanied by considerable costs and dangers. Many of the traditional ways of doing business in Europe will become untenable, and companies that are unable to adapt to the new realities will suffer greatly. Competition throughout the Continent will become much tougher even as it becomes much fairer. The shields and barriers provided by local currencies will disappear, and every company will be judged by common standards of operating efficiency, product and service quality, and marketing ability. Those that don't measure up will either fail or be acquired.

Preparing for this new era of competition requires every company to take a fresh look at the way it is organized and managed. The need for a pan-European perspective on products, prices, supply chains, and financing will conflict with the old model of organizing around country-specific business units. DaimlerChrysler, for instance, has a number of units that operate in individual countries. We are currently examining whether or not it makes strategic sense to manage some of these businesses more centrally. Before the euro, such organizational consolidation would have been more difficult. With the euro, it will be not only possible but, in many instances, essential.

Back in 1997, when we announced our commitment to the euro, we stressed that a single currency should be viewed not only as a challenge but also as an opportunity. That perspective has guided us in all our preparations since then. Approximately 1,500 of our employees are involved in euro-related projects, and we expect to spend DM 200 million on the changeover. That represents a big investment, but it's an investment that we hope will prepare us to compete effectively in the new landscape right from the start. As we enter the age of the euro, we are convinced that those companies that are best able to see and seize the new opportunities will gain the lion's share of the benefits.

Toward a New Corporate Culture
by L.M. de Kool

L.M. DE KOOL *is the chief financial officer of Sara Lee/DE in Utrecht, the Netherlands.*

Our company produces a variety of packaged consumer goods that are sold in retail shops throughout Europe and around the world. Much of our success over the years can be traced to our philosophy of decentralization. Our businesses are managed locally by executives who are given the freedom to make operating decisions based on their deep knowledge of the local marketplace.

For us, as for other highly decentralized companies, the launch of the euro presents an important organizational and even philosophical challenge. By bringing down barriers to cross-border trade—by making Europe in effect more homogeneous—the euro makes a pan-European perspective crucial for efficient and effective operations. The need for a pan-European view comes into direct tension, however, with our traditional, locally focused organizational and managerial structure. How we resolve that tension will to a large extent determine our success in the new Europe.

To understand why a pan-European perspective is so important, you have to understand how the single currency fundamentally changes the rules of marketing. In the past, similar or even identical products and brands often had very different positionings and price points in different countries. There were many good reasons for these country-by-country variations—different customer preferences, different supply-and-demand dynamics, different cost structures, different competitive forces, different tax schemes—and for consumers the variations were never an issue since they were largely hidden by the existence of local currencies with fluctuating exchange rates.

The euro suddenly makes all these price variations transparent—at both the wholesale and the retail level. Our trade customers as well as our end-consumers will demand that any differences in cross-border prices be rational and defensible. We may need to show, for example, that differences in the cost of doing business in two countries require us to set prices at different levels. Or we may need to show that performance differences among retailers in different countries warrant varying trade terms. The ability to provide such explanations will hinge on having clear pan-European product and brand strategies. Local managers will not be able to simply position and price a product based on their evaluation of local market conditions. Their decisions will need to fit cleanly into a broad European product strategy. Otherwise, retailers and consumers will rebel.

To accommodate these strategies, some companies are changing the way they're organized. They're moving to more centralized forms of management. At Sara Lee/DE, we're taking a different approach. We believe our decentralized structure remains a crucial source of competitive advantage. We are therefore focusing on changing our culture, not our organizational structure.

We are seeking, in particular, to shift the way our local managers view their roles within the broader company. To be successful, they will no longer be able to look at themselves as operating with complete autonomy; rather, they will have to see themselves as operating within a federation of businesses that, while independent, share common responsibilities. One of those responsibilities will be to work together to establish pan-European positioning and pricing strategies. Information sharing and consensus building will become more and more important as everyone focuses less on the differences among markets and more on the commonalities. In all cases, however, business strategies will be developed from the bottom up. The role of the corporate center will be to act as a timekeeper, ensuring that the company's efforts stay on track, and as a referee, helping to resolve disputes.

The glue of our new culture will be information. Business managers will need access to performance data in standardized form in order to have a common basis for conversation. In addition, because major European retailers will seek to do business with us on a continental level, our key account managers will need to have comprehensive information about our relationships with retailers across Europe. To ensure the availability of such information, we are accelerating a number of information standardization efforts, including the implementation of a European enterprise-resource-planning system.

Although Sara Lee/DE will not be changed fundamentally by the launch of the euro—we will continue to be guided by our decentralized management philosophy—the shift to a new, more cooperative culture promises to be a difficult challenge. Some of our people may not be able to shed the old ways of thinking and acting and, as a result, will find themselves without a place in our organization. But for those who embrace the new culture—who agree to converse, cooperate, and compromise—the future will bring new chances to excel.

Beyond the Currency Question
by Alan Spall and Richard Sykes

ALAN SPALL *is the group chief financial officer and* RICHARD SYKES *is the group vice president of information technology at Imperial Chemical Industries (ICI), an international coatings, specialty chemicals, and materials manufacturer based in London.*

The impact of the euro in its early years will be shaped by commercial forces. During the transition period from 1999 to 2002, national currencies will continue to exist, and companies will be free to choose which currency or currencies to use. The decision to use the euro will thus be driven by the demands and dynamics of the marketplace, not by legal or political fiat.

In this light, the fact that the United Kingdom is not adopting the euro makes little difference to the way we operate. In practical terms, the currency question is moot. Much intercompany business within the United Kingdom has long been conducted in currencies other than sterling. And where U.K.-sourced goods and services are bought and sold as part of wider European supply chains, there has always been a natural tendency to hedge currency risk by pricing in a common currency, such as the deutsche mark. (A similar phenomenon operates in the oil industry, where the U.S. dollar is the natural trading currency across the globe.) The euro simply provides a new, more stable common currency.

For all intents and purposes, then, ICI exists within the euro zone, and in formulating our responses to the new currency, we, too, have been guided by the marketplace. Because our businesses sell a broad variety of products in a broad range of wholesale and retail markets, we have not tried to impose a single corporate policy regarding the euro. Rather, we have given our business managers considerable leeway in deciding what makes sense for their products and operations.

The impact of the single currency on a particular product will hinge on the product's positioning. By establishing a common basis for price comparisons across the Continent, the euro will in effect penalize commodity products while rewarding products that have been successfully branded or otherwise differentiated. The market positioning of products in our Quest unit—fragrances and flavorings for the food and consumer-product industries—is based, for example, on their distinctive aesthetic and technical characteristics, not just on their price. Their differentiation provides a shield against the price-leveling effects of the euro. The advent of the single currency does not challenge Quest's existing strategy; it confirms it.

At the operating level, the euro provides new opportunities for consolidation and cost reduction. Our polyurethanes business, for example, has spent much of the 1990s restructuring its operations. Early in the decade, it abandoned its traditional, nationally focused structure and reorganized itself as a single pan-European entity. Achieving the

shift was difficult—it required the consolidation of manufacturing capacity, the streamlining of supply and distribution networks, and ex-
haustive negotiations with tax authorities in several countries—but it
enabled the unit to eliminate some 125,000 internal transactions a
year. The euro will now allow a further streamlining of the unit's European currency flows into a single cash stream. Rather than pooling
each day's cash in national currencies and within national borders and
banking systems, it will move to a single pan-European pooling, increasing the effectiveness and efficiency of its cash management. At
the same time, the single currency is likely to strengthen the unit's
productivity by speeding the pan-European rationalization of purchased services. We should see, for example, the rapid development of
competitively priced, end-to-end distribution services that ignore national boundaries.

While each business will be responsible for managing its own response to the euro, the challenge at the corporate level will be to ensure that the group maintains the right portfolio of businesses. To that
end, the launch of the euro is best viewed within the broader context
of globalization—as part of the ongoing trend toward open markets
around the world. The adoption of a single currency removes the historical barriers to European competition that were raised by local currencies and volatile exchange rates. In essence, it levels the European
playing field.

For a diversified, international manufacturer like ICI, the imperative
arising from globalization is to concentrate on those businesses that
can insulate themselves from ruthless competition. If you only compete on price, you're in big trouble. In recognition of this fact, ICI has
for several years been shifting its business portfolio away from its traditional commodity chemicals products and toward more specialized
goods that can be differentiated in the market. The euro makes this
shift all the more important—and all the more beneficial. By concentrating on differentiated goods, a manufacturer can reap gains on both
ends of its business. On the demand side, it will be able to protect its
products from price erosion. And on the supply side, it will be able to
capitalize on the increased price competition by purchasing commodity materials and services more cheaply.

For ICI, as for many manufacturers, the launch of the euro does not
represent a moment of discontinuity. It represents the continuation of
a trend—globalization—that has been reshaping the business landscape for years.

6
Asia's New Competitive Game

Peter J. Williamson

Many businesses venturing into Asia for the first time are surprised to find that their toughest competitors in the region are neither their familiar Western rivals nor well-known Japanese companies; they are lesser-known Asian companies based in other Asian countries. (See "The Emerging Asian Competitors.") And Western businesses are chagrined by their Asian competitors' use of an unusual but highly effective set of tactics and strategies—unorthodox approaches that often turn textbook management thinking on its head and help the companies that use them to enter and win share quickly in the region's still underdeveloped markets. What are the rules of Asia's new competitive game? Although specific strategies differ by industry, home country, and company culture, I have identified eight general rules that should be studied closely by Westerners intent on succeeding in the region.

It Is Better to Be Always First Than Always Right

Senior managers in emerging Asian multinationals argue that by being the first mover into markets, they can enjoy the advantages of having first pick of partners, sites, and other resources. First movers also are able to establish their products and brands quickly and cheaply—well before marketing channels become cluttered with competing messages. Although this strategy will lead to some mistakes, its practitioners point out that it gives them time to make corrections.

Latecomers may make fewer errors, but when they do err, they will lack the time to recover. As one CEO of a large Asian company puts it, "When you go in early, you're not always right, but you have time to correct. If you're a latecomer, you have to hit a hole in one. There isn't any time for detours and mistakes; unless you get it right the first time, you'll never catch up."

At the headquarters of Charoen Pokphand (CP) in Bangkok, for example, financial analysts and journalists have been lining up recently to learn how a company whose roots are in chicken feed has done so well operating in 26 of China's 30 provinces in businesses as diverse as motorcycles, petrochemicals, and telecommunications. Chairman and CEO Dhanin Chearavanont points out that CP's success is no overnight miracle: soon after China opened its doors in the late 1970s, the company began to explore opportunities. He says that his was the first foreign company to invest in both China's now-booming Shenzhen development zone and its Shantou region. Early entry allowed the company time to build its experience and capabilities while demonstrating that it was a reliable long-term investor that would ride out the sometimes volatile cycles generated by China's rapid pace of change. In around 1984, when a solid platform was in place, the company's growth was able to take off. Competitors that had waited until it became crystal clear that China would not turn back the clock were already far behind CP on the learning curve. The latecomers lacked a solid launching pad. They also risked being labeled fair-weather friends.

The Emerging Asian Competitors

The fast-growing and powerful new competitors in Asia can be classified into six basic groups. The first, the so-called overseas Chinese, typically consist of single families that own a mix of interests in publicly listed and privately held companies, with those interests often linked through complex cross-shareholdings. The overseas Chinese are based in Hong Kong, Indonesia, Malaysia, Taiwan, and Thailand. Many of the companies are diversified conglomerates that include an in-house bank and that form vertically integrated networks stretching from raw materials to distribution. From this base, they are building pan-Asian and global positions through overseas investments and networks of joint ventures and partnerships, often involving other overseas Chinese groups.

Representative Asian Corporations

Estimated group revenue (in billions of dollars)*

The Overseas Chinese

Salim Group (Indonesia)	11.5
Formosa Plastics (Taiwan)	9.5
Charoen Pokphand (Thailand)	9.0
Acer (Taiwan)	5.7
Siam Cement Group (Thailand)	5.5
Astra International (Indonesia)	4.5
Cheung Kong (Hong Kong)	4.0
Sun Hung Kai & Company (Hong Kong)	2.6
Perlis Plantations (Malaysia)	2.3

The Korean *Chaebol*

Samsung Electronics Company	83.8
Hyundai Motor Corporation	75.0
LG Group	65.0

Bumiputra Groups

Technology Resources Industries (Malaysia)	3.0
Renong Group (Malaysia)	1.7

Singapore Inc.

Singapore Telecom	2.5
Keppel Corporation	1.5

People's Republic of China Groups

CITIC Pacific	1.6
China Everbright Group	1.0

The National Champions

Sime Darby (Malaysia)	4.0
San Miguel Corporation (Philippines)	2.5

---

*Because they are structured as groups of affiliates, sometimes controlled by a family trust, few Asian groups consolidate their accounts. As a consequence, these figures have been estimated by aggregating the sales of listed subsidiary companies.

The second group is composed of Korean *chaebol*—family-led conglomerates such as Hyundai Motor Corporation, Samsung Electronics Company, Daewoo Corporation, and LG Group—which each boast sales of between $50 billion and $85 billion. They are diversified across an array of mainly manufacturing industries. The chaebol already have substantial manufacturing and distribution investments in the United States and Europe, to which they have been adding strategic stakes in high-technology companies. More recently, the leading chaebol have been investing heavily in Eastern Europe, Latin America, and Asian frontier markets such as Vietnam, where Western multinationals are less entrenched.

Third are a number of large business groups now being built by ethnic Malay entrepreneurs. (These are often dubbed *bumiputra* companies, *bumiputra* translating as "sons of the soil.") They include Technology Resources Industries, which built a mobile-telephone company in Malaysia capitalized at more than $2 billion and which subsequently acquired a controlling interest in the national carrier Malaysia Airlines for $720 million. The Renong Group, which won a $2.4 billion construction and operating contract for Malaysia's north-south highway, controls 12 other publicly listed companies, and recently acquired the State's pharmaceutical interests, is another example. Diversified Resources, a third example, is involved in financial services and construction and property development. It also holds a 32% stake in Hicom Holdings, which itself controls five listed engineering companies, including the one that manufactures Malaysia's Proton cars.

Fourth are the so-called *Singapore Inc.* companies, backed by the Singaporean government, which are active across Asia. Last year alone, the companies invested in projects worth a total of $19 billion. Some of the largest companies are those in which the government holds substantial equity stakes, including the Keppel Corporation, which is involved in shipyard and engineering facilities in the Philippines, property development in Indonesia and the Philippines, and joint venture investments in Vietnam and Myanmar; DBS Land, the property development arm of DBS Bank; and Sembawang Resources, a shipbuilding and engineering concern. Also, a consortium of Singaporean companies have a 65% share in the $20 billion Singapore-Suzhou industrial-township development project, which will create a new city for 600,000 people in mainland China.

Chinese state-owned enterprises compose the fifth powerful group in the Asian competitive game. The 1996 United Nations World Investment Report records that by the end of 1995, Chinese state-owned companies had invested a cumulative $20 billion directly in enterprises outside China. The International Monetary Fund estimates that China is now the eighth-largest source of foreign investment outflows in the world. China's flagship offshore vehicle, CITIC Pacific, is the tenth-largest company listed on the Hong Kong stock exchange. Among its many interests are a 25% stake in Cathay Pacific Airways, 28.5% of Dragon Airlines, 10% of Hongkong Telecom, and 20% of credit card issuer Manhattan Card in Hong Kong. The company also has stakes in power stations, infrastructure, shopping complexes, and industrial enterprises. CITIC Pacific is ultimately controlled by the China International Trust and Investment Corporation, itself chaired by Rong Yiren, vice president of the People's Republic of China.

Among the other important commercial arms of the Chinese government competing in Asian markets are China Merchants Holdings, China Resources Holdings, China Everbright Group (involved in financial services, manufacturing, property, and pharmaceuticals), Cosco (China Ocean Shipping Company), and Bank of China. The Chinese government also has invested in Australia, Canada, and the United States. Pulp and paper mills, North American forestry, steel mills, South African mining and manufacturing, and aluminum smelting and iron ore in Peru all have caught China's eye.

Finally, for the sixth group, there are a number of national champions from smaller countries that increasingly are competing on a pan-Asian basis. For example, San Miguel Corporation (based in the Philippines), with sales exceeding $2.5 billion, is the number one brewer in both the Philippines and Hong Kong. It also has substantial brewing interests in China, Indonesia, and Vietnam, as well as a string of wine-and-spirits, packaging, and food businesses in the Philippines. Sime Darby, based in Malaysia and the largest conglomerate in Southeast Asia, controls a network of 200 companies with 32,000 employees. The company has recently picked up its pace of growth and international expansion.

Each of the six groups brings its own distinctive combination of resources, capabilities, and networks of business and government relationships to today's Asian marketplace. With few exceptions, all should be prominent on every Western manager's radar screen.

To justify their early entry into markets, many Asian companies imagine a worst-case scenario, make sure they can survive it, and hope that, should the worst come to pass, an upside will develop later on. For Western-trained managers brought up on risk-adjusted net-present value, the idea of simply putting a floor under the nightmare scenario and then plunging in is anathema. But when the Indonesian corporation Raja Garuda Mas (RGM) decided to build a $250 million pulp plant at the depth of the worst recession in pulp prices for more than a decade, that was exactly its approach.

Looking to pioneer the use of fast-growing forests in northern Sumatra, RGM's subsidiary Indorayon asked, Would the plant be able to cover its interest costs if it were forced to sell its first output at very low prices (35% below normal) when the plant was due to start regular production five years later? Once satisfied that it could cover the interest costs, it went ahead. Today Indorayon is one of the largest and most successful pulp manufacturers in the world. CP applied the same logic when it first entered the Chinese market for processed animal feed in 1981. Having established that it could export the feed from its operations in Shenzhen to Hong Kong and still make a profit even if its China gambit did not work out, CP decided to proceed.

Asian companies enter so-called frontier markets in Asia—places such as Cambodia, Myanmar, and Vietnam—well before Western companies do. Between 1993 and 1994, two Singaporean companies established joint ventures that took over Myanmar's entire domestic and international aviation industry. Myanmar Airways International, which has been operating since August 1993, is 60% owned by Singapore's QAF (a diversified company whose core business is baking Gardenia brand bread) and 40% by the Burmese government. Backed by QAF's initial investment of $10 million, Myanmar Airways International is confident that it can obtain the landing rights to 37 countries as tourism and business traffic expand. Meanwhile, another Singaporean company, Techmat Holdings, invested $40 million in Myanmar's other major airline, Air Mandalay, and now owns 60% of the operation. While Western companies remain on the sidelines, these Asian companies now have a firm grip on the industry and its future potential for growth.

Equally significant is the fact that, by 1996, Taiwanese companies' cumulative investment in Vietnam was 50% higher than the combined investment of all European Union countries and three times higher than the total investment of either Japan or the United States. Meanwhile, in Cambodia, the ABC Stout and Tiger beer brands of the Singapore-based Asia Pacific Breweries have established themselves as market leaders. The $50 million joint-venture brewery being built near Phnom Penh by Asia Pacific Breweries (itself a joint venture between the Singaporean company Fraser & Neave and the Dutch company Heineken) was described by one of Cambodia's prime ministers as "the first great investment in our country." It will be the company's second brewery in Indochina, the first being a $42.5 million plant in Ho Chi Minh City, Vietnam.

Some observers see this penchant for being the first mover as an appetite for reckless gambling, but they are overlooking a number of factors. First, because emerging Asian competitors are close to the markets they serve, they have a capacity for rapid decision making and solid risk management that many Western companies lack. Second, as mentioned earlier, pioneers have time to make mistakes and to learn from them. Third, when a market is just opening up, partners and governments aren't in a position to demand hundreds of millions of dollars in investment or the latest proprietary technology. Therefore, it is more feasible to start with a low-cost bet as an early entrant. Later on, when the market is obviously established and investors are lining up to come in, the risks associated with each dollar of investment may have gone down, but the stakes required to play have often gone up.

Control the Bottlenecks in the Chain

By controlling the bottlenecks in the supply chain, companies gain the leverage to command a high share of the total available profit. Bottlenecks may occur when proprietary technologies, specialized skills, distribution networks, or raw materials are limited. If companies invest in enough capacity in controlling raw materials, components, or distribution, they can influence their competitors' volume growth and cost structures. This leverage is especially great in emerging markets that experience severe bottlenecks owing to their rapid growth.

The production of color television sets in China demonstrates the effectiveness of identifying and controlling bottlenecks in Asian growth. When it became clear that China's huge potential market for color television sets was taking off, foreign and domestic assemblers flocked into the business. Between 1986 and 1990, some 85 new assembly plants sprang up. But there was a severe bottleneck in the chain: good-quality cathode-ray tubes (picture tubes) were in short supply locally, their import was restricted, and the technology to produce quality tubes in efficient large-scale plants simply wasn't available to most of the new competitors. Just a handful of companies controlled the local production of top-grade picture tubes, one of them a joint venture between Japan's giant Matsushita Electric Industrial Corporation and a Chinese state-owned enterprise. That venture was large enough to supply not only its own needs but also those of its competitors. As the market surged, the venture enjoyed the luxury of being able to decide which of its competitors to supply with tubes—and at what price.

Taiwan's Acer is using a similar approach in the personal computer business. Taking advantage of low barriers to entry, new competitors have poured into the business of assembling personal computers, offering cutthroat prices and driving down margins. But this growing assembly capacity has created bottlenecks in other links in the industry's value chain: in sourcing key component technologies; in manufacturing critical components reliably at high volumes; and in brand building, logistics, and channel management. Acer's strategy is to focus its investment on those bottlenecks through the use of a combination of global brand building, advanced logistics and distribution, and highly efficient design and manufacturing of components. The goal is to participate in the most profitable parts of the chain and to control the key inputs into competitors' businesses simultaneously.

Build Walled Cities

At the core of most of the large emerging Asian multinational companies lies a walled city: one or more industries in which the company holds a dominant position. The Indonesian company Salim Group, for example, dominates Indonesia's cement industry, controls more than 60% of flour milling, and has an estimated 85% of the market in noodles. (See "Profile of a Leading Asian Conglomerate.") Charoen Pokphand of Thailand controls more than 50% of large-scale production of animal feed in its home country. Those positions are strongly defended against competitive incursions, often with the aid of exclusive licenses or concessions granted by governments. Walled cities provide a strong and reliable source of free cash flow for investment in international expansion and a base of experience from which to build up systems, staff, and know-how that can be shared across activities.

Profile of a Leading Asian Conglomerate

Soedono Salim (or Liem Sioe Liong) is an ethnic Chinese entrepreneur based in Indonesia who has built a pan-Asian business conglomerate. By reinvesting cash flow from dominant shares in flour milling and cement into other businesses, Salim has made his empire a force to be reckoned with by any company aiming to do business in the region. Businesses under the Salim umbrella include:

Indocement Tunggal Prakarsa
Largest cement producer in Southeast Asia.
Listed in Jakarta.

Indofood Sukses Makmur
World's largest producer of instant noodles.
Controls the world's largest flour miller.
Has substantial shares of the milk, snack food, and baby food markets in
  Indonesia.
Listed in Jakarta.

First Pacific Company
Conglomerate with international operations in trading and distribution.
Has telecommunications interests in China, Hong Kong, Indonesia, and the
  Philippines.
Has property and financial services interests.
Listed in Hong Kong.

Metro Pacific Corporation
Philippines-based conglomerate with interests in property, retailing, packaging,
  and consumer goods manufacturing.
Listed in Manila.

Berli Jucker
Conglomerate with interests in trading and distribution, glass manufacturing,
  steel production, consumer goods, and engineering in Thailand.
Listed in Bangkok.

United Industrial Corporation
Singapore-based property development company.
Has additional interests in shipping agencies, the manufacture of printed cir-
  cuit boards, and the distribution of detergents and consumer goods.
Listed in Singapore.

Bank Central Asia
Indonesia's largest private-sector bank.
Has more than 300 branches.

Indomobil
Indonesia's second-largest automobile assembler.

As trade barriers between Asian markets come down and the process of cross-border economic integration continues, however, the
nature of these walled cities is changing. Traditionally, walled cities

Exhibit 6-1   Where 30 Leading Asian Multinationals Do Business

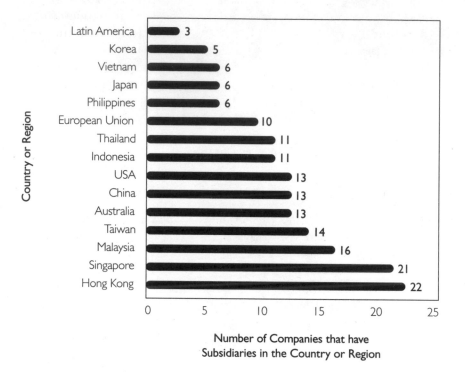

Number of Companies that have
Subsidiaries in the Country or Region

were built around dominant positions in a national home market. Now, however, emerging Asian multinationals have their sights set on the dominance of specialized, pan-Asian product segments. (See Exhibit 6-1 "Where 30 Leading Asian Multinationals Do Business.") Salim Group's plan to build a pan-Asian and ultimately global position in oleochemicals involves, for example, a $450 million facility in the Philippines, a $230 million plant on Batam Island off Singapore, major plants in China and Malaysia, the acquisition of 50% of the leading Australian producer of oleochemicals, and the purchase of a controlling interest in an existing operation in Germany.

Such actions are motivated by more than a simple desire for market share. The attitude is perhaps best summed up by the Chinese proverb "Better to be the head of a chicken than the tail of a cow." The objective is to choose a defensible segment defined by product group, technology, or geography (the head of the chicken) and to shape its future by setting the rules of the game and taking advantage of emerging opportunities. In a fortunate few cases, the defensible segment also will be large. But growth through dominance in multiple smaller opportunities will always be preferable to being a follower in a large business driven by others (the tail of the cow).

Bring Market Transactions In-House

The Asian preference for controlling the sources of supply, distribution, and even ancillary services has been a powerful force behind the high levels of vertical integration in the region and the formation of conglomerates. It reflects the fact that markets for inputs (such as raw materials and energy) and services (such as distribution, logistics, and financing) are poorly developed in many Asian nations. The billion-dollar Taiwanese food company President Enterprises, for example, has its own farms, food processing, one of the world's largest tin-plate operations for making cans, and an extensive in-house distribution network for its products—a structure that current Western management thinking would usually dismiss as unwieldy inefficiency. Yet President Enterprises is one of the fastest-growing and most profitable food companies in the world, with hopes of rivaling General Foods, Nestlé, and Unilever in the next decade.

With more than $4.5 billion in sales, Formosa Plastics, one of Taiwan's biggest companies, offers another good example. It is vertically integrated in the polyvinyl chloride (PVC) plastics industry from basic feedstocks right through to finished goods. As for conglomerates, consider the multibillion-dollar empire of Chinese Malaysian entrepreneur Robert Kuok, which extends into areas as diverse as sugar plantations, tin mining, the Shangri-La luxury hotel chain, TV broadcasting, and Hong Kong's major English-language daily newspaper, the *South China Morning Post.*

Vertical integration and horizontal diversification are prospering in Asia at a time when most Western companies are nearing the end of a long and sometimes painful process of refocusing on core activities. To support a high degree of focus on core activities, Western corporations must rely on suppliers and service providers to undertake those activities that are necessary but noncore. Many companies are reluctant to take on such noncore activities even when there is no suitable local source for them—an unwillingness that leaves their competitiveness impaired.

Emerging Asian multinationals, by contrast, actively seek involvement in upstream and downstream industries, either directly or through partnerships. They prize the greater security that comes from internalizing upstream or downstream activities: vertical integration can insulate them from the instability of fluctuating prices of inputs or intermediate goods. (For a detailed discussion of this topic, see Chapter 2 "Why Focused Strategies May Be Wrong for Emerging Markets.") More generally, in a world in which recourse to the law can be difficult and trust plays a pivotal role, these companies prefer to rely on an interdependent network, often bolstered by cross shareholdings and family or ethnic ties, than on impersonal markets.

As more and more Asian companies expand beyond their home nation, the desire to bring market transactions in-house is being reflected in the increasing number of cross-border Asian alliances. In 1996, for example, intra-Asian joint ventures outnumbered U.S.-Asian deals by almost four to one.[1]

Leverage Your Host Government's Goals

Asian governments typically see themselves in a long-term race to accelerate their economic development in the face of competition from highly developed economies on the one hand and from countries with lower labor costs on the other. Although they recognize the benefits of taking advantage of the "invisible hand" of the market to drive growth, they are far from convinced of the advantages of opening their markets to unfettered competition. Frequently the proverbial hand needs very visible guidance. Datak Seri Mahathir Mohamad, prime minister of Malaysia, put it this way in a 1996 speech given in Bangkok: "But for the right and the ability to regulate the economy in favor of locals in certain areas, while allowing and even providing incentives for foreign investment in other areas, it is doubtful that Malaysia would be as prosperous as it is today. . . . Without these powers to give unequal treatment, it is likely that Malaysia will become another basket case."

As a result of this mentality, Asian governments commonly award monopoly rights, concessions, and protection to companies whose investment commitments are carefully aligned with national goals. Emerging Asian multinationals are keenly aware of the advantages of aligning their strategies with those of their hosts. As one CEO of a large Asian corporation says, "Western delegations keep coming here talking about free trade and opening up our markets as if this must be good for us. Frankly, we aren't convinced. We have clear national goals to grow certain new, strategic industries. Asian multinationals often have a better understanding of how to align their investments with those goals."

Charoen Pokphand's successful entry into the poultry business in China illustrates the dovetailing of corporate and governmental goals. Since the late 1970s, the Chinese government has sought to maintain employment and provide economic growth in rural areas to stem the tide of people migrating to the cities. By creating income opportunities in the countryside, the government also wants to moderate disparities that might lead to political unrest. In addition, it hopes to improve protein intake and general health among the population. Given those policies, it is not surprising that more than 80 Chinese regions have welcomed the expansion of Chia Tai (as Charoen Pokphand is called in China) and its efficient poultry operations.

Over the past 25 years, industrialization of chicken farming has pushed up the per capita consumption of chicken tenfold and driven down the real (inflation-adjusted) cost of processed chicken by 65%. Urban consumers now get better nutrition and higher quality at lower prices, and China has a new source of exports that subsistence farmers could never have created. Western investors, meanwhile, have shied away from investing in agriculture, which has attracted just 4% of all foreign direct investment in China over the past 15 years. But with the right relationships established, Charoen Pokphand's agribusiness has spawned invitations to establish new ventures as diverse as motorcycles and telecommunications. The message is clear: making the government your silent partner is an important part of the new Asian game.

Organize Your Company Like a Network of Personal Computers

In ethnic Chinese capitalism, out of which the majority of the new Asian competitors have sprung, the extended family has been at the core of a cooperative business network. As businesses have grown, the core group has been extended to include loyal lieutenants who are treated as quasifamily for the purposes of managing more complex and dispersed corporate empires. Even today, such families as Hsu of Taiwan's Far Eastern group, Wang of Formosa Plastics, Li of Cheung Kong, and the Quek and Kwek families of Hong Leong Industries in Malaysia and the Hong Leong Group in Singapore are running their companies like family dynasties, often under a powerful patriarch. Even when the demand for funds necessitates public listings, these are engineered to maintain family control.

As the millennium approaches, business based on family ties is giving birth to a new type of organization. Instead of building either a centralized bureaucracy or a set of independent, far-flung subsidiaries to manage increasing complexity and geographic spread, Asia's new competitors are building extended networked organizations that rely on continual sharing of information among all their business units. In such organizations, information flows in many directions between nodes, each of which may act as an information supplier at one moment and a receiver at the next. The process of information sharing is similar to the process by which data flow in a network of computers as opposed to in a centralized mainframe computer system. This style of sharing is especially important for Asian companies, for which key technologies and market intelligence are relatively hard to come by.

One of the companies that typify this new style of organization is Acer, which is driven by the vision of its chairman and CEO, Stan Shih. The structure of Acer's client-server organization is familiar: strategic business units (SBUs), each responsible for a group of products, and regional business units (RBUs), each responsible for a geographic area.

At Acer, each SBU and RBU has independent capabilities. RBUs, for example, are not simply distributors. They have the capability to assemble a product that has been locally customized to meet local needs, augmenting standard technologies and components in what Acer calls the fast-food model of the computer supply chain. Shih believes that as they develop, RBUs should move from being wholly owned subsidiaries of Acer to becoming minority-owned affiliates of the network, thereby ensuring that they develop as truly local competitors. In addition to acting as clients for the SBUs' products, the RBUs act as servers, providing local market intelligence and informing the SBUs and RBUs of local best practices.

Maintaining excellent multilateral communication among different groups within a company becomes more difficult when the groups are linked to the parent company only by minority shareholdings. But according to Shih, the advantage in such situations is that each group must continually prove the worth of its role in the network, an effort that reduces the risk of complacency. If the benefits of the linkages do not justify the costs, the subsidiary organization will be spun off.

The primary Hong Kong affiliate of Liem Sioe Liong's Salim Group, First Pacific Company (FPC), offers a good example of successful management of a network of affiliates. The Liem investors hold a 59% controlling interest in FPC, a \$4 billion business that is listed on the Hong Kong and Amsterdam stock exchanges. Liem provided the initial capital commitment from which FPC acquired its core of international trading and commodities groups and financial services businesses. FPC serves as Salim Group's window on the world and is managed by an independent-minded, multinational management team led by Manuel Pangilinan, a Filipino with an M.B.A. from a top U.S. business school. As FPC developed, it built a major presence in the Asian telecommunications industry. The company was structured as a network of majority interests and minority participations, including Pacific Link in Hong Kong, IndoLink in Indonesia, SMART in the Philippines, and Escotel in India. Each acted as a client and a server within the network, despite the differing levels of FPC's equity stake and the diversity of the participants. Pangilinan has observed that codifying and putting to use the experience gained from dealing with all the partners will gain FPC a considerable competitive advantage.

Make Commercialization the Equal of Invention

A decade ago, the most advanced technologies were out of reach for many Asian companies. The Western technological lead was often large enough to guarantee sales—even if customers had to put up with high prices, poor service, or prototype-style products. Today the technological gap between Europe, Japan, the United States, and the rest of Asia has closed. Increasingly, leading Asian players are developing direct links with companies on the technological forefront. In recent years, for example, Korea's Samsung Electronics Company has acquired 51% of the CAD/CAM software company Lux (which is based in Japan) and 42% of U.S. personal-computer maker AST Research. In addition, Samsung has purchased two U.S. companies: Harris Microwave Semiconductor, which specializes in optical semiconductors and gallium arsenide chips, and Integrated Telecom Technology, which is a leader in technology for automated teller machines.

The emerging Asian competitors excel at bringing technologies pioneered at cutting-edge technology companies into development and production—and doing so at a very low cost. A spokesperson for a leading Taiwanese electronics company puts it this way: "We are not in a position to set standards and take huge risks, but we have the capacity to develop leading-edge products faster and at lower cost than our competitors here or overseas once standards are set." Sim Wong Hoo, chairman of Creative Technology in Singapore, expresses the same idea when he says, "We did not invent sound in PCs, but we managed to standardize sound in PCs."

What You Don't Know, You Can Learn

Because today's competitive game in Asia is won by the speedy, it is essential for companies to master new skills, understand new technologies, and build new capabilities more quickly than their rivals. In order to succeed, companies need to seek not only share of market but also share of knowledge—knowledge of cutting-edge products and processes.

Traditionally, industry analysts placed their Asian bets on the companies with the largest existing market shares or the biggest war chests of resources. Yet by those criteria, many of today's budding Asian multinationals would have been overlooked even recently, because their origins are quite humble. Although some have grown gradually, others have become leaders in their sectors with astonishing speed. In 1989, First Pacific of Hong Kong did not have any experience in telecommunications; today more than 25% of First Pacific's profits come from that sector. How was this achieved? First Pacific concluded that technical know-how was not the main barrier to entry in telecommunications; rather, it was learning how to navigate through the regulatory and competitive environments in Hong Kong, Indonesia, and the Philippines and how to build a base of business contacts. Because First Pacific already had experienced people and an extensive network in place, it had only to learn the "hard" technology before Western competitors learned the "soft" side of regulatory and industry dynamics. As it turned out, learning the "hard" technology was the more straightforward task—and that gave First Pacific an advantage in the race.

Competing on the basis of their capacity to learn is fundamental to the way Asia's emerging competitors do business. Sukanto Tanoto, chairman of the Raja Garuda Mas group in Indonesia, one of the world's largest wood-pulp producers, says, "They underestimated our learning capacity; originally we knew little about pulp, but we learn fast. We asked endless questions of our consultants and suppliers, so by the end of the day we knew—and adapted—it all."

An obvious response for Western companies faced with the new and often unfamiliar rules of the Asian competitive game is to enter into some form of joint venture with an Asian company. But as Asian companies have grown, they also have begun to rewrite the ways in which joint ventures are formed and managed, presenting Western competitors with yet another challenge as they try to gain a foothold in the fast-changing region.

Traditionally, Western companies formed joint ventures with Asian companies in order to gain access to local markets, and the partnerships were often unequal. The Asian partner provided access to local distribution and political networks. The foreign company contributed the products, systems, technology, manufacturing expertise, and the majority of the cash investment—and therefore expected to be dominant in the relationship. Today, having accumulated formidable stocks of capital, resources, systems, and technical skills, large Asian companies no longer need to play second fiddle in joint ventures. Not satisfied with being merely distributors and local representatives, they are seeking new roles in their partnerships with Western and Japanese companies.

Asia's new style of partnerships falls into one of two basic categories: *specialized infilling* and *operating partnerships.* In a specialized-infilling relationship, the Asian company already has a strong base in a business, often focused on the standard, mass-production end of the market. But for the business to grow its profits, it needs to expand its offerings and add more value—which requires access to specialized designs, systems, or specific technologies that can be used to fill in the gaps in existing capabilities. For such purposes, Asian companies seek partnerships with smaller Western or Japanese companies that have a unique technology or a differentiated product to offer. And whether its partner is large or small, Asian infillers will favor a licensing arrangement or other specific agreement over a full-blown joint venture, with the Asian company typically being the lead player.

In operating partnerships, the large Asian company's goal is to expand into new businesses, new geographical regions, or both. It requires a Western partner with a full range of technologies, products and systems, and extensive operating experience. The Asian partner will provide access to a pan-Asian network of relationships with suppliers, buyers, and other Asian alliance partners; experience in operating with different governments and market environments; and probably a significant investment stake. The operating structure is likely to be an ongoing joint venture in which the parties are equals.

Sime Darby, for example, has a strong base in electronics and basic manufacturing, and has pursued licensing agreements and other types of infilling partnerships with a number of small Scandinavian companies. By contrast, in oil, gas, and technical services—areas in which it needs partners with a depth of operating experience—it has entered into full joint ventures with major international players. Likewise, Charoen Pokphand and Honda have agreements whereby Honda provides infilling capabilities for some of CP's core manufacturing businesses. In brewing and telecommunications, however, where CP is a relative newcomer and needs to access both breadth and depth of experience and technology, it has operating partnerships—in these cases equity joint ventures—with Heineken and Nynex Corporation.

Increasingly, Asian companies also look beyond the borders of their home country and no longer restrict the ambit of their joint ventures or partnerships to the domestic market. This means that Western companies will more and more frequently face the challenge of selecting an Asian partner to work with in multiple countries. Rather than dealing with a series of subordinate local partners, they must learn to build strong cross-border synergies with a single Asian multinational partner.

Because established Asian players are now engaging in specialized infilling, often through licenses or technical agreements, Western companies are finding it more difficult to profit fully from Asia's ongoing boom. Licensing offers Western companies only a small portion of the new wealth being generated in Asia because much of the added value—and the profits—lie elsewhere in the overall supply chain. In order to make Asia contribute significantly to their company's bottom line, Western managers must decide either to bundle their technology and systems with operating experience that can add real value to an Asian partnership (thereby allowing their company to demand a greater share of the returns) or to go it alone as direct competitors in the Asian game. The former strategy places increased pressure on the employees of the Western company, who must learn to transfer their experience and knowledge to a new market. The alternative strategy—becoming a direct competitor—means deciding how, as a Western company, one can add something unique to today's new Asian game.

There is hope, however, because despite their formidable competitive strengths, emerging Asian companies have yet to catch up with their Western competitors in some critical areas—areas that can be a source of leverage for Western companies competing in the region. Many emerging Asian companies have brands that are poorly developed outside the boundaries of their home country—a problem exacerbated by the lack of attention being paid to marketing in some industries. Furthermore, because many Asian markets were dominated until recently by standard, mass-produced products, many indigenous companies have limited experience in handling high levels of variety, customization, and differentiation. And although some cutting-edge Asian companies such as Acer are learning to decentralize their operations, other companies in the region tend to be highly centralized and hierarchical—a fact that impedes their ability to build effective multinational organizations. Furthermore, although those same companies have access to the most modern technologies and can set technical standards, most companies are much more limited in that regard. Finally, many Asian companies possess poorly developed logistics, distribution, and service systems, especially across borders.

Those shortcomings should be a source of encouragement for Western managers intent on improving their performance in the region. But these managers must recognize that competing does not mean simply transferring technology, assets, and know-how into Asia. The issue is not Can we supply booming Asian markets? but rather How do we win share against an increasingly powerful set of locals with the inside track? Historically, many Western managers have been unwilling to consider the potential benefits of "unorthodox" Asian business tactics. But in the future, winning share in Asia will depend on understanding—and then changing—the unique dynamics of Asian industries. Western companies will have to set new rules of competition, reach previously excluded consumers, attack Asian control of value-chain bottlenecks, offer more product variety and customization, and leverage pan-Asian brands and operating scale. Regardless of whether Westerners try to go it alone or form partnerships with local companies; they will be forced to learn the rules of the new Asian competitive game. Then they will have to decide whether to keep or break them.

Note

1. Based on data from *M&A Asia/Asian M&A Reporter,* January 1997, p. 31.

PART

III

Corporate Strategies

7

The Right Mind-set for Managing Information Technology

M. Bensaou and Michael Earl

Although most executives in the West recognize the importance of information technology, their experience with it as a strategic business tool is often frustrating. Invite any group of senior executives in the United States or Europe to list their complaints about IT and they will typically identify five problems:

- IT investments are unrelated to business strategy.
- Payoff from IT investments is inadequate.
- There's too much "technology for technology's sake."
- Relations between IT users and IT specialists are poor.
- System designers do not consider users' preferences and work habits.

These problems are not new. Such lists have been circulating for the past 15 years, and companies have spent millions of dollars on consulting fees trying to resolve the problems—with little to show for their money. The problems are now so entrenched that top managers are adopting extreme attitudes and deploying extreme policies. Some outsource as many IT activities as possible, in the often mistaken belief that outsiders can manage the function better. Others cling to the vain hope that a new generation of "power users" will come to the rescue by developing creative software built around laptops and Internet browser software. We've even heard one executive declare that somebody should "just go ahead and blow up the IT function."

Why is there such confusion? Because information technology is at once exalted and feared. On the one hand, managers insist on elevating IT to the level of strategy; on the other, they recognize that integrating IT with business goals is only marginally easier than reaching the summit of Everest. It can be done, but it's difficult—and the cost of failure is high.

We believe that Western managers should back away from the immediate problems. They need to reflect on how they are framing the underlying IT-management issues. Too many executives in the West are intimidated by the task of managing technology. They tiptoe around it, supposing that it needs special tools, special strategies, and a special mind-set. Well, it doesn't. Technology should be managed— controlled, even—like any other competitive weapon in a manager's arsenal.

We revamped our own thinking in the course of a research project designed to compare Western and Japanese IT management. We were startled to discover that Japanese companies rarely experience the IT problems so common in the United States and Europe. In fact, their senior executives didn't recognize the problems when we described them. When we dug deeper into 20 leading companies that the Japanese themselves consider exemplary IT users, we found that the Japanese see IT as just one competitive lever among many. Its purpose, very simply, is to help the organization achieve its operational goals.

Where a Western CIO might spend time trying, often fruitlessly, to develop an IT strategy that perfectly mirrors the company's business strategy, a Japanese executive would skip that step entirely and base IT investment decisions on simple and easily quantified performance-improvement goals. Where a Western manager might go for a leading-edge application in the almost mystical belief that it would deliver competitive advantage, a Japanese manager would look at performance goals and choose the technology—whether old or new—that would help him achieve those goals. (See Exhibit 7-1 "How Japanese and Western Managers Frame IT Management.")

By now, some CEOs and CIOs may be shaking their heads in disbelief. In visits to Japan, they have found anything but a model to copy. After all, Japanese companies' expenditures on IT are perhaps half that of Western companies. Adoption of many modern technologies has been slow. The ratio of personal computers per capita in Japan compared with the United States, for example, is one to six, and computer use in offices is patchy. In short, the prevailing wisdom is that Japanese companies lag behind the West in IT and that Japanese

Table 7-1 How Japanese and Western Managers Frame IT Management

Issue	Western framing	Japanese framing
How do we decide what information systems our business needs?	**Strategic alignment** We develop an IT strategy that aligns with our business strategy.	**Strategic instinct** We let the basic way we compete, especially our operational goals, drive IT investments.
How will we know whether IT investments are worthwhile?	**Value for money** We adapt capital-budgeting processes to manage and evaluate IT investments.	**Performance improvement** We judge investments based on operational performance improvements.
When we're trying to improve a business process, how does technology fit into our thinking?	**Technology solutions** We assume that technology offers the smartest, cheapest way to improve performance.	**Appropriate technology** We identify a performance goal and then select a technology that helps us achieve it in a way that supports the people doing the work.
How should IT users and IT specialists connect in our organization?	**IS user relations** We teach specialists about business goals and develop technically adept, business-savvy CIOs.	**Organizational bonding** We encourage integration by rotating managers through the IT function, colocating specialists and users, and giving IT oversight to executives who also oversee other functions.
How can we design systems that improve organizational performance?	**Systems design** We design the most technically elegant system possible and ask employees to adapt to it.	**Human design** We design the system to make use of the tacit and explicit knowledge that employees already possess.

managers could learn from U.S. and European practices. Some Japanese executives believe that themselves.

A second look reveals that the prevailing wisdom is wrong. In fact, we found five principles of IT management in Japan that struck us as powerful, important, and universal.

From Strategic Alignment to Strategic Instinct

The concept of strategic alignment arose in the West because many organizations discovered they were developing information systems that did not support their business strategies. Development projects were often given priority according to technical criteria rather than business imperatives, and funding commonly went to projects sponsored by groups with the most clout—often the finance function—rather than to projects with the most strategic importance. The solution to these evils was to develop an IT strategy. Thus IT vendors, consultants, and academics invented and sold planning techniques that aimed first at discovering a company's competitive strategy and second at suggesting an IS portfolio to support it. Strategic alignment would then be assured.

Unfortunately, the goal remained elusive. Business strategies were rarely as clear as expected; IT opportunities were poorly understood; the organization's parts had different priorities; and the IT strategies that were eventually drawn up often seemed devoid of common sense. So strategic alignment still heads CIO agendas—and the consulting gravy train still makes frequent runs.

The Japanese executives we interviewed had never considered developing a special IT strategy. They are far more comfortable thinking instead about operational goals. Information technology, seen in that context, is just a competitive lever that helps them reach those goals; it is not fundamentally different from quality, customer service, or new product development.

Consider the case of Seven-Eleven Japan, a company that has invested aggressively and successfully in IT for many years. One could argue that the company's strong performance rests on its IT investments. Yet when we asked executives for the strategic logic underlying those investments, all we got was a long list of incremental improvements dating back to 1974. In each case, an operational objective that reflected a customer need had driven the improvement. Executives, looking back, could describe with great specificity how those customer needs were met. Thus the company has spent more than 20 years learning how to satisfy its customers better; we can label that process "strategic" after the fact, but that's not a term the company's managers would volunteer.

Since Seven-Eleven Japan's inception, founder Toshifumi Suzuki has been obsessed with convenience, quality, service, and the continual application of IT to capture customers' needs better. The company has built an information system that rivals any in the West for just-in-time logistics excellence and deep knowledge of the company's customers. Japanese consumers place a high premium on freshness, for example, and the company started making multiple daily deliveries as early as 1978, modeling itself on Toyota's groundbreaking just-in-time system. Now stores receive four batches of fresh inventory each day. The stores' fresh food changes over entirely three times per day, which allows managers to change their physical layout throughout the day, as the flow of customers shifts from housewives to students to salarymen.

This just-in-time system allows the stores to be extraordinarily responsive to consumers' shifting tastes. If a particular kind of *bento* (take-out lunch box) sells out by noon, for example, extra stock can be in the stores by early afternoon. If it's raining, bentos won't be in high demand, so the number delivered will go down—but the system will remind operators to put umbrellas on sale next to the cash register. This level of responsiveness is made possible by a sophisticated point-of-sale data-collection system and an electronic ordering system that links individual stores to a central distribution area.

Seven-Eleven Japan's early investment in those systems, and its constant additions to them, have paid off handsomely. The company is now the largest and most profitable retailer in Japan. Since its creation in the early 1970s, it has continually increased the number of stores, as well as each store's average profit margin and average daily sales, and it has reduced the average turnover time of its stock. Seven-Eleven Japan has been so successful that it recently took over its troubled parent, the Southland Corporation, owner of the U.S. 7-Eleven chain.

What is striking about this example is that investment in IT follows a logic of strategic instinct rather than strategic alignment—although in hindsight, alignment appears to be there. Seven-Eleven Japan's focus on customer satisfaction, product quality, and service makes sense to customers, suppliers, and store managers. These focal points drive not only IT investment but also logistics, sales, store management, and relationships with suppliers and wholesalers. Furthermore, the strategic instinct driving the investments legitimizes a process of ongoing learning in which a small initiative can evolve into an ever bigger one: bolder and better ideas emerge and are developed in a process of learning by doing; that is, by making strategy in small steps.

As we're framing it, strategic instinct almost always reflects a fundamental, down-to-earth source of competitiveness (usually related, in Japan, to operational excellence or customer knowledge). It combines the "what" and the "how" of competitive strategy—both defining strategic intent and envisioning its implementation. That source of competitiveness is the determining factor in decisions made throughout the company. It drives business development even when—as is often the case—there is no formal business strategy in place at all. And it is why IT is seen not as something special, different, and problematic, but rather as part of a fully integrated picture.

From Value for Money to Performance Improvement

Appraising the return on IT investments has never been simple in the West. Both costs and benefits can seem uncertain. Many companies have introduced investment management processes akin to capital budgeting, hoping to legitimize IT projects and ensure management commitment to them. In other companies, CEOs and CFOs periodically demand audits of projects, investigations into how much value IT investments have delivered, and one-off accounting of the total corporate expenditure on IT.

Such concerns about affordability and return on investment are neither irrational nor improper. After all, information technology should not be exempt from the pursuit of shareholder value, and in some industries the cost of IT is so high that it *is*, properly, a strategic question. However, the cumulative and pervasive value-for-money mind-set can be destructive. It can bias investment decisions toward cost-saving automation projects; it can deter ideas for revenue-generating IT applications; and it can lead to the dangerously late adoption of IT infrastructure improvements. It also carries an implicit message that IT is something to be exploited only when benefits are obvious and certain.

In Japanese corporations, IT projects are not assessed primarily by financial metrics; audits and formal approval for investments are rare. Instead, because operational performance goals drive most IT investments, the traditional metric is performance improvement, not value for money.

We recall an IT investment decision in a large Japanese food and drink company. Retailers were demanding the ever speedier replenishment of stock, so the company had to improve its supply chain management. In the course of reexamining their logistics, group managers concluded that they couldn't solve the problem without a new information system. Once they'd reached that conclusion, the next steps were never in doubt. The managers involved—the directors of logistics, supply and purchasing, IT, and planning—simply developed new system requirements and approved the expenditure. There was no concern about whether the new project had been part of a capital budget or IT plan, or whether it met a threshold rate of return. If supply chain improvement was vital, so was the system: end of story.

The fact that investment decisions are not financially based doesn't mean they're fuzzy. In many companies, the operational performance goals are articulated with fine-grained specificity. Seven-Eleven Japan has translated its focus on convenience, quality, and service into five areas of special concern: item selection, item-by-item control, new product development, quality or freshness of products, and value-added services. If an IT investment supports improvement in one of those areas, it not only justifies itself but also can be validated easily by operational efficiency measures.

The Japanese preference for continuous improvement and incremental advances means that a lot of IT spending comes in small steps. However, major investments are also driven by broad operational-performance goals. Matsushita, for example, has been pursuing order-of-magnitude reductions in the lead times for product development and for order taking and fulfillment. Those operational goals recently drove an investment by the company of 32 billion yen in a telecommunications network that will link 140 overseas production sites and sales offices by 1999. The goals also include financial targets that the networked businesses are expected to achieve.

What underpins this performance-improvement principle is the idea of *gemba*, or support for people on the front line, whether they are in manufacturing, supply, or sales. The front line is where investment can be made most effectively—investment in IT or training or simply in the tools to do the job. Such a core value makes the justification of systems intuitive. Very often a business case is never explicitly documented or argued: a gemba case is obvious. Only one sort of audit follows: Are we improving performance as targeted and, if not, what must we do?

The principle of performance improvement is not so easily applied in the domain of organizational computing. But, as we shall see, another Japanese principle comes into play there.

From Technology Solutions to Appropriate Technology

Executives in the West often complain about the phenomenon of "technology for technology's sake." Indeed, some IT vendors and consultants pride themselves on offering "technology solutions." But most would-be customers want to know what the problem or opportunity is first.

The dynamics of the technology-solutions philosophy are clear. Vendors need to create markets for new technologies. IT specialists want to try out the latest and greatest technology toys. Users can't necessarily judge what's possible until they use a new technology, so they depend on the judgment of IT specialists. And sometimes, especially in the United States, people are proud of adopting new technologies ahead of the rest of the world. That bias can lead to wonderful results: the growth of the Internet and the World Wide Web, for example. But it has a dark side, too. Most executives can recall more than one system that was too advanced for the needs of the company and other systems that were redesigned even though they were still perfectly adequate.

So on the one hand, we see IT pioneers in the West introducing and adopting leading-edge technology that often yields early-mover advantages. On the other hand, we see unnecessary investments and many new developments in technology that promise a lot but deliver little. It is a curious mix but may be the inevitable outcome of a society devoted to technological advancement.

Japan has an equally curious mix. The Japanese run some of the best-designed, most technologically advanced factories in the world. Managers and scholars from around the world visit these factories to observe legendary uses of advanced manufacturing technology, robotics, computer-integrated manufacturing, and flexible manufacturing systems. And, as we have seen, some Japanese retail companies are extremely sophisticated in their collection and use of data on customer needs and habits. Increasingly, manufacturing companies are, too. Kao, the leading Japanese cosmetics and soap company, stores all customer complaints (and the advice the customers received) in a database; that database is a major source of ideas for engineers in the new-product-development group.

Most Japanese offices, on the other hand, are low tech. PCs are scarce, and they're outnumbered by "dumb" terminals; decision-support and executive-information systems are mostly alien concepts; and e-mail and groupware adoption is slow. There are some readily apparent explanations for those absences. Until recently, computers have not coped well with the kanji characters of the Japanese writing system. Most managers are not used to keyboards. And the IT vendor marketplace has not been open to international competition. We would argue, however, that there is a more important underlying reason.

The Western bias is toward technology for technology's sake. The Japanese bias, in contrast, is toward adopting appropriate technology. Managers identify the task to be accomplished and the desired level of performance; then they select a technology that will help the company achieve that level in a way that suits the people doing the work. Once again, the operational goal drives the choice of technology. Three cases demonstrate the point.

In factories, operational goals can often be achieved best through the aggressive use of advanced manufacturing technologies—often, but not always. A typical Japanese factory has a lot of high-tech areas alongside a few low-tech islands where human judgment is still needed.

NSK, one of the world's leading bearings and auto components manufacturers, is a good example. It has highly integrated technology systems, but certain areas are still low tech. For simulation and analysis in component design, engineers use the company's flexible-engineering information-control system and an array of databases and expert systems. But the engineers themselves develop and approve final designs. Similarly, the company's salespeople can search a database and narrow the range of products that they might suggest to a customer, but they make the final judgment about what to offer. (Once they've made that decision, they can immediately obtain a blueprint of the appropriate product design from a fax machine connected to the expert system.) And quality engineers use handheld terminals to monitor quality data, which is automatically recorded from in-line sensors and inspection machines. Although they are well supported technically, they are still walking around the factory, using their eyes and ears to assess progress. A high-tech solution would have been to place the engineers in a separate room, monitoring quality data remotely. All these IT systems are linked to a budgetary control system; during board meetings, senior executives can access the various databases from on-line terminals.

In nonfactory settings, the Japanese use advanced or even conventional technologies more tentatively. In a study of IT use in buyer-supplier relations in Japan and the United States, one of the authors of this article found that parties from both countries exchanged order and quotation data in electronic form. However, U.S. companies used electronic data interchange (EDI) extensively, whereas most Japanese companies still relied on tapes, disks, and courier mail. The Japanese companies had judged the use of EDI to be premature. They wanted to construct effective partnerships first, and then consider how IT could help. In other words, they didn't assume that advanced forms of electronic communication were advantageous.

Finally, consider one technology tool that's often used in Western companies—executive information systems—and another that has been advocated for years—decision support systems. In Japanese corporations, few executives use these systems directly. Why? Because they don't fit well with how decisions get made in Japan. Typically, a top manager in Japan will float an initial idea to a broad group of people throughout the company. They will then discuss and analyze the idea until a consensus about its value emerges. Some employees may raise objections, and their criticisms will lead to modifications in the original idea. Other critics may be co-opted with promises of future concessions. These informal negotiations are a highly valued, central part of Japanese decision-making culture. The extensive discussion period means that executive-information and decision-support systems have so far not been appropriate technologies in Japan.

Organizational decision making in Japan is starting to change, however. Many office settings have not felt much market pressure to change until recently. World-class competitors could overlook low office productivity because they were growing so quickly and because they faced little competition from imported goods. In practice, the result has been far muddier operational goals in white-collar settings than in factories.

Economic and competitive pressures have focused managers' attention on white-collar productivity. As a result, technology is replacing people in some aspects of information processing. And major electronics companies such as Toshiba, Fujitsu, and NEC have introduced electronic networks to speed up decision making. The networks enable managers to share information more efficiently, to send and receive documents and proposals, to schedule meetings, and to vote on proposals. But serious efforts are being made to preserve the face-to-face discussions between key stakeholders.

From IS User Relations to Organizational Bonding

Although the IT function in Western companies is often relatively decentralized, users frequently perceive it as centralized. They think that specialists are remote and have too much control. And they complain that IT people know nothing about the business. "By the time we educate the IT people about the real world, they've left the company," said one line manager we know.

Indeed, the labels "user" and "specialist," while accurate, also help create two cultures. Differences in vocabulary only exacerbate the divide. As one European CIO remarked to us recently, "When an executive says 'Okay, show me how we can use IT strategically,' the IT folks start talking about data architecture."

Western companies have introduced bridging devices to solve these problems, with mixed results. People who serve in liaison roles that are designed to close the gap often end up as middlemen who only keep the two sides apart. Creating hybrid managers—people who are knowledgeable about business and IT—sounds appealing, but the hybrids soon discover they're stuck in a career cul-de-sac.

Once again, a first look at the organization of IT in Japan seems far from promising. The IT function has low status; it is not a place in which to make one's reputation. Career IT specialists tend to be regarded as engineers rather than businesspeople. Often the IT department is run as an "offshore bureau"; that is, it is not structurally integrated with the rest of the organization. And there are few high-profile CIOs.

On closer examination, however, we found four characteristics of Japanese companies that encourage integration, or organizational bonding, between IT and the business.

First, many Japanese managers spend two or three years, usually against their wishes, in an IT department as part of a job rotation scheme. The postings help them develop knowledge that will prove useful in subsequent jobs. They provide managers not only with technological know-how but also with knowledge about how to get things done in IT and about who can help with what. The rotations can be seen as an institutionalized version of Western companies' creation of hybrid managers.

Second, when IT projects are in progress, IT specialists are usually colocated with the users and managers for whom the application is being developed. Colocation improves communication and understanding between users and specialists; it is another way of encouraging bonding.

Third, the senior executives in charge of IT are usually in charge of one or two other functions as well—often finance and planning. This practice prevents IT from being isolated within the company. We recall the case of a Japanese beverage company that urgently needed a new order-processing system. No elaborate planning study was done, no formal capital-expenditure proposals were drawn up, and there was no bargaining between the interested parties about who should pay for what. The directors of IT, finance, and planning sorted it out very quickly. How? They were the same person. Many conflicts between departments can be avoided when senior managers have overlapping responsibilities; integration and bonding can occur quite naturally.

Finally, Japanese IT departments rely heavily on their vendors for advice. Japanese companies seldom use off-the-shelf packaged software; they usually develop applications in-house, working closely with a dedicated vendor. For example, Seven-Eleven Japan has since its creation entrusted the software and hardware design of its integrated information system to the Nomura Research Institute, the second-largest systems integrator in Japan.

Such long-term relationships can constrain experimentation and the adoption of radically new and diverse technologies. But they ensure a committed partnership on large projects, and they help users and specialists develop a mutual understanding of appropriate technologies. The relationships are another means of organizational bonding.

We stress organizational bonding because none of the distinguishing features noted above is structural in nature. That is, they do not depend on setting up committees, creating new liaison roles, or tinkering with the degree of centralization—all devices that are favored in the West. The focus is on proximity, cross training, shared understanding, and relationships. And once again, the Japanese are not treating IT as something that requires special handling.

From Systems Design to Human Design

In the West, system development tends to focus more on the business process being supported or redesigned than on the people who will use the product. Perhaps as a result, people often find new systems difficult to use, counterintuitive, and annoying. Moreover, if you asked people the radical question, How much have IT systems increased job satisfaction? you'd soon learn that IT systems have deskilled and routinized far more work than they have enriched. Our point is not that job enrichment should be the goal of IT development, but rather that specialists often leave no room in their systems for human judgment or understanding when they become overly focused on technological "solutions."

In Japan, building systems is not an end in itself; enhancing the contribution of people is the higher goal. That's why the principle of "human design" is central to the way the Japanese use IT. If a system automates work that people can do better, it is not considered a good system—and the potential for that result is raised explicitly when an IT project is under consideration.

Consider again the question of whether decision support technologies should be used in organizational decision making. Two aspects of Japanese organizational behavior militate against the practice. The first is the belief that broad participation and consensus not only facilitate commitment but also produce better decisions.

The second is the Japanese reliance on social and experiential processes of knowledge creation.[1] Japanese executives are deeply aware of the importance of tacit knowledge—knowledge that cannot be fully communicated with words and numbers, such as things we don't know we know and things we can't easily explain. Information technology, of course, is much better suited to processing explicit knowledge than tacit knowledge. That's why, when difficult problems arise in development projects, Honda uses brainstorming camps rather than "data mining," computer-aided design, or simulations.

Matsushita's process for developing an automatic bread-making machine illustrates the Japanese awareness of tacit knowledge. The project development team found that when they x-rayed and analyzed dough kneaded by a master baker, they didn't learn much. Rather than continue down an unpromising technological path, team members—led by the head of software development—apprenticed themselves to the best master baker in Osaka. By observing the traditional craft of kneading and twisting dough, and by learning it themselves, they discovered the secret of making good bread.

Because of this very Japanese concern for capturing human knowledge—and also, incidentally, commitment—the process of system design usually involves nonspecialists. When production systems at NSK were being designed, the president announced that the heads of sales, production, and design, as well as the plant managers, would be required to help design and promote the system.

We believe that Seven-Eleven Japan has been so successful not because of its IT systems (though they are world class) but because of its substantial investment in training and supporting front-line workers in the use of those systems. Chairman Suzuki is very clear about the paramount importance of using information intelligently: "It is not enough to exchange information. The information has no value unless it is understood and properly integrated by the franchises and allows them to work better."

Seven-Eleven Japan's franchise operators receive far more training about inputting and interpreting data than do store managers in any other franchise system we know of. In addition, the company has 1,000 operational field counselors who provide the human backup to the distribution system. Each counselor supervises six or seven stores, which he visits two or three times a week to exchange information, criticism, and suggestions. Through this face-to-face contact, franchise operators learn to analyze local data, develop ideas about what they should be ordering, and test their ideas against corporate headquarters' suggestions. The company spends more than $1 million per year on weekly meetings that bring all the field counselors together in Tokyo.

Respect for people also explains why Japanese companies use extensive prototyping and opt for continuous improvement in systems development: Both approaches require the subtleties of human judgment. Both allow systems to be adjusted so that they fit job and work design better. And both are more responsive to user ideas and suggestions than is conventional, formal system development.

It's interesting to remember that Toyota's influential quality circles began as a grassroots movement: factory workers were simply trying to improve the quality of their work life. That their movement was encouraged and co-opted by management suggests how central people are in this incremental approach to system design. Indeed, the subsequent TQM movement may have influenced Japan's evolutionary approach to systems design.

The philosophy that underpins the principle of valuing people is *chowa*, or harmonization, which is a powerful idea in Japanese culture. In the specific case of managing IT, chowa means that technology should fit the people using it rather than the other way around.

Can the West Really Reinvent IT Management?

When considering the five principles outlined here, executives may say, "But we do some of this already. Is this really so different?" We agree that some Western companies are attempting to put into practice some of the ideas we have explored. For example, many companies have thrown out long-term IS planning. And many IT professionals could tell you that their biggest success came at a time when most of the organization's IT resources were focused on a single project that everyone believed was critical to the business. Very often the project started in a small way and grew because of its obvious value. But such experiences have not developed into a principle of strategic instinct. Indeed, many companies still wonder what sort of IT strategy-making process they should adopt.

Some companies do take nonfinancial dimensions into account in IT project appraisals; others admit to unanticipated benefits from some of their IT investments. However, most find it hard to break out of the value-for-money mind-set or to realize that some IT investments have a straightforward support role in business; namely, enabling performance improvement.

Many companies would claim that they avoid leading-edge technologies, stating that "leading edge is bleeding edge." However, the principle of appropriate technology is subtly different: sometimes the most advanced form of IT makes sense, and sometimes simpler, older forms will do. Sometimes high tech should cohabit with low tech.

Other companies continue to experiment with bridge building between the IT function and IT users. What they do not usually recognize is that the integration of IT with the organization has to be from top to bottom and systemic, not structural. In other words, bridges will collapse as long as there's one IT culture and another business culture, but the principle of organizational bonding will keep them strong and stable.

Western companies have tried experimenting with sociotechnical systems development, with ergonomics and "user friendliness," and with less technocratic approaches to information processing. However, those approaches lack a key ingredient: they treat people only as users of systems and do not value them as complements—and even alternatives—to systems.

Another challenge to our ideas is that the Japanese management of IT is culturally specific. Of course, it's not wise—it's probably not possible—simply to overlay practices from one culture onto a very different one. Western managers learned that lesson in the early 1980s, during their first attempt to imitate Japanese manufacturing techniques. However, it is possible to learn from other cultures if it's understood that first some translation is required. Ultimately, Western managers learned a great deal from Japanese manufacturing, but first they needed to differentiate between underlying principles that can be transferred (like lean manufacturing) and culturally specific practices that may or may not work in a different setting (like daily quality circles).

Indeed, we believe that the vogue for benchmarking and copying best practices can be dangerous. Business practices are heavily influenced by national culture, industry traditions, and company-level characteristics. It makes more sense to focus instead on *best principles*. If you understand why a practice works and what distinguishes it fundamentally from conventional practice, you can probably identify the underlying principle involved. That universal idea can then be transported and applied to fit a local context. Certainly the five principles described here can be transferred. There's nothing culturally specific about choosing appropriate technology or about developing an IT system to support well-articulated operational goals.

It's tempting to think about our five IT-management principles at a cultural or national level. "Americans value individualism, so appropriate technology in the United States will support independent decision making," for example. However, we suspect that the principles can best be interpreted, adopted, and customized at the company level, because that's where competitive strategy is developed and played out.

We set out, very simply, to compare Japanese and Western IT-management practices. To our surprise, we found principles—strategic instinct, performance improvement, appropriate technology, organizational bonding, and human design—that we believe are hidden strengths in many Japanese corporations. And these strengths should serve them extremely well as they search for new levels of competitiveness.

At the moment, Western managers are not inclined to think in terms of learning from Japan—or anywhere else. But that could be a grave error. All appearances to the contrary, this may be a more dangerous time for U.S. businesses than it is for Japan's. The Japanese know they have to find new ways to compete. U.S. managers, in contrast, are in danger of supposing they'll be on top of the international heap forever.

It's time for senior managers to regain control of technology in their companies: to abandon the dangerous idea that IT requires special, technocratic means of management. As many executives have begun to suspect, the IT management traditions that have evolved over the last 40 years are flawed. Powerful IT vendors, management consultants, and specialists developed those ideas and profited from them. In the end, even those constituencies have begun to doubt their gospels. It is time for Western companies to rethink how they manage technology. The principles underlying Japanese practice provide an excellent foundation.

Note

1. This concept and the illustrations that follow are drawn from Ikujiro Nonaka and Hirotaka Takeuchi, *The Knowledge-Creating Company* (New York: Oxford University Press, 1995).

8

Group Versus Group: How Alliance Networks Compete

Benjamin Gomes-Casseres

Collaboration in business is no longer confined to conventional two-company alliances, such as joint ventures or marketing accords. Today we see groups of companies linking themselves together for a common purpose. Consequently, a new form of competition is spreading across global markets: group versus group.

Call them networks, clusters, constellations, or virtual corporations, these groups consist of companies joined together in a larger, overarching relationship. The individual companies in any group differ in size and focus, but they fulfill specific roles within their group. Furthermore, within the network or group, companies may be linked to one another through various kinds of alliances, ranging from the formality of an equity joint venture to the informality of a loose collaboration.

A prime example of such an alliance group was built between 1987 and 1991 by Silicon Valley start-up Mips Computer Systems, which has since been acquired by Silicon Graphics. Mips developed a huge network of alliances to promote its new microprocessor technology. And networks exist in other industries, too, where they are often created to maximize joint volume in order to exploit economies of scale. For example, Swissair's alliances with Delta Air Lines, Singapore Airlines, and SAS sought to increase bookings on transatlantic and European-Asian flights and to combine the procurement and maintenance of airplanes. In automobiles, General Motors' network of partners, which includes Toyota, Isuzu, Suzuki, and Saab, competes globally with a group of Ford partners, consisting of Nissan, Mazda, Kia, and

Jaguar. In the multimedia field, an array of alliance groups has sprung up in the past two years as the computer and communications industries have converged. Computer companies have joined with consumer electronics companies, cable TV operators, telecommunications providers, and entertainment companies to develop new products and services.

Are alliance groups the wave of the future or a passing fad? Have they actually helped group members compete more effectively?

Too little empirical evidence exists as yet to answer these questions with complete assurance. But we do know enough, based on the experiences of the pioneers in group-based competition, to examine the questions that senior executives should be asking themselves before they organize, dive into, or decide to forgo these alliance networks. Networks offer obvious advantages to their members. However, those advantages come with costs that may not be so obvious.

The Growth of Group-Based Competition

How did this idea of networks of alliances arise? For one, there is the influence of the global economy. In the 1950s and 1960s, companies based in the United States were for the most part unchallenged in their technology, marketing skills, and ability to manage large-scale businesses. In the global environment of the 1980s and 1990s, however, companies all over the world have matched or approximated the achievements of those U.S.-based companies. The change is dramatic in industries like computers, where newcomers can ride the wave of new technologies, and in mature industries like automobiles, where new entrants can adapt more readily to changing market demands. As a result, it's essential for U.S. companies to develop relationships with peers abroad—if only to remain abreast of important external developments and perhaps to influence them.

Another recent factor favoring the formation of alliance groups is the growing complexity of products and services, and of their design, production, and delivery. It's the rare product today that doesn't contain components incorporating wholly distinct and specialized technologies. It's the rare service today whose performance doesn't combine several specialized skills. And it's the rare business today that doesn't rely for its raw materials, marketing, or distribution on people with diverse technological or market-specific skills. Finding and assembling all those assets under a single roof is difficult, to say the least. Often, it's not even desirable. Because the greatest advantages of specialization and of scale are often realized at the component rather than at the system level, companies may do best to focus on the component level while forming ties to one another in order to manage system-level interdependence.

In response to these changes in the competitive environment, companies have created networks of alliances in order to command competitive advantages that individual companies or traditional two-company alliances cannot. Networks have distinct advantages in three kinds of situations in particular.

First, network competition is growing in battles over technical standards. In emerging industries, various technologies may contend for market share. The outcome of this battle often depends on the number of companies adopting each technology. Alliance networks can help contending companies promote their technologies and gain the critical mass required to persuade more businesses to use their design. To do that, they must persuade enough "sponsors" to join their group. They also count on a snowball effect to help them: the more machines they sell incorporating their technology, the more software will be written for that technology, which in turn will help sell more machines, and so on.

Second, the increasing importance of global scale has created a fertile ground for alliance networks. Linking with local companies in various markets may help a company spread its costs over larger volumes or give it access to skills and assets in different nations. While networks of wholly owned subsidiaries can also be used, regulatory barriers or the need for rapid expansion sometimes preclude this option. Consider alliance groups in the airline industry. Deregulation in the United States, the rise of the hub-and-spoke system, and the economic integration of Europe increased the value of scale and scope in the industry during the 1980s and 1990s. Only those companies able to spread their operations over multiple national markets earn a profit. In addition, airlines with large domestic feeder networks can expect higher load factors on long intercontinental flights. Smaller carriers, such as Swissair, had no choice but to link up with other airlines.

Third, new technologies are creating links between industries that were formerly separate. Networks allow specialists in each field to cooperate and exploit new opportunities much faster than if each were to try to acquire the industry-specific skills and assets of the others.

For example, consider the networks of alliances emerging in the multimedia field, where computer technology is merging with telecommunications, video, and audio technologies. Several groups of companies have been formed to develop personal digital assistants (PDAs). Apple developed its Newton using chips from Advanced RISC Machines and with design and manufacturing help from Sharp; Apple is now licensing its technology to other companies. AT&T joined with Olivetti, Marubeni, and Matsushita in launching EO, a start-up company that developed the PDA to be sold by the partners. Casio and Tandy developed their own PDA that uses software from GeoWorks; and Amstrad worked with Eden for its version of the product.

The Characteristics of Alliance Groups

The idea that individual companies can gain competitive advantage from banding together is not new. Japanese companies have long done so in their *keiretsu*, and U.S. and European companies did so in the cartels they created after World War I. Today's alliance groups, however, are something different.

Keiretsu companies have long-standing and broad-based relationships with one another. They tend to help one another in various ways and in multiple fields of business. In contrast, alliance groups are more focused, their purposes more strategic, and the roles of their members more narrowly tailored. Interwar cartels differ even more starkly from alliance groups. U.S. and European companies in the sugar, rubber, nitrogen, steel, aluminum, magnesium, incandescent lamp, and chemical industries banded together in industrywide cartels with the aim of allocating world markets. Their purpose was to suppress competition. In contrast, more than one group usually exists in any industry, and competition between or among the groups can be fierce.

An alliance group, then, is a collection of separate companies linked through collaborative agreements. Not all the companies in a group have to be linked directly to all the others. Some may be related only by virtue of their common ties to another network company or to a single sponsoring company. For example, the Mips group was structured precisely in this way, as were competing groups formed by Sun Microsystems, IBM, and Hewlett-Packard (HP). All groups were created to promote the RISC (reduced instruction-set computing) technology of the sponsoring company. (See Exhibit 8-1 "The Structure of the RISC Groups.") There may be an overarching collaborative agreement to which all network members are party; most of the RISC groups had such agreements in place. But the point is that a constellation of alliances can consist of few or many companies. Indeed, alliance groups vary by size, pattern of growth, composition, internal competition, and governance structure. What's appropriate for one network might be wholly inappropriate for another.

SIZE

Alliance networks often grow out of the need to gain scale economies or market share. That was precisely Mips's objective in creating its RISC group. Mips sought to challenge the likes of Intel, Motorola, Sun, and others, each of which was developing its own design for a RISC chip to be used in workstations. Mips turned to partnerships. Seeking strength in numbers, it licensed NEC, Siemens, Toshiba, LSI Logic, and two smaller companies to produce its chips; it persuaded Digital Equipment Corporation (DEC), Silicon Graphics, Bull, Nixdorf, Olivetti, and others to agree to use them; and it struck up working relationships with a host of software companies, system integrators, and computer resellers.

As Mips's network of alliances grew, Compaq and Microsoft joined in, and the group launched a joint effort to develop a new standard for personal computers, the Advanced Computing Environment (ACE). Within months, more than 150 companies had signed on to help. Suddenly, Intel, IBM, Apple, HP, and Sun were on notice. To defend their own technologies, IBM, Motorola, and Apple joined together in a group around the PowerPC chip, and Sun and HP strengthened and expanded their respective groups. Intel independently redoubled its efforts to develop the Pentium chip, which would compete with the RISC chip of Mips and others. Within a year, the Mips juggernaut had been checked. Mips itself was soon acquired by Silicon Graphics, and the ACE initiative died. But group-based competition in the industry continues. The Mips network survives, and competition among it and the groups headed by IBM, HP, and Sun remains strong.

When the competition among networks centers on the establishment of an industry standard, the number of companies in the

Exhibit 8-1   The Structure of the RISC Groups: Early 1992

Each group in the RISC computer field was composed of a mix of companies and types of alliances. The company at the center of each group usually designed the RISC technology, licensed the semicondutor companies to produce chips, and supplied systems on an OEM basis to the resellers. The link between the central company and the system manufacturers was often less formal: the latter simply committed to using the RISC design in their systems. Finally, some of the companies were linked to one another through equity investments.

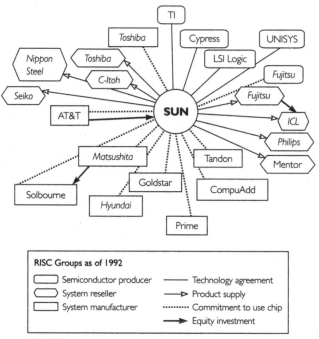

RISC Groups as of 1992

Semiconductor producer	—— Technology agreement
System reseller	——▷ Product supply
System manufacturer	········· Commitment to use chip
	——➤ Equity investment

Non-U.S. companies in italics

network and their combined share of the total market are critical to success. Sun recruited a large number of companies to its technology. Mips's competing network of alliances contained fewer, larger members. In their collective strengths, these two networks were roughly evenly matched, but IBM neutralized the numerical advantage of Mips and Sun when it joined with Apple. The two personal computer giants together could promise a potentially huge market share for PowerPC, the RISC technology microprocessor that IBM developed with Motorola.

Exhibit 8-1   (continued)

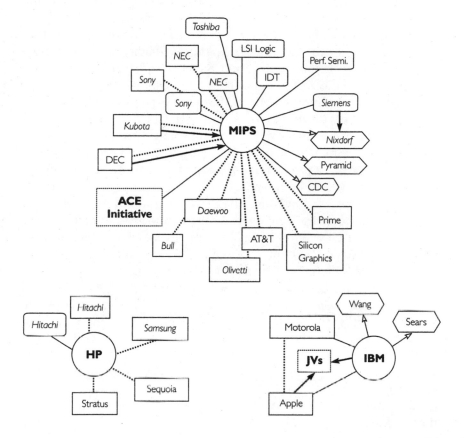

Overall size may be less important in alliance networks driven by the convergence of two or more industries like those in the multimedia field. The idea here is to link complementary technologies or markets. Still, when the dissimilar partners in these alliance networks can exploit economies of scale in their own industries, a greater volume of joint business can help the network in its common purpose.

PATTERN OF GROWTH

Most alliance networks don't spring into existence fully formed; they are built piece by piece. Both the rate of growth and the sequence in which particular members join can affect a network's competitive success. For instance, Kubota, a Japanese machinery producer seeking to diversify into computers, provided Mips with capital at a critical stage and thereby supported the network's early growth. DEC's subsequent decision to join the group gave Mips credibility at a crucial time and led to the decision of NEC and Siemens to become Mips allies. This impressive core group then pulled other companies into the Mips orbit. Later, the addition of Microsoft and Compaq was critical to the launching of the ACE initiative.

Mips's experience suggests that groups can experience runaway growth that ultimately may not be sustainable. While the rapid growth of ACE was a public relations coup for Mips, the large number of companies involved hampered the effectiveness of the group. Competing interests existed even among the core group of ACE founders, and additional conflicts emerged as new companies joined. Consequently, Mips itself was pulled in different directions, and the network soon showed signs of fractures.

IBM pursued a more cautious growth strategy in building the network of alliances that would develop and market the PowerPC. First, it collected its main players by creating close alliances with Apple and Motorola. Apple's earlier ties with Motorola (its computers used Motorola chips) helped cement the three-way network. This triad was charged with developing the new semiconductor, hardware, and software technologies needed for the PowerPC. Only then did IBM fan out to find other players, such as Bull.

Two general principles about the process of growth emerge from these examples. First, to attract new members, a network must show a potential for joint benefits. Some companies will see the potential early, but more skeptical companies may have to be convinced and will only join later in the network's development. Often, the very fact of network growth will attract cautious latecomers. Second, previous relationships between allies and potential allies can be important in attracting new members. Sometimes this means that an ally of an ally will join the group or that an enemy of the enemy will sign on.

COMPOSITION

In networks of companies in converging industries, more important than network size or business volume or even market share is composition—ensuring that the network covers all technologies or markets crucial to the product. The mix of companies in these groups tends to reflect the new opportunities that convergence offers for combining technologies. But even in well-established industries, where the intention is to match the skills assembled by competing networks, composition can be important to a network's success. Both the Ford and GM alliance networks, for instance, contain members with comparable skills and specialties—strong Japanese companies (Mazda with Ford, and Toyota with GM), European luxury-car makers (Jaguar and Saab), and European truck makers (Fiat and Volvo).

In standards battles, too, network composition matters. The leading companies in RISC technology designed their networks to include all the capabilities they thought they needed to compete. The differences in the mix of companies in these networks depended on the capabilities of the RISC designer itself. Neither Mips nor Sun fabricated its own semiconductor chips, so both allied themselves with a handful of semiconductor producers. Beyond that, however, the composition of their respective networks reflected the organizers' different needs. Sun was already successful at making and selling its own workstation systems, accounting for the bulk of RISC workstation sales in its network. Sun thus concentrated on adding OEM resellers and software producers to its network. Mips, in contrast, recruited more systems manufacturers and vendors. In order to help attract these systems companies, Mips even committed to limiting its own sales of finished systems. The composition of IBM's RISC network is different still. With little need for additional semiconductor and systems manufacturing capability beyond that of the triad core—IBM, Apple, and Motorola—IBM concentrated on adding software partners instead.

INTERNAL COMPETITION

The level of internal competition depends both on how many members perform similar functions and on the structure of the relationships among the members. Mips and Sun approached this issue very differently in their respective networks.

Mips licensed six semiconductor producers worldwide to make its R3000 microprocessor. This degree of duplication was intentional, as it helped assure customers that they would not become dependent on a single source. But, with it, Mips tried to minimize competition among its alliance partners: it licensed 6, not 60, producers and, in selecting them, tried to minimize potential rivalries in each company's geographic market. Sun, on the other hand, did little to discourage competition among its semiconductor suppliers. It tended to use a different supplier for each successive generation of its chip and let the suppliers compete each time for its business. Finally, HP emphasized complementarity among a smaller number of allies than MIPS had. "This enables the partners to work together more smoothly rather than focus primarily on competing among themselves," explains Jim Bell, president of HP's Precision RISC Organization, which helps coordinate HP's alliances in the RISC field.

Internal competition has two opposing effects on performance. To a point, it increases group flexibility, drives innovation, and ensures security of supply. But it can fragment a part of the business so much that none of the members reaches efficient scales or earns a sufficient return to reinvest in growth. The line between just enough and too much competition is a fine one. Furthermore, different companies within any given network will have different opinions about where that line should be drawn. Companies subject to internal competition will opt for more order. Other network members may benefit, at least in the short run, from competition among suppliers or buyers inside the network.

GOVERNANCE STRUCTURE

Cooperation between companies is never automatic. The structure of the partnership must provide incentives for performance. Without some sort of collective governance, a group risks becoming no more than a haphazard collection of alliances.

One characteristic of a network's governance structure is the degree to which it is managed as a collective. At one extreme, many formal consortia have governing bodies composed of representatives from member companies, with no individual member in control. Sun's RISC group, for example, has created Sparc International to coordinate some of its efforts; IBM and its partners have created the Power Open Association; and HP has created the Precision RISC Organization. But alliance networks may also function without joint management, as Mips's RISC group did. In these networks, member companies maintain a relationship to the lead company, thereby creating the larger group. The lead company usually provides the management for these multiple partnerships.

Group-Based Versus Company-Based Advantages

Who wins and who loses *among* competing alliance groups depends on the competitive advantages that each group of companies collectively builds. Who wins and who loses *within* a group is a related, but very different, matter. The executive who is considering joining or forming a network must be able to distinguish between group- and company-based advantages.

Group-based advantages help determine the success of the collective in relation to other groups. Company-based advantages, taken together, help the network compete by providing it with the components needed for success. Taken individually, these same company-based advantages help determine the position and power of each company within the network. In other words, if the network-based advantages create the total pie available to members, the company-based advantages affect how the pie is divided.

While group- and company-based advantages are thus intertwined, the balance between the two may in itself be a distinct element of a network. In some networks—Sun's, for example—a host of second-tier companies surrounds the central company that holds key advantages and owns the bulk of the collective business. In other networks—IBM's, for instance—a number of core companies holds complementary but equally critical advantages and shares the business more evenly. Both arrangements can work, and the choice may simply reflect the size of the organizing company or the companies in the core group.

These distinctions between group and company-based advantages suggest three questions that managers should address as they design an alliance network:

Is the whole greater than the sum of its parts? An alliance group works best when the individual partnerships complement one another or, at least, when they don't conflict. The network structure should provide incentives for member cooperation, not dissent.

Who controls the group? The company that founds the group does not always remain in control. Small companies, in particular, run the risk of losing control to larger partners or to subgroups of partners within the network unless they own a critical part of the group's value chain. How the network is governed and how control is shared influence the effectiveness of the whole and the fate of individual members.

Where is competitive advantage created? The performance of a company within the group depends both on competitive advantages created by the group as a whole and on advantages of the company compared with other group members. The group-based advantages, in turn, depend on key characteristics of the group—size, composition, governance, internal competition, and processes of growth. Each company will gain competitive advantage according to the group it joins and the role it plays within that group.

The Hidden Costs of Alliance Groups

While increasing size may be an indication of a network's growing strength and success, size often comes at some expense. Companies building or participating in alliance networks should therefore weigh the benefits of greater size against three types of constraints.

Organizational constraints are internal to the company and weigh heaviest on the lead, or central, company in a network. Every new alliance requires top management's attention, especially in the early stages of planning, partner search, and negotiation. Every new alliance increases the difficulties of coordinating operations as more partners have to be consulted. In this sense, a network of alliances becomes more difficult to manage the more members it has. When partners have conflicting interests—in other words, when there is internal competition—the task of managing a network becomes still more difficult. When he was CEO of Mips in 1991 and trying to manage partnerships with NEC, Siemens, LSI Logic, Performance Semiconductor, and Integrated Device Technology, Robert Miller observed, "Keeping five companies on the same strategic path can be difficult; it takes diplomacy, time, and energy at the senior level."

While managers of large networks of alliances are currently struggling with how best to manage them, several models are beginning to show promise. Some companies have put a top executive in charge of overseeing external strategic relations. These managers are often able to give their personal attention to only a small portion of the alliances within the network. Often they concentrate on alliances involving equity investments while developing guidelines for the decentralized control of looser relationships.

Other companies allocate alliance responsibility along functional lines, such as marketing alliances under marketing executives or technology alliances under R&D departments. Still others require business units to manage their own relationships. Particularly critical alliance networks are sometimes managed by specific senior-executive "champions," who may sit on the boards of joint ventures or otherwise take direct responsibility for alliance negotiation and management.

Collective governance structures such as IBM's Power Open Association and Sun's Sparc International may help maintain network cohesion. However, the burden of negotiating with new partners and monitoring existing agreements usually falls to the central company within the network. Therefore, top-level executives of the central company must always bear in mind that mismanagement can erode the group-based advantages that size and variety generate.

Strategic gridlock is external to the company, because it stems from crowding in the alliance field. As more partnerships are formed in a given business or country, there are likely to be fewer partners available for new deals. This constraint is particularly troublesome in oligopolistic industries, in which only a few strong companies compete world-wide. In the RISC field, for example, the early movers, Mips and Sun, tied up important partners in Europe and Japan. Fortunately for IBM and DEC, by the time they decided to create their respective RISC networks, Mips's once extensive network had begun to decline and the ties among its members to weaken. As a result, IBM could attract Bull and Wang, and DEC could lure Olivetti.

These external limits on alliance strategies are not easy to manage, and most companies are trying one of three approaches: preemption, avoidance, or compartmentalization. First, partner scarcity often provokes companies to take preemptive strikes early in order to secure their first choices. As soon as alliances come to be seen as potentially useful in entering or dominating a field, leading companies may leap to create partnerships, sometimes on short notice and with a minimum of planning. Second, companies may avoid, when possible, taking on partners that might involve conflicts of interest with existing alliances. Mips sought semiconductor partners that did not have their own RISC projects, thereby eliminating Motorola and Advanced Micro Devices as potential partners. Third, companies limit the scope of collaboration in each alliance—for example, by limiting its geographic territory. This kind of compartmentalization solution minimizes overlap, leaving each alliance to operate more or less independently of the others. But the approach sacrifices the benefits that can spring from

integration among alliances. Indeed, compartmentalization almost ensures that the value of a network will not exceed the value of the sum
of its parts.

Dependence is inherent in networks. In all alliances, the allying
companies lose some control. To the extent that I rely on you, my
freedom to act independently of you is reduced. Cumulatively, the
growth of a network of alliances may gradually and inexorably link
an individual company's destiny to that of the network. If that occurs,
the company may have to subordinate its own decisions to those of
the network. And, ironically, even if the network is growing and capturing market share, the company may have to share a progressively
greater portion of network profits just to attract or retain alliance
partners.

Organizational constraints, strategic gridlock, and dependence all
contributed to the decline of Mips and its once-promising network of
alliances. But of the three constraints, dependence took the greatest
toll. To gain more sponsors, Mips had to share potential profits from its
technology with partners. Furthermore, Mips's fate came to depend
on the success of ACE, which in turn hinged on the actions of several
key members, including DEC and Compaq. The limits on Mips's ability to appropriate returns from its technology weakened the company's financial condition, which cast doubt on Mips's ability to survive and discouraged potential new allies. It also forced Mips to cut
back on R&D, eroding its technological advantage. As soon as DEC
and Compaq reduced their commitment to ACE in 1992, the group
fell apart. Mips, as an independent company, went down with it. It
was then acquired by Silicon Graphics.

Latecomers to the RISC field are trying to avoid the problems that
plagued Mips. HP, DEC, and IBM, entering the race after Mips and Sun
had already created their large constellations, are building smaller and
more manageable groups. Silicon Graphics, which inherited the Mips
network, has refocused on nurturing a few key alliances in targeted
market segments.

What the Pioneers Have Learned

Because even pioneers in the field are still learning how to initiate,
build, and manage networks of alliances, much of what they are
learning is specific to their own experience. Still, a few general lessons
have emerged:

Groups are only as strong as the alliances within them: manage individual relationships carefully. There is no shortcut to designing and implementing partnerships. Even when no new money is being spent, the task requires the same depth of analysis that managers typically apply to major investment decisions. (See Rosabeth Moss Kanter, "Collaborative Advantage: The Art of Alliances," HBR, July–August 1994).

Effective groups are worth more than the sum of the alliances within them: manage the group as a whole. Anything less than explicit group management constitutes a lost opportunity to create competitive advantage. Opportunity costs can turn into real costs if a network is left untended and uncultivated.

The sky is not the limit in alliance groups: expand with caution. The pressure to forge links with new partners is often great, particularly when one's competitors are doing so daily. However, beware of falling prey to a faddish exuberance. Expand an alliance network only when it makes strategic sense. Even then, do so with the organizational constraints mentioned above in mind.

Where you sit in which network determines what you get: position your company strategically within and among alliance groups. This is the essence of network competition. Managers need to pay attention to both group- and company-based sources of competitive advantage.

A lack of commitment is the flip side of flexibility: be sure that the network strategy is sustainable for your company. Alliance groups can fall apart just as rapidly as they are formed. When rivalry among networks is great, competitors will think nothing of picking off the members of a network teetering on dissolution.

Managers who follow these guidelines will avoid some of the pitfalls of their predecessors. And their experiences, in turn, will help refine old ideas and develop new ones about how to manage competition among groups.

9

Making the Most of Foreign Factories

Kasra Ferdows

Many companies are not tapping the full potential of their foreign factories. They establish and manage their foreign plants to benefit only from tariff and trade concessions, cheap labor, capital subsidies, and reduced logistics costs. Therefore, they assign a limited range of work, responsibilities, and resources to those factories.

But there are companies that expect much more from their foreign factories and, as a result, get much more out of them. They use them not only to gain access to the usual incentives but also to get closer to their customers and suppliers, to attract skilled and talented employees, and to create centers of expertise for the entire company. These factories perform functions beyond mere production—functions such as after-sales service and product engineering. For example, Hewlett-Packard Company's factory in Guadalajara, Mexico, not only assembles computers but also designs computer memory boards. 3M's operations in Bangalore, India, manufacture software and write that software, as well. In Singapore, workers have designed and manufactured two popular pagers for Motorola. And Alcatel Bell's factories in Shanghai are two of the most innovative plants in its worldwide manufacturing network.

The difference between the two approaches lies in the way managers have answered a seemingly simple, but fundamental, question: How can a factory located outside a company's home country be used as a competitive weapon not only in the markets that it directly serves but also in *every* market served by the company? I have found in the research I have conducted over the past five years that if managers do not consider manufacturing to be a source of competitive advantage, they are likely to establish foreign factories with a narrow strategic scope; they then provide those factories with limited resources. In contrast, if managers regard manufacturing as a major source of competitive advantage, they generally expect their foreign factories to be highly productive and innovative, to achieve low costs, and to provide exemplary service to customers throughout the world.[1]

Expecting More from Foreign Factories

It is difficult if not impossible to prove quantitatively how much any factor, let alone an attitude or approach, is responsible for a company's overall success. Nevertheless, after decades of studying and working with multinationals, I am convinced that the companies that treat their foreign plants as a source of competitive advantage are rewarded in the form of higher market share and greater profits. Moreover, I believe that because of increasing global competition, the gap between the companies that treat their foreign plants as a source of competitive advantage and those that do not is widening. Indeed, managers with a limited view of what a foreign factory can or should achieve are falling out of step with three current realities of global business.

First, declining tariffs are reducing the importance of establishing foreign factories as a means of overcoming trade barriers. Tariffs have declined worldwide from an average of 40% in 1940 to 7% in 1990. Trade pacts—GATT, the European Union, NAFTA, Mercosur, and others—are accelerating that reduction. GATT has recently propelled governments from Indonesia to Argentina to issue their first multiyear schedules for reducing tariffs.

This trend is making life difficult for factories that have owed their existence to tariff barriers. For example, faced with declining tariffs in Australia, Nissan closed its plant in Clayton, Victoria, in 1992. In addition, tariff cuts in many South American and Asian countries figured prominently in Procter & Gamble's decision to close many of the 30 plants it has shut since 1993 as part of its Strengthening Global Effectiveness program.

Second, the increasing sophistication of manufacturing and product development and the growing importance of having world-class suppliers are causing more multinationals to place less emphasis on low wages when they are choosing foreign manufacturing sites. According to the latest data compiled by the United Nations Conference on Trade and Development, in 1994 ten industrialized countries—the United States, the United Kingdom, France, Germany, Spain, Canada, Australia, Holland, Belgium, and Italy—received half of the world's foreign direct investments and accounted for two-thirds of the world's accumulated stock of foreign direct investments. The largest recipient was the United States: by 1994, foreign multinationals had more than $500 billion invested in the United States, up from $80 billion in 1980. That cumulative investment nearly equaled the total amount that multinationals had invested in the world's 154 developing countries. Britain, with $214 billion, was the second-largest recipient, followed by France and Germany.

None of these recipients offers cheap wages, materials, or capital costs. Clearly, leading manufacturers recognize that low wages, grants, and subsidies do not necessarily mean low total costs. Indeed, the low wages available in many countries, after adjusting for productivity, lose their attraction. For example, although manufacturing wages in India and the Philippines are much lower than those in the United States, their average manufacturing labor cost is higher after adjustments are made for productivity.

When superior manufacturers do establish plants in developing countries, they take care to locate their factories in the areas that have the most advanced infrastructure and workers' skills rather than in the areas that offer merely the lowest wages. For example, 3M chose Bangalore as a manufacturing site. Land is more expensive and wages are higher there than in many other places in India; but Bangalore offers the advantages of skilled labor and suppliers, as well as sophisticated competitors. Similarly, Xerox chose to produce copiers and toner in Shanghai, and Motorola located its pager-manufacturing facility in the port city of Tianjin. Shanghai and Tianjin are two of China's higher-cost cities. Companies like Xerox and Motorola accept the additional cost of locating their factories in these places. To achieve a higher level of productivity than other companies commonly achieve, they plan to run their plants with more sophisticated production processes.

Third, the pressure to transfer ideas from development to production ever more quickly and efficiently is pushing companies to forge a close working relationship between those two functions. Many companies are concentrating production and development in the same organizational and geographical unit. This trend marks a departure from the conventional wisdom, which holds that the role of the foreign plant is to produce what has been designed and developed at corporate headquarters. Managers who adopt this view believe that because the resources needed to design and develop products are expensive, dividing them into small fragments and spreading them across multiple locations is not economical.

Superior manufacturers, however, have resolved this dilemma by turning their factories into specialists. For example, a company that makes printers might structure its manufacturing network so that one site develops and manufactures integrated circuit boards, a second power supplies, and a third toner and cartridges. Each of these units becomes the custodian of specialized development and manufacturing knowledge for the entire company.

Why spread these specialized units around the globe? Why not keep them in one location or close to one another? Why not keep them in the home country? Because a company would miss opportunities to collect and digest the expertise that other regions have to offer. A ceramics producer operating a factory in New York's "Ceramic Valley," the area around Corning where many companies in the ceramics industry are located, is bound to learn more about the latest advances in technology than a producer that operates elsewhere. For similar reasons, a manufacturer of medical instruments is likely to benefit from having a factory in Minnesota's "Medical Lane" near the Mayo Clinic; a maker of watches or watch components from having a factory in the area of Switzerland and France around Jura; and a textile machinery producer from having a factory in northern Italy.

Defining the Six Strategic Roles

Because each foreign factory inevitably has its own unique history and challenges, articulating its strategic role can be difficult. Classifying the different roles can help reduce this complexity. Start by answering two basic questions about each factory: What is the primary strategic reason for the factory's location? and What is the scope of its current activities? Based on the answers to these questions, managers can use a framework I developed to categorize plants and to determine how to expand their roles. (See "Charting the Strategic Roles of Foreign Factories.")

Charting the Strategic Roles of Foreign Factories

Offshore Factory

An offshore factory is established to produce specific items at a low cost—items that are then exported either for further work or for sale. Investments in technical and managerial resources are kept at the minimum required for production. Little development or engineering occurs at the site. Local managers rarely choose key suppliers or negotiate prices. Accounting and finance staffs primarily provide data to managers in the home country. Outbound logistics are simple and beyond the control of the plant's management.

Source Factory

The primary purpose for establishing a source factory is low-cost production, but its strategic role is broader than that of an offshore factory. Its managers have greater authority over procurement (including the selection of suppliers), production planning, process changes, outbound logistics, and product-customization and redesign decisions. A source factory has the same ability to produce a product or a part as the best factory in the company's global network. Source factories tend to be located in places where production costs are relatively low, infrastructure is relatively developed, and a skilled workforce is available.

Server Factory

A server factory supplies specific national or regional markets. It typically provides a way to overcome tariff barriers and to reduce taxes, logistics costs, or exposure to foreign-exchange fluctuations. Although it has relatively more autonomy than an offshore plant to make minor modifications in products and production methods to fit local conditions, its authority and competence in this area are very limited.

Contributor Factory

A contributor factory also serves a specific national or regional market, but its responsibilities extend to product and process engineering as well as to the development and choice of suppliers. A contributor factory competes with the company's home plants to be the testing ground for new process technologies, computer systems, and products. It has its own development, engineering, and production capabilities. A contributor factory also has authority over procurement decisions and participates in the choice of key suppliers for the company.

Outpost Factory

An outpost factory's primary role is to collect information. Such a factory is placed in an area where advanced suppliers, competitors, research laboratories, or customers are located. Because every factory obviously must make products and have markets to serve, virtually all outpost factories have a secondary strategic role—as a server or an offshore, for example.

Lead Factory

A lead factory creates new processes, products, and technologies for the entire company. This type of factory taps into local skills and technological resources not only to collect data for headquarters but also to transform the knowledge that it gathers into useful products and processes. Its managers have a decisive voice in the choice of key suppliers and often participate in joint development work with suppliers. Many of its employees stay in direct contact with end customers, machinery suppliers, research laboratories, and other centers of knowledge; they also initiate innovations frequently.

According to this framework, foreign factories can fall into any of six categories. An *offshore* factory is established to gain access to low wages or other factors integral to low-cost production. Its responsibilities are limited to the low-cost production of specific items that are then exported either for further work or for sale. Such a factory is not expected to be innovative; its managers follow the instructions, methods, and plans handed down to them; and they rely on others to provide the expertise in new processes, products, and technologies. A *source* factory also is established to gain access to low-cost production; but unlike an offshore factory, it has the resources and the expertise to develop and produce a part or a product for the company's global markets. A *server* factory is a production site that supplies specific national or regional markets. A *contributor* factory both serves a local market and assumes responsibility for product customization, process improvements, product modifications, or product development. An *outpost* factory is established primarily to gain access to the knowledge or skills that the company needs. Finally, a *lead* factory has the ability and knowledge to innovate and create new processes, products, and technologies for the company.

Some factories combine two or more of these roles. For instance, a factory may be a server for a specific region and an offshore site for the production of certain components. Indeed, any type of factory may have a secondary strategic role—such as providing an operational hedge against currency risks, acting as an alternate source of supply for a critical component, or preempting competitors in a national or regional market. Nevertheless, this simple framework is helpful in articulating the strategic contributions of most foreign factories.

Determining the Strategic Role

After assessing each factory's current role, the next step is to determine the future role that the company's leaders would like each to play. Sometimes internal events drive the decision to change a factory's role. For example, a merger adds new factories to the network; the product mix changes; or other factories in the company's global network become bigger or smaller.

At other times, external events drive the need for change. For example, as the details of the 1992 European Union were unfolding in the late 1980s, manufacturers that had plants scattered across many European countries were forced to question why they needed so many server factories; and those that had plants in only a few countries were forced to ask how they were going to supply new markets or cope with new competitors in their existing markets. Today Mercosur and NAFTA are raising similar questions for manufacturers in South America and North America.

More subtle external factors also may create the need for change. Increasing wages, declining tariffs, and a growing local market may prompt a company to turn an offshore factory into a server. For example, European and U.S. electronics manufacturers turned some offshore factories in Malaysia into servers after increases in Malaysian wages had reduced their production cost advantage and growing local demand had provided an alternative to the European and North American markets. In contrast, the rising productivity, product quality, and dependability of a factory in China, combined with low wages and government incentives to export, may prompt a company to turn a server factory originally built to supply the Chinese market into an offshore factory for supplying low-cost components to other markets.

A company's business strategy should determine the decision to change a factory's strategic role. I devised a strategic matrix to help managers visualize such changes. (See Exhibit 9-1 "The Roles of Foreign Factories: A Strategic Matrix.") In order to increase

Exhibit 9-1   The Roles of Foreign Factories: A Strategic Matrix

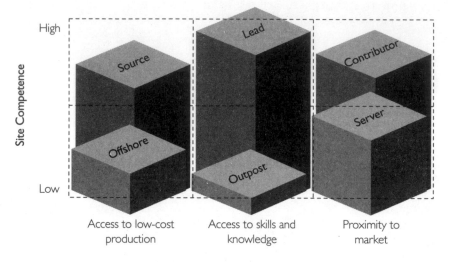

Strategic Reason for the Site

manufacturing's strategic contribution, a company generally must upgrade the role of its foreign factories, moving them up the matrix. Alternatively, it may choose to keep a given factory in its current role, to move it horizontally across the matrix (from source to contributor, for example), to move it down the matrix, or, if it is already at the bottom of the matrix, to close or divest it. Different moves present different challenges.

In the easiest case, a factory is in a low position—an offshore, an outpost, or a server—and remains there. Almost every foreign factory starts in the lower part of the matrix. And some companies, for sound reasons, keep many of their factories in those positions. Coca-Cola Company, for example, has many bottling plants that are servers and are likely to remain in that role. Because of high transportation costs, Coca-Cola will always need hundreds of bottling plants around the world, each of which serves a relatively small geographic market. These plants receive concentrated Coke syrup and, following specific methods and adhering to strict standards, add water and other ingredients to make the final product. Even minor adjustments in the formula to adapt the product to local tastes require approval from regional or corporate headquarters. Of course, a plant kept in a limited strategic role may still have to improve its performance. Indeed, good manufacturers are relentless in their quest for improving the quality, cost efficiency, dependability, and flexibility of all their production operations no matter their strategic scope.

Moving a plant horizontally across the matrix usually requires a substantial overhaul of its organization, control systems, and equipment. A major European pharmaceuticals company discovered just that when it decided to change the role of a plant in Turkey. The factory had been operating as a server. The company, however, decided in the early 1990s that it wanted the plant to operate as an offshore as well and produce some drugs for export. It quickly became clear that the factory needed new equipment to meet the packaging and labeling requirements of different European countries. Its fairly rudimentary outbound logistics system had to be redesigned completely; its cost accounting methods had to be changed to conform to the methods used in the rest of the company; and new channels of communication with sales offices in other countries had to be developed, which required improving the staff's foreign language skills.

Upgrading the Strategic Role

Moving a plant up the matrix means giving it a broader, upgraded strategic role in the company's network of factories. Superior manufacturers have a larger portion of their global factories in the higher source, contributor, and lead positions than average manufacturers do. The challenges involved in upgrading a plant are substantial. But the rewards are substantial, too. Indeed, it often takes years and a tremendous investment of resources for factories to ascend to these positions; but these plants ultimately provide their companies with a formidable strategic advantage. (See Exhibit 9-2 "Paths to Higher Strategic Roles.")

Consider Hewlett-Packard's successful plant in Singapore, which was established in 1970 as an offshore plant. It took about a decade and the investment of substantial resources for the factory to become a source plant for calculators and keyboards, and another decade for it to assume a lead position for keyboards and inkjet printers. (See "How Hewlett-Packard Upgraded the Strategic Role of Its Factory in Singapore.")

Exhibit 9-2   Paths to Higher Strategic Roles

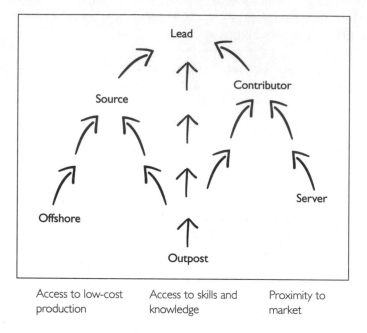

Access to low-cost   Access to skills and   Proximity to
production   knowledge   market

Primary Strategic Reason for the Site

Site Competence

↑   + Become global hub for product or process knowledge

↑   + Supply global markets

↑   + Assume responsibility for product development

↑   + Make product-improvement recommendations

↑   + Assume responsibility for process development

↑   + Assume responsibility for the development of suppliers

↑   + Make process-improvement recommendations

↑   + Assume responsibility for procurement and local logistics

↑   + Maintain technical processes

↑   + Assume responsibility for production

How Hewlett-Packard Upgraded the Strategic Role of Its Factory in Singapore

The story of Hewlett-Packard's factory in Singapore illustrates many of the critical managerial decisions involved in upgrading a factory's strategic role. The factory was built in 1970 to produce simple labor-intensive components at a low cost. It is now one of HP's global centers for the design, development, and manufacture of a number of critical products and components, including keyboards and inkjet printers.

The Initial Decision: Valuing the Intangibles
HP's first important decision was selecting a site for the factory. Even though HP was looking for a location that would make low-cost production possible, it chose Singapore over cheaper Asian locations because the city offered several intangible, long-term benefits: a better-educated workforce that spoke English, a more stable government, and a more developed infra-structure. One of HP's managers' basic beliefs was that factories should be able to operate in the same place for a very long time. (HP has never closed any of its factories worldwide.) The ability of each factory to attract and keep qualified people, they felt, was the key to keeping the factories vital.

HP negotiated hard with Singaporian officials for the best deals on taxes, tariffs, and other subsidies. But those deals were tactical matters and not the basic reason for choosing Singapore as the plant's site.

Early Years: Becoming a Better Offshore Plant
During its early years, the plant succeeded because wages, taxes, and employed capital were relatively low in Singapore. But neither HP's corporate leaders nor its local managers were content to depend solely on those advantages. From the start, the factory embarked on a quality-improvement program and gradually reduced waste and improved efficiency.

In 1973, HP transferred the manufacture of the HP-35, a simple calculator, from a factory in the United States to the Singapore plant in order to reduce production costs. It was the first complete product entrusted to the plant. The plant managed to cut the cost of the calculator substantially, which prompted HP to transfer other items to it. Each subsequent success triggered the transfer of ever more sophisticated products and components. By the late 1970s, the factory was producing many items, including keyboards, solid-state displays, and integrated circuits. (All these items, however, were still designed, developed, and initially produced in the United States.) By generating quick paybacks, the plant induced HP to make new investments in it and, as a result, kept raising its profile within the company.

From Offshore to Source

The quest to reduce costs and improve production quality had inevitably directed managers in Singapore to pay more attention to improving the design of products to make them easier and less expensive to manufacture. A case in point is the HP41C, a sophisticated hand-held calculator. HP transferred the manufacture of this calculator to Singapore because the plant could produce it at a lower cost. Managers in Singapore set out to reduce its costs by half—an ambitious goal that could be achieved only by redesigning the product. The redesign involved reducing the number of integrated circuit boards in the product from two to one, but the Singapore staff lacked the necessary expertise. Because both local managers and corporate managers were convinced that developing this expertise could aid the factory's cost-reduction efforts in general, they agreed to send 20 of the plant's engineers to the United States for a year to learn how to design application-specific integrated circuits for the product—an expertise they then brought back to Singapore.

The results were phenomenal. The plant slashed the production cost of the HP41C by 50% and, using the knowledge it had acquired, reduced the production costs of other models substantially. In 1983, HP shifted the entire production of the line of calculators to Singapore. In addition, HP's executives, impressed by the plant's prowess in redesigning products and processes, decided to shift some development and engineering work to Singapore.

HP also transferred a senior U.S. manager with extensive experience in the company's manufacturing and R&D organizations to Singapore that year. He started a small R&D group with three engineers. By the time he returned to the United States in 1986, the group had grown to 35 people, and its workload had increased significantly as it proved its worth.

Consider the group's success in improving the production of keyboards. The engineers investigated several new production processes that offered the possibility of reducing costs substantially while improving quality. One such technology was a new "dye sublimation" process that would allow the factory to imprint letters on 120 key caps in one step. The R&D group's success with this and other technologies helped convince top-level managers to give it a bigger challenge: the design of HP's next generation of keyboards. In 1986, after the plant had successfully designed and produced the new keyboard, HP gave it sole responsibility for developing and supplying all HP keyboards. The Singapore plant also increased its cost advantage by developing a pool of Asian suppliers. In general, Asian suppliers offered lower prices than their U.S. counterparts. More important, they worked closely with the plant to deliver parts just-in-time, to improve quality, and to share development expenses.

Because of the plant's accomplishments, HP transferred the job of manufacturing the all-important thermal inkjet printer, the Thinkjet, to Singapore in 1984—a mere four months after the printer, HP's first inkjet product, had been introduced in the United States. Reducing the line's production cost was strategically critical, and HP executives had faith that the Singapore plant could do it. It did not disappoint them. The factory slashed the printer's production cost by 30% in a few months: one-third of the reduction was the result of efficient production, low wages, and low taxes; one-third was the result of improving the product's design; and the final third was the result of switching to Asian suppliers.

By the mid-1980s, the plant had assumed a much broader strategic role in HP's global network of factories. In addition to continuing to offer low wages, low taxes, and efficient production, it could redesign and develop products, conduct joint development with suppliers, and distribute its products globally. The Singapore plant was no longer merely an offshore. It had turned into a source.

From Source to Lead

As the strategic role of the plant broadened, local managers continued to initiate new projects and HP's top management assigned more global responsibilities to the plant. Progress was not always smooth. For example, in 1989, an ambitious attempt to develop and produce a low-cost inkjet printer jointly with HP's Vancouver division failed. It was a major setback, but local managers quickly rebounded by successfully proposing that the plant be given the job of modifying for the Japanese market a new DeskJet printer just introduced in the United States. The project would signal the first time the Singapore operation would have full responsibility for a business: the redesign, production, distribution, and marketing of a product in a new market.

Despite the factory's demonstrated capabilities, this was a risky proposition. Any problems or stumbles could tarnish HP's reputation in a critical market. The project also was risky for managers in Singapore. The stakes were high, and the work involved new activities and a long-term commitment of resources. (It was clear that the first model would have to be followed quickly by other new models.) The plant would have to develop expertise in new functions and a fast-changing technology.

The first product, introduced in 1991, was not well received in Japan. But instead of retreating, the managers in Singapore suggested that they redesign another recently introduced inkjet printer, the DeskJet 505. This product was a success, and the plant has since continued to develop new, and generally smaller, inkjet printers for the Japanese and other markets. In the process, it has acquired considerable expertise in producing smaller inkjet printers and is now a lead plant. It is HP's global center for the design, development, and manufacture of portable printers for markets worldwide.[2]

Even though factories may start at different positions on the matrix, the managerial approaches to upgrading their strategic roles have several imperatives in common.

FOCUS ON THE INTANGIBLE BENEFITS

Each company has its unique reasons for manufacturing outside its home country. (See Exhibit 9-3 "Why Manufacture Abroad?") Some benefits—such as a reduction in labor, capital, and logistics costs—are tangible and easy to measure; others—such as learning from foreign research centers, customers, and suppliers—are intangible and difficult to measure.

How a company treats the intangible benefits says a great deal about the role of manufacturing in its corporate strategy. If manufacturing plays a negligible strategic role, the tangible benefits usually dominate the decision to manufacture abroad. As a company upgrades the strategic role of its manufacturing operations, however, it stresses the intangibles more.

Consider Lego, the Danish toy maker. Many U.S. toy makers have moved their factories from Japan to Taiwan to Singapore to Thailand and now to China, attracted by the marginal cost advantages in those countries. In contrast, Lego has continued to produce most of its toys and molds in Denmark, Germany, Switzerland, and the United States. Why hasn't Lego moved its production to low-cost countries? The answer lies in the way it treats the intangible benefits of location. Lego depends on its factories to develop unique capabilities in injection molding and mold design and to advance the company's knowledge of plastic materials. Highly industrialized countries that offer skilled technicians, sophisticated suppliers, research centers, and universities allow Lego to accomplish those ends more easily.

It is hard to argue against opting for immediate, tangible benefits by promising probable, intangible benefits in the future. But more

Exhibit 9-3 Why Manufacture Abroad?

Most tangible

Reduce direct and indirect costs
Reduce capital costs
Reduce taxes
Reduce logistics costs
Overcome tariff barriers
Provide better customer service
Spread foreign exchange risks
Build alternative supply sources
Preempt potential competitors
Learn from local suppliers
Learn from foreign customers
Learn from competitors
Learn from foreign research centers
Attract talent globally

Most intangible

attention to the intangibles can launch a factory on a path to expanding the scope of its capabilities.

CULTIVATE COMPETENCIES

At HP, managers of the Singapore factory knew that the company's leaders expected them to expand the factory's competences and to upgrade its strategic role. Similar expectations made it possible for the managers of NCR's factory in Dundee, Scotland, and Sony's factory in Bridgend, Wales, to upgrade their strategic roles. The NCR plant started in the 1960s as a server for a variety of products, such as mainframe computers and cash registers. Like many other traditional foreign plants, it stayed in the server position for years. But in the early 1980s, it embarked on a new path that moved it into a contributor position for automated teller machines by the mid-1980s and into a lead position for ATMs by the early 1990s. (See "From Server to Lead: NCR in Dundee, Scotland.") The Sony plant in Bridgend started in 1974 as a server, supplying television sets and components to Europe. By the mid-1980s, it had expanded its role to contributor; and it continues to become a still stronger and more effective contributor. (See "From Server to Contributor: Sony in Bridgend, Wales.")

From Server to Lead: NCR in Dundee, Scotland

Established in the 1960s to serve Western Europe, NCR's factory in Dundee, Scotland, had by the early 1990s turned itself into a world-class manufacturer of automated teller machines. Since then, the factory has helped the company maintain its number one position in the worldwide ATM market.

At the end of the 1970s, the factory seemed doomed. NCR's plants in the Dundee area had plummeted from six, with a combined workforce of 6,000, to one, with a workforce of 700. The remaining factory, which made such products as mainframe computers and cash registers, was vertically integrated and unfocused.

Then in the early 1980s, like many beleaguered multinationals, NCR restructured itself along business units. The company's leaders challenged its plants to become world-class manufacturers. The mandate was clear: help create businesses that are competitive on a worldwide scale or face closure. Dundee aimed to become number one in the self-service banking-transaction business.

Dundee's managers established two priorities: upgrade manufacturing performance and speed up the product-development cycle. By the mid-1980s, both initiatives were in full swing. To improve manufacturing performance, the factory launched total quality management, just-in-time procurement and production, cell production, and a variety of other continuous-improvement programs. It also started to develop closer relationships with local suppliers. To speed up product development, it built up a strong R&D department. (By 1990, 250 of its 1,400 employees were in R&D.) The factory also created a special competence in developing new products and ramping up their production quickly. By 1985, Dundee had become more efficient and had expanded its strategic role. Once a mediocre server, the plant had transformed itself into an effective contributor. It was a second source for the development and production of ATMs not only for the European market but also for markets worldwide.

Throughout the last years of the 1980s, Dundee continued its push to improve its manufacturing and product-development capabilities. Self-financing its growth, it established closer links to end customers (it visited bankers and had them visit Dundee); local educational establishments (it funded a department of mechatronics, or mechanical and electronic engineering, at the University of Dundee, for example); and suppliers (80% of supplies came from local sources). By 1990, Dundee had become NCR's lead plant for ATMs, with primary responsibility for developing and manufacturing the products that the billion-dollar business needed. The plant continued to play this role after AT&T's acquisition of NCR in the early 1990s, and it promises to be one of the pillars of the newly independent company that AT&T spun off in 1996.

From Server to Contributor: Sony in Bridgend, Wales

Sony built a new factory in Bridgend, Wales, in 1973. Pursuing a strategy that its chairman, Akio Morita, called "global localization" (that is, thinking globally when making local decisions), Sony had given the plant a charter to produce television sets and components for the European market. Bridgend started as a server plant, buying many subassemblies from Sony in Japan. At that time, critics assumed it was one of the so-called screwdriver assembly factories that Japanese manufacturers were establishing in foreign countries to overcome trade barriers. But the plant would prove that it was much more than a limited assembly plant.

In the plant's early years, quality was a concern. So the plant embarked on a program of improvement that would lead eventually to a zero-defect campaign. By the early 1980s, the plant had invested in quality-management and education programs and had installed the most up-to-date production processes and systems, including just-in-time manufacturing supported by manufacturing resource planning (MRP II). Bridgend also stepped up its efforts to reduce its dependence on Sony Japan by producing more parts itself and purchasing more from European suppliers. In 1986, it extended its zero-defect program to suppliers. Close cooperation with its 140 suppliers enabled the factory to institute a "no incoming inspection" policy for their parts in 1989. By then, European-made parts comprised nearly 90% of the content of its products; the mechanical parts the factory used came from the United Kingdom—primarily from Wales.

The Bridgend factory also worked on customizing product design for the European market. In 1984, as part of an effort to strengthen its design capability, it introduced four common platforms for 80 different models of television sets. Sony also set up a local engineering-and-development facility in the same year. Within three years, local people comprised all the full-time staff.

By 1988, 185 engineers were working in the plant—a large number, considering that the site employed a total of 1,500 people. The engineers worked on design and development projects for six months and then produced the new designs in the next six months—a cycle that meshed with the cycle of television sales. In the first, quiet part of the year, the engineers and many other employees focused on developing and learning how to manufacture new models. By the time the sales cycle started to climb to its November peak, the entire staff—including the engineers—began focusing on production. While the factory was ramping up production, engineers learned valuable lessons about designing products so that they could be manufactured more easily and inexpensively, and with fewer defects. Engineers then could put those lessons into practice when they developed new models.

Since 1988, the plant has designed and developed most of the products it has produced. Today it exports more than three-quarters of the 200 models it produces. It continues to be a strong and valuable contributor plant in Sony's global network.

A factory's long journey up the matrix requires the development of a variety of competencies that are acquired in three stages.

STAGE 1: IMPROVING THE INSIDE. Many companies demand continuous improvement in their factories' performance. The ways in which factories can enhance their performance include improving the plant's physical layout, machinery, work design, and production quality; providing employee training and education; instituting innovative work processes, such as cells and self-managed teams; and adopting computer-assisted manufacturing and just-in-time production processes.

If a factory is not improving internally as fast as it should, then its strategic role will probably be downgraded. An offshore, outpost, or server in such a position is not likely to survive in the long run. In contrast, improved production efficiency and quality usually permit a plant to take on bigger assignments; and managers of high-performing factories naturally want to expand their influence beyond their factories' walls.

STAGE 2: DEVELOPING EXTERNAL RESOURCES. Moving up the matrix from offshore, outpost, or server roles to either source or contributor roles requires developing additional competencies. While HP's factory in Singapore was improving the management of its workforce, equipment, and production techniques, it also started to pay more attention to the way it worked with parties outside the factory. HP's success in reducing costs, particularly in the late 1970s and early 1980s, hinged on overhauling its group of suppliers located in and outside Singapore and on requiring them to deliver on a just-in-time basis. The NCR factory in Dundee increased its locally supplied items from

50% in the mid-1980s to 80% in the late 1980s; and the Sony factory in Bridgend started out importing many components from suppliers in Japan but gradually developed its own supplier base in Europe.

The managers of those plants also realized that achieving ongoing cost reductions would require changes in product design. For example, Sony's Bridgend factory designed and developed four common platforms for the various television systems used in Europe. NCR's Dundee plant redesigned major sections of the teller machines it built to make them easier to manufacture. And HP's Singapore factory reduced the number of components in its calculators by redesigning the product, including its application-specific integrated circuits.

To tackle these challenges, the factories had to expand their internal and their external capabilities. In order to develop direct lines of communication to R&D centers inside their companies, as well as ties to vendors of new technologies outside their companies, they had to add development engineers and technicians to their staffs. They also had to develop logistics skills so that they could take and fulfill orders from retailers, distributors, and, in some cases, end customers located in several different countries. They had to develop the capacity to answer customers' inquiries, to receive orders in several languages and from incompatible computer systems, to arrange international shipments, and to handle an expanded number of models and parts.

STAGE 3: TAKING ON A GLOBAL MANDATE. Moving into a lead position requires competencies that go beyond those needed for a company's current production operations; it requires the ability to generate new knowledge for the company's future manufacturing activities. To become a lead factory, the HP plant not only had to develop the ability to design and manufacture inkjet printers but also had to transform itself into a global center of knowledge about the printers for the entire company. Similarly, the NCR plant had to go beyond merely being an efficient producer of ATMs; it also had to learn how to develop and manufacture the next generation of the devices and transform itself into the custodian of that expertise for the company.

Instead of focusing primarily on pruning overhead costs, these factories focused on growth. They created and refined new products and processes that had a broad impact on their companies' competitiveness. To that end, managers at these factories constantly sought to expand their pool of skilled employees. They continuously added such people as process and development engineers, sales and lab technicians, computer experts, logistics managers, human resource professionals, quality managers, and cost accountants. The atmosphere inside the factories was dynamic, engaging, and challenging—precisely the conditions that attract highly qualified individuals.

Because it entails a substantial investment of time and resources, as well as changes in a factory's culture and management style, the decision to upgrade a factory to a lead position should not be made lightly. It demands a serious commitment by both corporate and plant management.

CREATE A ROBUST NETWORK

Plant closures, major shifts of production from one country to another, and buying and selling plants are all expensive. Such factors lead to instability in a company's global network of plants and make it difficult for the average foreign plant to develop the competencies it needs to upgrade its strategic role. How can a company avoid such instability? Superior manufacturers do it by creating robust networks.

A robust network is one that can cope with changes in the competitive environment without resorting to extreme measures. For example, as currencies fluctuate, a company with a less robust network would shift production among its factories rapidly and dramatically in order to keep its production costs down. A company in which manufacturing plays a negligible strategic role expects little from a factory beyond, say, low-cost production and, as a result, invests little in the plant. In contrast, a superior manufacturer invests more in its factory and expects more benefits from the factory's smooth operation; typically, the factory is better at coping with adverse competitive conditions. As a result, the savings from switching production are smaller for the superior manufacturer, and the benefits from not switching are greater. In short, such manufacturers are far less trigger-happy than manufacturers with less robust networks.

A robust network by definition contains many factories in upgraded strategic roles (sources, contributors, and leads). The more robust the network, the more secure the network. Security is a necessary condition for cultivating the development of a site's competencies, which in turn allows the factory to expand its strategic role and its ability to deal with adverse conditions. And the cycle continues.

Nurturing Growth Abroad

What are the guidelines for a company that wishes to get more from its foreign factories? To start, review periodically the strategic role of each plant in the global network. As part of this assessment, construct a map of the existing network and the current roles of each factory, and compare it with a map of the desired network based on the company's evolving business strategy. Such a comparison is likely to reveal gaps in the network (for example, which factory will supply the planned expansion into the East Asian market) and scenarios for changes in the roles of existing factories.

More important than these periodic checkups is what one does between them. The most critical task is to increase the capacity of foreign factories to absorb and create knowledge. Technicians, engineers, designers, as well as experts in such areas as procurement, logistics, and quality help a foreign factory accomplish that task. It is no coincidence that superior manufacturers distribute more of their technical resources around the globe.

Maintaining a critical mass of precious resources in one location while at the same time avoiding a duplication of work within the network can present managers with a dilemma. The solution lies in specialization. Whenever feasible, a foreign factory's ultimate mission should include developing a world-class specialty. It is not always necessary to specify the exact nature of the specialty for each factory; specifying a tentative direction or area of growth is often sufficient. Top-level managers should draw up broad guidelines, give factories a chance to expand their capabilities, and ensure that there is no major duplication of work within the network. For their part, each plant's managers should focus on cultivating the appropriate site competence—whether that means managing internal operations more efficiently or building external resources or taking on a global mandate.

Of course, it's the responsibility of the company's leaders to make sure that each foreign plant has managers with the appropriate skills. While the factory is playing one of the lower strategic roles and management is focused on improving the operations inside the factory, a specialist from headquarters is the most suitable plant manager. But when the factory's role is being upgraded and the focus shifts to the management of suppliers, customers, and others outside the factory, then someone with a more general management background who is familiar with local conditions is more appropriate. An upgraded server or a contributor plant needs a manager with superior local knowledge, including proficiency in the local language; a source plant needs a manager with the technical expertise required to optimize the plant's performance; and a lead plant needs a manager who not only has a deep technical background and is familiar with the local conditions but also knows the company intimately. A careful plan for the recruitment, development, and assignment of managers to foreign factories must always accompany the plans for upgrading the role of manufacturing.

Nurturing the growth of foreign plants demands a commitment sustained over many years, especially on the part of corporate management. There are many obstacles and temptations along the way. First, many managers fear relying on a foreign factory for a critical skill, and they impose a ceiling on how far a foreign factory can develop. Second, the tradition of treating a foreign factory as a cost center can turn it into a cash cow and deprive it of the investment it needs to elevate itself. Superior manufacturers know that the journey of improvement is taken step by step, and every new step requires more resources. Third, the urge to shift production in direct response to fluctuations in the value of foreign currencies is often hard to resist and creates instability for a foreign plant's management. Fourth, alluring government incentives that attempt to convince companies to locate their plants far from centers of technology, sophisticated markets, or advanced suppliers can be difficult to ignore.

Overcoming such obstacles is difficult during ordinary times; and during a period of downsizing, the task is daunting. Far from headquarters, managers of foreign factories often feel particularly vulnerable when the company engages in aggressive outsourcing and other cost-cutting campaigns. Valuable momentum built over several years can easily be destroyed by a wrong signal from the top.

The real mastery of superior manufacturers is their ability to overcome these obstacles and maintain an environment conducive to growth. They nurture such an environment because it is profitable. Not every one of their foreign factories has to become a lead. But they stack the deck in a way that gives their plants a fighting chance to move in that direction. Superior manufacturers are convinced that a foreign factory can be a potent strategic asset.

Notes

1. My research includes a four-year study of the role of foreign factories owned by ten large multinational manufacturing companies: Apple, Digital Equipment, Electrolux, Ford, Hewlett-Packard, Hydro Aluminum, IBM, Olivetti, Philips, and Sony. My observations and conclusions also are based on my work as a consultant to 12 large multinational manufacturing companies and on data from several surveys that I helped conduct. Those surveys included a questionnaire about the configuration of the global manufacturing networks of companies in the pharmaceuticals, food-processing, and paper-machinery industries. They also included the Global Manufacturing Futures Surveys, a series of biannual surveys of the management practices of some 600 large manufacturers in North America, Europe, and Japan that Boston University, INSEAD, and Waseda University have been conducting since 1982.

2. The information in this insert is based on my work with the Hewlett-Packard Company and on the Harvard Business School case study, "Hewlett-Packard: Singapore" (HBS case no. 694–035).

10
Building Effective R&D Capabilities Abroad

Walter Kuemmerle

An increasing number of companies in technologically intensive industries such as pharmaceuticals and electronics have abandoned the traditional approach to managing research and development and are establishing global R&D networks in a noteworthy new way. For example, Canon is now carrying out R&D activities in 8 dedicated facilities in 5 countries, Motorola in 14 facilities in 7 countries, and Bristol-Myers Squibb in 12 facilities in 6 countries. In the past, most companies—even those with a considerable international presence in terms of sales and manufacturing—carried out the majority of their R&D activity in their home countries. Conventional wisdom held that strategy development and R&D had to be kept in close geographical proximity. Because strategic decisions were made primarily at corporate headquarters, the thinking went, R&D facilities should be close to home.

But such a centralized approach to R&D will no longer suffice—for two reasons. First, as more and more sources of potentially relevant knowledge emerge across the globe, companies must establish a presence at an increasing number of locations to access new knowledge and to absorb new research results from foreign universities and competitors into their own organizations. Second, companies competing around the world must move new products from development to market at an ever more rapid pace. Consequently, companies must build R&D networks that excel at tapping new centers of knowledge and at commercializing products in foreign markets with the speed required to remain competitive. And more and more, superior manufacturers are doing just that. (See Exhibit 10-1 "Laboratory Sites Abroad in 1995.")

In an ongoing study on corporate strategy and the geographical dispersion of R&D sites, I have been examining the creation of global research networks by 32 U.S., Japanese, and European multinational companies.[1] The most successful companies in my study brought each new site's research productivity up to full speed within a few years and quickly transformed knowledge created there into innovative products. I found that establishing networks of such sites poses a number of new, complex managerial challenges. According to my research, managers of the most successful R&D networks understand the new dynamics of global R&D, link corporate strategy to R&D strategy, pick the appropriate sites, staff them with the right people, supervise the sites during start-up, and integrate the activities of the different foreign sites so that the entire network is a coordinated whole.

Adopting a Global Approach to R&D

Adopting a global approach to R&D requires linking R&D strategy to a company's overall business strategy. And that requires the involvement of managers at the highest levels of a company.

CREATING A TECHNOLOGY STEERING COMMITTEE

The first step in creating a global R&D network is to build a team that will lead the initiative. To establish a global R&D network, the CEOs and top-level managers of a number of successful companies that I studied assembled a small team of senior managers who had both technical expertise and in-depth organizational knowledge. The technology steering committees reported directly to the CEOs of their respective companies. They were generally small—five to eight members—and included managers with outstanding managerial and scientific records and a range of educational backgrounds and managerial responsibilities. The committees I studied included as members a former bench scientist who had transferred into manufacturing and had eventually become the head of manufacturing for the company's most important category of therapeutic drugs; a head of marketing for

Exhibit 10-1   Laboratory Sites Abroad in 1995

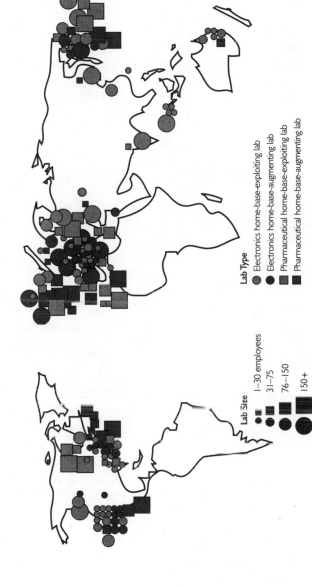

Lab Type

- Electronics home-base-exploiting lab
- Electronics home-base-augmenting lab
- Pharmaceutical home-base-exploiting lab
- Pharmaceutical home-base-augmenting lab

Lab Size

1–30 employees

31–75

76–150

150+

memory chips who had worked before in product development in the same electronics company; and an engineer who had started out in product development, had moved to research, and eventually had become the vice president of R&D. Members of these committees were sufficiently senior to be able to mobilize resources at short notice; and they were actively involved in the management and supervision of R&D programs. In many cases, members included the heads of major existing R&D sites.

CATEGORIZING NEW R&D SITES

In selecting new sites, companies find it helpful first to articulate each site's primary objective. (See Table 10-1 "Establishing New R&D Sites.") R&D sites have one of two missions. The first type of site—what I call a *home-base-augmenting site*—is established in order to tap knowledge from competitors and universities around the globe; in that type of site, information flows *from* the foreign laboratory *to* the central lab at home. The second type of site—what I call a *home-base-exploiting site*—is established to support manufacturing facilities in foreign countries or to adapt standard products to the demand there; in that type of site, information flows *to* the foreign laboratory *from* the central lab at home. (See Exhibit 10-2 "How Information Flows Between Home-Base and Foreign R&D Sites.")

The overwhelming majority of the 238 foreign R&D sites I studied fell clearly into one of the two categories. Approximately 45% of all laboratory sites were home-base-augmenting sites, and 55% were home-base-exploiting sites. The two types of sites were of the same average size: about 100 employees. But they differed distinctly in their strategic purpose and leadership style.[2] (See "Home-Base-Augmenting and Home-Base-Exploiting Sites: Xerox and Eli Lilly.")

Home-Base-Augmenting and Home-Base-Exploiting Sites: Xerox and Eli Lilly

The particular type of foreign R&D site determines the specific challenges managers will face. Setting up a *home-base-augmenting site*—one designed to gather new knowledge for a company—involves certain skills. And launching a *home-base-exploiting site*—one established to help a company efficiently

Table 10-1 Establishing New R&D Sites

Types of R&D Sites	Phase 1 Location Decision	Phase 2 Ramp-Up Period	Phase 3 Maximizing Lab Impact
Home-Base-Augmenting Laboratory Site Objective of establishment: absorbing knowledge from the local scientific community, creating new knowledge, and transferring it to the company's central R&D site	• Select a location for its scientific excellence • Promote cooperation between the company's senior scientists and managers	• Choose as first laboratory leader a renowned local scientist with international experience – one who understands the dynamics of R&D at the new location • Ensure enough critical mass	• Ensure the laboratory's active participation in the local scientific community • Exchange researchers with local university laboratories and with the home-base lab
Home-Base-Exploiting Laboratory Site Objective of establishment: commercializing knowledge by transferring it from the company's home base to the laboratory site abroad and from there to local manufacturing and marketing	• Select a location for its proximity to the company's existing manufacturing and marketing locations • Involve middle managers from other functional areas in start-up decisions	• Choose as first laboratory leader an experienced product-development engineer with a strong company wide reputation, international experience, and knowledge of marketing and manufacturing	• Emphasize smooth relations with the home-base lab • Encourage employees to seek interaction with other corporate units beyond the manufacturing and marketing units that originally sponsored the lab

Exhibit 10-2 How Information Flows Between Home-Base and Foreign R&D Sites

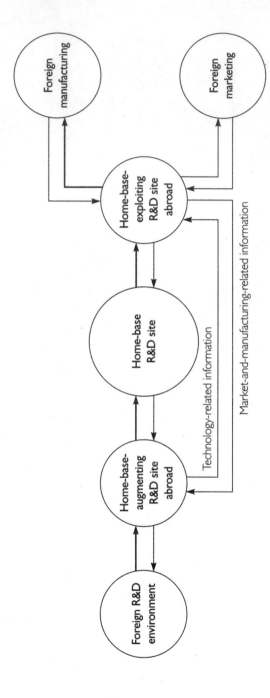

commercialize its R&D in foreign markets—involves others. The cases of Xerox and Eli Lilly present an instructive contrast.

Xerox established a home-base-augmenting laboratory in Grenoble, France. Its objective: to tap new knowledge from the local scientific community and to transfer it back to its home base. Having already established, in 1986, a home-base-augmenting site in Cambridge, England, Xerox realized in 1992 that the research culture in continental Western Europe was sufficiently different and complementary to Great Britain's to justify another site. Moreover, understanding the most advanced research in France or Germany was very difficult from a base in Great Britain because of language and cultural barriers. One senior R&D manager in the United States notes, "We wanted to learn firsthand what was going on in centers of scientific excellence in Europe. Being present at a center of scientific excellence is like reading poetry in the original language."

It was essential that managers from the highest levels of the company be involved in the decision-making process from the start. Senior scientists met with high-level managers and entered into a long series of discussions. Their first decision: to locate the new laboratory at a center of scientific excellence. Xerox also realized that it had to hire a renowned local scientist as the initial laboratory leader. The leader needed to be able to understand the local scientific community, attract junior scientists with high potential, and target the right university institutes and scholars for joint research projects. Finally, Xerox knew that the laboratory would have an impact on the company's economic performance only if it had the critical mass to become an accepted member of the local scientific community. At the same time, it could not become isolated from the larger Xerox culture.

Xerox considered a number of locations and carefully evaluated such aspects as their scientific excellence and relevance, university liaison programs, licensing programs, and university recruiting programs. The company came up with four potential locations: Paris, Grenoble, Barcelona, and Munich. At that point, Xerox also identified potential laboratory leaders. The company chose Grenoble on the basis of its demonstrated scientific excellence and hired as the initial laboratory leader a highly regarded French scientist with good connections to local universities. Xerox designed a facility for 40 researchers and made plans for further expansion. In order to integrate the new laboratory's scientists into the Xerox community, senior R&D management in Palo Alto, California, allocated a considerable part of the initial laboratory budget to travel to other Xerox sites and started a program for the temporary transfer of newly hired researchers from Grenoble to other R&D sites. At the same time, the Grenoble site set out to integrate itself within the local research community.

In 1989, Eli Lilly considered establishing a home-base-exploiting laboratory in East Asia. The company's objective was to commercialize its R&D more effectively in foreign markets. Until then, Eli Lilly had operated one home-base-augmenting laboratory site abroad and some small sites in industrialized countries for clinical testing and drug approval procedures. But in order to exploit Lilly's R&D capabilities and product portfolio, the company needed a dedicated laboratory site in East Asia. The new site would support efforts to manufacture and market pharmaceuticals by adapting products to local needs. To that end, the management team decided that the new laboratory would have to be located close to relevant markets and existing corporate facilities. It also determined that the initial laboratory leader would have to be an experienced manager from Lilly's home base—a manager with a deep understanding of both the company's local operations and its overall R&D network.

The team considered Singapore as a potential location because of its proximity to a planned Lilly manufacturing site in Malaysia. But ultimately it decided that the new home-base-exploiting laboratory would have the strongest impact on Lilly's sales if it was located in Kōbe, Japan. By establishing a site in the Kōbe-Osaka region—the second-largest regional market in Japan and one that offered educational institutions with high-quality scientists—Lilly would send a signal to the medical community there that the company was committed to the needs of the Japanese market. Kōbe had another advantage: Lilly's corporate headquarters for Japan were located there, and the company was already running some of its drug approval operations for the Japanese market out of Kōbe. The city therefore was the logical choice.

The team assigned an experienced Lilly researcher and manager to be the initial leader of the new site. Because he knew the company inside and out—from central research and development to international marketing—the team reasoned that he would be able to bring the new laboratory up to speed quickly by drawing on resources from various divisions within Lilly. In order to integrate the new site into the over-all company, some researchers from other Lilly R&D sites received temporary transfers of up to two years to Kōbe, and some locally hired researchers were temporarily transferred to other Lilly sites. It took about 30 months to activate fully the Kōbe operation—a relatively short period. Today the site is very productive in transferring knowledge from Lilly's home base to Kōbe and in commercializing that knowledge throughout Japan and Asia.

CHOOSING A LOCATION FOR THE SITE

Home-base-augmenting sites should be located in regional clusters of scientific excellence in order to tap new sources of knowledge. Central to the success of corporate R&D strategy is the ability of senior researchers to recognize and combine scientific advancements from different areas of science and technology. Absorbing the new knowledge can happen in a number of ways: through participation in formal or informal meeting circles that exist within a geographic area containing useful knowledge (a knowledge cluster), through hiring employees from competitors, or through sourcing laboratory equipment and research services from the same suppliers that competitors use.

For example, the Silicon Valley knowledge cluster boasts a large number of informal gatherings of experts as well as more formal ways for high-tech companies to exchange information with adjacent universities, such as industrial liaison programs with Stanford University and the University of California at Berkeley. In the field of communication technology, Siemens, NEC, Matsushita, and Toshiba all operate laboratory sites near Princeton University and Bell Labs (now a part of Lucent Technologies) to take advantage of the expertise located there. For similar reasons, a number of companies in the same industry have established sites in the Kanto area surrounding Tokyo. Texas Instruments operates a facility in Tsukuba Science City, and Hewlett-Packard operates one in Tokyo.

After a company has picked and established its major R&D sites, it might want to branch out. It might selectively set up secondary sites when a leading competitor or a university succeeds in building a critical mass of research expertise in a more narrowly defined area of science and technology outside the primary cluster. In order to benefit from the resulting miniclusters of expertise, companies sometimes establish additional facilities. For that reason, NEC operates a small telecommunications-oriented R&D facility close to a university laboratory in London, and Canon operates an R&D facility in Rennes, France, close to one of France Telecom's major sites.

Home-base-exploiting sites, in contrast, should be located close to large markets and manufacturing facilities in order to commercialize new products rapidly in foreign markets. In the past, companies from industrialized countries located manufacturing facilities abroad primarily to benefit from lower wages or to overcome trade barriers. Over time, however, many of those plants have taken on increasingly complex manufacturing tasks that require having an R&D facility nearby in order to ensure the speedy transfer of technology from research to manufacturing. A silicon-wafer plant, for example, has to interact closely with product development engineers during trial runs of a new generation of microchips. The same is true for the manufacture of disk drives and other complex hardware. For that reason, Hewlett-Packard and Texas Instruments both operate laboratories in Singapore, close to manufacturing facilities.

The more complex and varied a manufacturing process is, the more often manufacturing engineers will have to interact with product development engineers. For example, in the case of one of Toshiba's laptop-computer-manufacturing plants, a new model is introduced to the manufacturing line every two weeks. The introduction has to happen seamlessly, without disturbing the production of existing models on the same line. In order to predict and remedy bugs during initial production runs, development engineers and manufacturing engineers meet several times a week. The proximity of Toshiba's laptop-development laboratory to its manufacturing plant greatly facilitates the interaction.

Establishing a New R&D Facility

Whether establishing a home-base-augmenting or a home-base-exploiting facility, companies must use the same three-stage process: selecting the best laboratory leader, determining the optimal size for the new laboratory site, and keeping close watch over the lab during its start-up period in order to ensure that it is merged into the company's existing global R&D network and contributes sufficiently to the company's product portfolio and its economic performance.

SELECTING THE BEST SITE LEADER

Identifying the best leader for a new R&D site is one of the most important decisions a company faces in its quest to establish a successful global R&D network. My research shows that the initial leader of an R&D site has a powerful impact not only on the culture of the site but also on its long-term research agenda and performance. The two types of sites require different types of leaders, and each type of leader confronts a particular set of challenges.

The initial leaders of home-base-augmenting sites should be prominent local scientists so that they will be able to fulfill their primary responsibility: to nurture ties between the new site and the local scientific community. If the site does not succeed in becoming part of the local scientific community quickly, it will not be able to generate new knowledge for the company. In addition to hiring a local scientist, there are a variety of other ways to establish local ties. For example, Toshiba used its memory-chip joint venture with Siemens to develop local ties at its new R&D site in Regensburg, Germany. The venture allowed Toshiba to tap into Siemens's dense network of associations with local universities. In addition, it helped Toshiba develop a better understanding of the compensation packages required to hire first-class German engineering graduates. Finally, it let the company gain useful insights into how to establish effective contract-research relationships with government-funded research institutions in Germany.

In contrast, the initial leaders of home-base-exploiting sites should be highly regarded managers from within the company—managers who are intimately familiar with the company's culture and systems. Such leaders will be able to fulfill their primary responsibility: to forge close ties between the new lab's engineers and the foreign community's manufacturing and marketing facilities. Then the transfer of knowledge from the company's home base to the R&D site will have the maximum impact on manufacturing and marketing located near that site. When one U.S. pharmaceutical company established a home-base-exploiting site in Great Britain, executives appointed as the initial site leader a manager who had been with the company for several years. He had started his career as a bench scientist first in exploratory research, then in the development of one of the company's blockbuster drugs. He had worked closely with marketing, and he had spent two years as supervisor of manufacturing quality at one of the company's U.S. manufacturing sites. With such a background, he was able to lead the new site effectively.

However, the best candidates for both home-base-augmenting and home-base-exploiting sites share four qualities: they are at once respected scientists or engineers and skilled managers; they are able to integrate the new site into the company's existing R&D network; they have a comprehensive understanding of technology trends; and they are able to overcome formal barriers when they seek access to new ideas in local universities and scientific communities.

Appointing an outstanding scientist or engineer who has no management experience can be disastrous. In one case, a leading U.S.

electronics company decided to establish a home-base-augmenting site in the United Kingdom. The engineer who was appointed as the first site leader was an outstanding researcher but had little management experience outside the company's central laboratory environment. The leader had difficulties marshaling the necessary resources to expand the laboratory beyond its starting size of 14 researchers. Furthermore, he had a tough time mediating between the research laboratory and the company's product development area. Eleven of the 14 researchers had been hired locally and therefore lacked deep ties to the company. They needed a savvy corporate advocate who could understand company politics and could promote their research results within the company. One reason they didn't have such an advocate was that two of the three managers at the company's home base—people who had promoted the establishment of the new R&D lab—had quit about six months after the lab had opened because they disagreed about the company's overall R&D strategy. The third manager had moved to a different department.

In an effort to improve the situation, the company appointed a U.S. engineer as liaison to the U.K. site. He realized that few ideas were flowing from the site to the home base; but he attributed the problem to an inherently slow scientific-discovery process rather than to organizational barriers within the company. After about two years, senior management finally replaced the initial laboratory leader and the U.S. liaison engineer with two managers—one from the United Kingdom and one from the United States. The managers had experience overseeing one of the company's U.S. joint ventures in technology, and they also had good track records as researchers. Finally, under their leadership, the site dramatically increased its impact on the company's product portfolio. In conjunction with the increase in scientific output, the site grew to its projected size of 225 employees and is now highly productive.

In the case of both types of sites, the ideal leader has in-depth knowledge of both the home-base culture and the foreign culture. Consider Sharp's experience. In Japan, fewer corporate scientists have Ph.D.'s than their counterparts in the United Kingdom; instead they have picked up their knowledge and skills on the job. That difference presented a management challenge for Sharp when it established a home-base-augmenting facility in the United Kingdom. In order to cope with that challenge, the company hired a British laboratory leader who had previously worked as a science attaché at the British embassy in Japan. In that position, he had developed a good understanding of the Japanese higher-education system. He was well aware that British and Japanese engineers with different academic degrees might have similar levels of expertise, and, as a result, he could manage them better.

The pioneer who heads a newly established home-base-augmenting or home-base-exploiting site also must have a broad perspective and a deep understanding of technology trends. R&D sites abroad are often particularly good at combining knowledge from different scientific fields into new ideas and products. Because those sites start with a clean slate far from the company's powerful central laboratory, they are less plagued by the "not-invented-here" syndrome. For example, Canon's home-base-augmenting laboratory in the United Kingdom developed an innovative loudspeaker that is now being manufactured in Europe for a worldwide market. Senior researchers at Canon in Japan acknowledge that it would have been much more difficult for a new research team located in Japan to come up with the product. As one Canon manager puts it, "Although the new loudspeaker was partially based on knowledge that existed within Canon already, Canon's research management in Japan was too focused on existing product lines and would probably not have tolerated the pioneering loudspeaker project."

Finally, leaders of new R&D sites need to be aware of the considerable formal barriers they might confront when they seek access to local universities and scientific communities. These barriers are often created by lawmakers who want to protect a nation's intellectual capital. Although foreign companies do indeed absorb local knowledge and transfer it to their home bases—particularly in the case of home-base-augmenting sites—they also create important positive economic effects for the host nation. The laboratory leader of a new R&D site needs to communicate that fact locally in order to reduce existing barriers and prevent the formation of new ones.

DETERMINING THE OPTIMAL SIZE OF THE NEW R&D SITE

My research indicates that the optimal size for a new foreign R&D facility during the start-up phase is usually 30 to 40 employees, and the best size for a site after the ramp-up period is about 235 employees, including support staff. The optimal size of a site depends mainly on a company's track record in international management. Companies that already operate several sites abroad tend to be more successful at establishing larger new sites.

Companies can run into problems if their foreign sites are either too small or too large. If the site is too small, the resulting lack of critical mass produces an environment in which there is little cross-fertilization of ideas among researchers. And a small R&D site generally does not command a sufficient level of respect in the scientific community surrounding the laboratory. As a result, its researchers have a harder time gaining access to informal networks and to scientific meetings that provide opportunities for an exchange of knowledge. In contrast, if the laboratory site is too large, its culture quickly becomes anonymous, researchers become isolated, and the benefits of spreading fixed costs over a larger number of researchers are outweighed by the lack of cross-fertilization of ideas. According to one manager at such a lab, "Once people stopped getting to know one another on an informal basis in the lunchroom of our site, they became afraid of deliberately walking into one another's laboratory rooms to talk about research and to ask questions. Researchers who do not know each other on an informal basis are often hesitant to ask their colleagues for advice: they are afraid to reveal any of their own knowledge gaps. We realized that we had crossed a critical threshold in size. We subsequently scaled back somewhat and made an increased effort to reduce the isolation of individual researchers within the site through communication tools and through rotating researchers among different lab units at the site."

SUPERVISING THE START-UP PERIOD

During the initial growth period of an R&D site, which typically lasts anywhere from one to three years, the culture is formed and the groundwork for the site's future productivity is laid. During that period, senior management in the home country has to be in particularly close contact with the new site. Although it is important that the new laboratory develop its own identity and stake out its fields of expertise, it also has to be closely connected to the company's existing R&D structure. Newly hired scientists must be aware of the resources that exist within the company as a whole, and scientists at home and at other locations must be aware of the opportunities the new site creates for the company as a whole. Particularly during the start-up period, senior R&D managers at the corporate level have to walk a fine line and decide whether to devote the most resources to connecting the new site to the company or to supporting ties between the new site and its local environment.

To integrate a new site into the company as a whole, managers must pay close attention to the site's research agenda and create mechanisms to integrate it into the company's overall strategic goals. Because of the high degree of uncertainty of R&D outcomes, continuous adjustments to research agendas are the rule. What matters most is speed, both in terms of terminating research projects that go nowhere and in terms of pushing projects that bring unexpectedly good results.

The rapid exchange of information is essential to integrating a site into the overall company during the start-up phase. Companies use a number of mechanisms to create a cohesive research community in spite of geographic distance. Hewlett-Packard regularly organizes an in-house science fair at which teams of researchers can present projects and prototypes to one another. Canon has a program that lets researchers from home-base-augmenting sites request a temporary transfer to home-base-exploiting sites. At Xerox, most sites are linked by a sophisticated information system that allows senior R&D managers to determine within minutes the current state of research projects and the number of researchers working on those projects. But nothing can replace face-to-face contact between active researchers. Maintaining a global R&D network requires personal meetings, and therefore many researchers and R&D managers have to spend time visiting not only other R&D sites but also specialized suppliers and local universities affiliated with those sites.

Failing to establish sufficient ties with the company's existing R&D structure during the start-up phase can hamper the success of a new foreign R&D site. For example, in 1986, a large foreign pharmaceutical company established a biotechnology research site in Boston, Massachusetts. In order to recruit outstanding scientists and maintain a high level of creative output, the company's R&D management decided to give the new laboratory considerable leeway in its research agenda and in determining what to do with the results—although the company did reserve the right of first refusal for the commercialization of the lab's inventions. The new site was staffed exclusively with scientists handpicked by a newly hired laboratory leader. A renowned local biochemist, he had been employed for many years by a major U.S. university, where he had carried out contract research for the company. During the start-up phase, few of the company's veteran scientists were involved in joint research projects with the site's scientists—an arrangement that hindered the transfer of ideas between the new lab and the company's other R&D sites. Although the academic community now recognizes the lab as an important contributor to the field, few of its inventions have been patented by the company, fewer have been targeted for commercialization, and none have reached the commercial stage yet. One senior scientist working in the lab commented that ten years after its creation, the lab had become so much of an "independent animal" that it would take a lot of carefully balanced guidance from the company to instill a stronger sense of commercial orientation without a risk of losing the most creative scientists.

There is no magic formula that senior managers can follow to ensure the success of a foreign R&D site during its start-up phase. Managing an R&D network, particularly in its early stages, is delicate and complex. It requires constant tinkering—evaluation and reevaluation. Senior R&D managers have to decide how much of the research should be initiated by the company and how much by the scientist, determine the appropriate incentive structures and employment contracts, establish policies for the temporary transfer of researchers to the company's other R&D or manufacturing sites, and choose universities from which to hire scientists and engineers.

Flexibility and experimentation during a site's start-up phase can ensure its future productivity. For example, Fujitsu established a software-research laboratory site in San Jose, California, in 1992. The company was seriously thinking of establishing a second site in Boston but eventually reconsidered. Fujitsu realized that the effort that had gone into establishing the San Jose site had been greater than expected. Once the site was up and running, however, its productive output also had been higher than expected. Furthermore, Fujitsu found that its R&D managers had gained an excellent understanding of the R&D community that created advanced software-development tools. Although initially leaning toward establishing a second site, the managers were flexible. They decided to enlarge the existing site because of its better-than-expected performance as well as the limited potential benefits of a second site. The San Jose site has had a major impact on Fujitsu's software development and sales—particularly in

Japan but in the United States, too. Similarly, at Alcatel's first foreign R&D site in Germany, senior managers were flexible. After several months, they realized that the travel-and-communications budget would have to be increased substantially beyond initial projections in order to improve the flow of knowledge from the French home base. For instance, in the case of a telephone switchboard project, the actual number of business trips between the two sites was nearly twice as high as originally projected.

Integrating the Global R&D Network

As the number of companies' R&D sites at home and abroad grows, R&D managers will increasingly face the challenging task of coordinating the network. That will require a fundamental shift in the role of senior managers at the central lab. Managers of R&D networks must be global coordinators, not local administrators. More than being managers of people and processes, they must be managers of knowledge. And not all managers that a company has in place will be up to the task.

Consider Matsushita's R&D management. A number of technically competent managers became obsolete at the company once it launched a global approach to R&D. Today managers at Matsushita's central R&D site in Hirakata, Japan, continue to play an important role in the research and development of core processes for manufacturing. But the responsibility of an increasing number of senior managers at the central site is overseeing Matsushita's network of 15 dedicated R&D sites. That responsibility includes setting research agendas, monitoring results, and creating direct ties between sites.

How does the new breed of R&D manager coordinate global knowledge? Look again to Matsushita's central R&D site. First, high-level corporate managers in close cooperation with senior R&D managers develop an overall research agenda and assign different parts of it to individual sites. The process is quite tricky. It requires that the managers in charge have a good understanding of not only the technological capabilities that Matsushita will need to develop in the future but also the stock of technological capabilities already available to it.

Matsushita's central lab organizes two or three yearly off-site meetings devoted to informing R&D scientists and engineers about the entire company's current state of technical knowledge and capabilities. At the same meetings, engineers who have moved from R&D to take over manufacturing and marketing responsibilities inform R&D members about trends in Matsushita's current and potential future markets. Under the guidance of senior project managers, members from R&D, manufacturing, and marketing determine timelines and resource requirements for specific home-base-augmenting and home-base-exploiting projects. One R&D manager notes, "We discuss not only why a specific scientific insight might be interesting for Matsushita but also how we can turn this insight into a product quickly. We usually seek to develop a prototype early. Prototypes are a good basis for a discussion with marketing and manufacturing. Most of our efforts are targeted at delivering the prototype of a slightly better mousetrap early rather than delivering the blueprint of a much better mousetrap late."

To stimulate the exchange of information, R&D managers at Matsushita's central lab create direct links among researchers across different sites. They promote the use of videoconferencing and frequent face-to-face contact to forge those ties. Reducing the instances in which the central lab must act as mediator means that existing knowledge travels more quickly through the company and new ideas percolate more easily. For example, a researcher at a home-base-exploiting site in Singapore can communicate with another researcher at a home-base-exploiting site in Franklin Park, Illinois, about potential new research projects much more readily now that central R&D fosters informal and formal direct links.

Finally, managers at Matsushita's central lab constantly monitor new regional pockets of knowledge as well as the company's expanding network of manufacturing sites to determine whether the company will need additional R&D locations. With 15 major sites around the world, Matsushita has decided that the number of sites is sufficient at this point. But the company is ever vigilant about surveying the landscape and knows that as the landscape changes, its decision could, too.

As more pockets of knowledge emerge worldwide and competition in foreign markets mounts, the imperative to create global R&D networks will grow all the more pressing. Only those companies that embrace a global approach to R&D will meet the competitive challenges of the new dynamic. And only those managers who embrace their fundamentally new role as global coordinators and managers of knowledge will be able to tap the full potential of their R&D networks.

Notes

1. In a systematic effort to analyze the relationship of global strategy and R&D investments in technologically intensive industries, I have been collecting detailed data on all dedicated laboratory sites operated by 32 leading multinational companies. The sample consists of 10 U.S., 12 Japanese, and 10 European companies. Thirteen of the companies are in the pharmaceutical industry, and 19 are in the electronics industry. Data collection includes archival research, a detailed questionnaire, and in-depth interviews with several senior R&D managers in each company. Overall, these companies operate 238 dedicated R&D sites, 156 of them abroad. About 60% of the laboratory sites abroad were established after 1984. I have used this sample, which is the most complete of its kind, as a basis for a number of quantitative and qualitative investigations into global strategy, competitive interaction, and R&D management.

2. My research on global R&D strategies builds on earlier research on the competitiveness of nations and on research on foreign direct investment, including Michael E. Porter, *The Competitive Advantage of Nations* (New York: The Free Press, 1990), and Thomas J. Wesson, "An Alternative Motivation for Foreign Direct Investment" (Ph.D. dissertation, Harvard University, 1993). My research also builds on an existing body of knowledge about the management of multinational companies. See, for example, Christopher A. Bartlett and Sumantra Ghoshal, *Managing Across Borders* (Boston: Harvard Business School Press, 1989).

11
The Right Way to Manage Expats

J. Stewart Black and Hal B. Gregersen

In today's global economy, having a workforce that is fluent in the ways of the world isn't a luxury. It's a competitive necessity. No wonder nearly 80% of midsize and large companies currently send professionals abroad—and 45% plan to increase the number they have on assignment.

But international assignments don't come cheap. On average, expatriates cost two to three times what they would in an equivalent position back home. A fully loaded expatriate package including benefits and cost-of-living adjustments costs anywhere from $300,000 to $1 million annually, probably the single largest expenditure most companies make on any one individual except for the CEO.

The fact is, however, that most companies get anemic returns on their expat investments. Over the past decade, we have studied the management of expatriates at about 750 U.S., European, and Japanese companies. We asked both the expatriates themselves and the executives who sent them abroad to evaluate their experiences. In addition, we looked at what happened after expatriates returned home. Was their tenure worthwhile from a personal and organizational standpoint?

Overall, the results of our research were alarming. We found that between 10% and 20% of all U.S. managers sent abroad returned early because of job dissatisfaction or difficulties in adjusting to a foreign country. Of those who stayed for the duration, nearly one-third did not perform up to the expectations of their superiors. And perhaps most problematic, one-fourth of those who completed an assignment left their company, often to join a competitor, within one year after repatriation. That's a turnover rate double that of managers who did not go abroad.

If getting the most out of your expats is so important, why do so many companies get it so wrong? The main reason seems to be that many executives assume that the rules of good business are the same everywhere. In other words, they don't believe they need to—or should have to—engage in special efforts for their expats.

Take the expat assignment process. Executives know that negotiation tactics and marketing strategies can vary from culture to culture. Most do not believe, however, that the variance is sufficient to warrant the expense of programs designed to select or train candidates for international assignments.

Further, once expats are in place, executives back home usually are not inclined to coddle their well-paid representatives. When people are issued first-class tickets on a luxury liner, they're not supposed to complain about being at sea.

Finally, people at the home office find it difficult to imagine that returning expats need help readjusting after just a few years away. They don't see why people who've been given an extended period to explore the Left Bank or the Forbidden City should get a hero's welcome. As a result of such thinking, the only time companies pay special attention to their expats is when something goes spectacularly wrong. And by then, it's too little, too late.

Of course, some companies do engage in serious efforts to make foreign assignments beneficial both for the employees and the organization. Very often, however, such companies consign the responsibility of expat selection, training, and support to the human resources department. Few HR managers—only 11%, according to our research—have ever worked abroad themselves; most have little understanding of a global assignment's unique personal and professional challenges. As a result, they often get bogged down in the administrative minutiae of international assignments instead of capturing strategic opportunities.

Over the past several years, we have concentrated on examining the small number of companies that have compiled a winning track record in the process of managing their expats. Their people overseas report a high degree of job satisfaction and back that up with strong performance. These companies also hold on to their expats long after they return home. GE Medical Systems, for example, has all but eliminated unwanted turnover after repatriation and has seen its international sales expand from 10% to more than 50% of its total sales during the last ten years.

The companies that manage their expats effectively come in many sizes and from a wide range of industries. Yet we have found that they all follow three general practices:

When making international assignments, they focus on knowledge creation and global leadership development. Many companies send people abroad to reward them, to get them out of the way, or to fill an immediate business need. At companies that manage the international assignment process well, however, people are given foreign posts for two related reasons: to generate and transfer knowledge, to develop their global leadership skills, or to do both.

They assign overseas posts to people whose technical skills are matched or exceeded by their cross-cultural abilities. Companies that manage expats wisely do not assume that people who have succeeded at home will repeat that success abroad. They assign international posts to individuals who not only have the necessary technical skills but also have indicated that they would be likely to live comfortably in different cultures.

They end expatriate assignments with a deliberate repatriation process. Most executives who oversee expat employees view their return home as a nonissue. The truth is, repatriation is a time of major upheaval, professionally and personally, for two-thirds of expats. Companies that recognize this fact help their returning people by providing them with career guidance and enabling them to put their international experience to work.

Let's explore the practices in turn, illustrating them with companies that have put them to good use over the past several years.

Sending People for the Right Reasons

For as long as companies have been sending people abroad, many have been doing so for the wrong reasons—that is, for reasons that make little long-term business sense. Foreign assignments in glamorous locales such as Paris and London have been used to reward favored employees; posts to distant lands have been used as dumping grounds for the mediocre. But in most cases, companies send people abroad to fill a burning business need: to fight a competitor gaining market share in Brazil, to open a factory in China, to keep the computers running in Portugal.

Immediate business demands cannot be ignored. But the companies that manage their expats effectively view foreign assignments with an eye on the long term. Even when people are sent abroad to extinguish fires, they are expected to plant forests when the embers are cool. They are expected to go beyond pressing problems either to generate new knowledge for the organization or to acquire skills that will help them become leaders.

Imagine a large Canadian company that wants to open a telephone-making plant in Vietnam. It would certainly send a manager who knows how to manufacture phones and how to get a greenfield facility up and running quickly. The manager's performance rating and compensation would reflect those objectives, but that's where most companies would stop. Companies that manage their expats effectively, however, would require more of the manager in Vietnam. Once the plant was established, he would be expected to transfer his knowledge to local professionals—and to learn from them, too. Together, they would be expected to generate innovative ideas.

Nokia, the world's second largest manufacturer of mobile phones, is a good example of a company that effectively uses international assignments to generate knowledge. Unlike most large technology companies, Nokia does not rely on a central R&D function. Instead, it operates 36 centers in 11 countries—from Finland to China to the United States. Senior executives scan their global workforce for engineers and designers who are likely to generate new ideas when combined into a team. They bring these people together in an R&D center for assignments of up to two years, with the explicit objective of inventing new products. The approach works well: Nokia continues to grab global market share by rapidly turning new ideas into successful commercial products, such as the Nokia 6100 series mobile telephones that were launched last year in Beijing and have quickly captured a leading position in markets around the world.

Other companies have more need to focus on the second reason for international assignments: to develop global leadership skills. Such companies would concur with a recent observation by GE's CEO: "The Jack Welch of the future cannot be like me. I've spent my entire career in the United States. The next head of GE will be somebody who has spent time in Bombay, in Hong Kong, in Buenos Aires." An executive cannot develop a global perspective on business or become comfortable with foreign cultures by staying at headquarters or taking short business trips abroad. Such intangibles come instead as a result of having spent more than one sustained period working abroad.

Indeed, the only way to change fundamentally how people think about doing business globally is by having them work abroad for several months at a time. Everyone has a mental map of the world—a set of ingrained assumptions about what people are like and how the world works. But our maps may not be able to point us in the right direction when we try to use them in uncharted territory. Consider the case of a tall American businessman who, during a recent trip to Japan, dined at a traditional restaurant. Upon entering, he bumped his head on the doorjamb. The next day, the same thing happened. It was only on the third time that he remembered to duck. People on international assignments hit their heads on doorjambs many times over the years. Eventually, they learn to duck—to expect that the world abroad will be different from the one they had imagined. Hard experience has rearranged their mental maps or, at the very least, expanded the boundaries on their maps.

It is with such a broadened view of the world that global leaders are made. A vice president for Disney, for example, was posted in 1993 to EuroDisney, the company's struggling theme park just outside Paris. Stephen Burke arrived in France with the same mental map of the company as the senior managers at home. He believed, for instance, that families and alcohol do not mix at Disney theme parks. But after living in France for several months, Burke came to see what an affront EuroDisney's no-alcohol policy was to most of its potential local customers. A glass of wine with lunch was as French as a cheeseburger was American. Further, Burke came to see that Disney's lack of focus on tour operators—a more important distribution channel in Europe than in North America—made it inconvenient to book reservations for complete vacation packages, which many Europeans prefer to arrange.

With his new perspective on the local market, Burke pushed hard to persuade Disney's top management to sell wine at its French park and to create complete vacation packages for tour operators. He succeeded. Because of those and other changes, attendance and hotel occupancy soon skyrocketed, and EuroDisney posted its first operational profit.

Burke told us afterward, "The assignment to EuroDisney caused me to challenge long-held assumptions that were based on my experiences and career at Disney. After living in France, I came to look at the world quite differently."

The two principal goals of international assignments—generation of knowledge and development of global leaders—are not mutually exclusive. But it is unlikely that an international posting will allow a company to achieve both goals in every case or to an equal degree. Not every employee going abroad has abundant knowledge to share or the right stuff to be the company's future CEO. What matters, however, is that executives explicitly know beforehand why they are sending a person overseas—and that the reason goes beyond an immediate business problem.

Just as important, it is critical that expats themselves know the rationale for their assignments. Are they being sent abroad to generate knowledge or to develop their leadership skills? At the effective companies we studied, this kind of information helps expats focus on the right objectives in the right measure. For example, a communications company recently transferred one of its top lean-manufacturing experts from Asia to the United States. His task was to help managers understand and implement the practices that had been perfected in Singapore and Japan. The company's senior executives did not expect him to hone his leadership capabilities because they did not believe that he would ascend the corporate ranks. Knowing the main purpose of his posting, the expert was able to focus his energy on downloading his knowledge to other managers. Moreover, he did not build up unrealistic expectations that he would be promoted after returning home.

Companies with foreign operations will always face unexpected crises from time to time. But the companies that reap the most from sending their people abroad recognize that international assignments can't just be about sending in the medics. They must also be about ensuring the organization's health over the long term.

Sending the Right People

Just as managers often send people abroad for the wrong reasons, they frequently send the wrong people. Not because they send people who don't have the necessary technical skills. Indeed, technical skill is frequently the main reason that people are selected for open posts. But managers often send people who lack the ability to adjust to different customs, perspectives, and business practices. In other words, they send people who are capable but culturally illiterate.

Companies that have a strong track record with expats put a candidate's openness to new cultures on an equal footing with the person's technical know-how. After all, successfully navigating within your own business environment and culture does not guarantee that you can maneuver successfully in another one. We know, for instance, of a senior manager at a U.S. carmaker who was an expert at negotiating contracts with his company's steel suppliers. When transferred to Korea to conduct similar deals, the man's confrontational style did nothing but offend the consensus-minded Koreans—to the point where suppliers would not even speak to him directly. What was worse, the man was unwilling to change his way of doing business. He was soon called back to the company's home office, and his replacement spent a year undoing the damage he left in his wake.

How do you weed out people like the man who failed in Korea? The companies that manage expats successfully use a variety of tools to assess cultural sensitivity, from casual observation to formal testing. Interestingly, however, almost all evaluate people early in their careers in order to eliminate some from the potential pool of expats and help others build cross-cultural skills.

Although the companies differ in how they conduct their assessments, our research shows that they seek the following similar characteristics in their expats:

A Drive to Communicate. Most expats will try to communicate with local people in their new country, but people who end up being successful in their jobs are those that don't give up after early attempts either fail or embarrass them. To identify such people, the most effective companies in our research scanned their ranks for employees who were both enthusiastic and extroverted in conversation, and not afraid to try out their fractured French or talk with someone whose English was weak.

Broad-Based Sociability. The tendency for many people posted overseas is to stick with a small circle of fellow expats. By contrast, successful global managers establish social ties to the local residents, from shopkeepers to government officials. There is no better source for insights into a local market and no better way to adjust to strange surroundings.

Cultural Flexibility. It is human nature to gravitate toward the familiar—that's why many Americans overseas find themselves eating lunch at McDonald's. But the expats who add the most value to their companies—by staying for the duration and being open to local market trends—are those who willingly experiment with different customs. In India, such people eat dal and chapatis for lunch; in Brazil, they follow the fortunes of the local jai alai team.

Cosmopolitan Orientation. Expats with a cosmopolitan mind-set intuitively understand that different cultural norms have value and meaning to those who practice them. Companies that send the right people abroad have identified individuals who respect diverse viewpoints; they live and let live.

A Collaborative Negotiation Style. When expats negotiate with foreigners, the potential for conflict is much higher than it is when they are dealing with compatriots. Different cultures can hold radically different expectations about the way negotiations should be conducted. Thus a collaborative negotiation style, which can be important enough in business at home, becomes absolutely critical abroad.

Consider the approach taken by the vice chairman of Huntsman Corporation, a private chemicals company based in Salt Lake City with sales of $4.75 billion. Over the last five years, Jon Huntsman, Jr., has developed an informal but highly successful method for assessing cultural aptitudes in his employees. He regularly asks managers that he thinks have global leadership potential to accompany him on international trips, even if immediate business needs don't justify the expense. During such trips, he takes the managers to local restaurants, shopping areas, and side streets and observes their behavior. Do they approach the strange and unusual sights, sounds, smells, and tastes with curiosity or do they look for the nearest Pizza Hut? Do they try to communicate with local shopkeepers or do they hustle back to the Hilton?

Huntsman also observes how managers act among foreigners at home. In social settings, he watches to see if they seek out the foreign guests or talk only with people they already know. During negotiations with foreigners, he gauges his managers' ability to take a collaborative rather than a combative approach.

Although time consuming and sometimes costly, Huntsman's approach to screening potential expats is actually remarkably efficient. He is able to assess candidates before the pressures of an impending international problem make a quick decision necessary. Consequently, he makes fewer expensive mistakes when choosing whom to send abroad.

Other companies, such as LG Group, a $70 billion Korean conglomerate, take a more formal approach to assessing candidates for foreign assignments. Early in their careers, candidates complete a survey of about 100 questions designed to rate their preparation for global assignments and their cross-cultural skills. Afterward, LG employees and their managers discuss how specific training courses or future on-the-job experiences could help them enhance their strengths and overcome their weaknesses. From this discussion, a personalized development plan and timetable are generated. Because LG's potential expats are given time to develop their skills, about 97% of them succeed in meeting the company's expectations when they are eventually sent on international assignments.

The surveys used by LG were purchased from an outside company and cost from $300 to $500 per person. Other organizations develop them in-house, with the help of their training or HR departments. In either case, the survey questions generally ask people not to evaluate their own characteristics but to describe their past behavior. For example, they might be asked when they had last eaten a meal from a cuisine that was unfamiliar to them.

A third approach to identifying potential expats is used by Colgate-Palmolive, which has about 70% of its sales outside the United States and decades of international experience. To fill its entry-level marketing positions, the company recruits students from universities or business schools who can demonstrate an ability to handle cross-cultural situations. They may have already worked or lived abroad and will at the very least have traveled extensively; they will often be able to speak a foreign language. In this way, Colgate-Palmolive leverages the investment that other companies have made in an employee's first experience abroad.

Colgate-Palmolive takes a similarly cautious approach once such promising young people are on staff. Instead of sending them on long assignments abroad, it sends them on a series of training stints lasting 6 to 18 months. These assignments do not come with the costly benefits that are provided to high-level expats, such as allowances for housing and a car. This strategy means the company can provide young managers with a broad range of overseas experience. One manager hired in the United States, for example, spent time in the Czech Republic and the Baltic states and recently became country manager in Ukraine—all before celebrating his thirtieth birthday.

Companies face a trade-off between the accuracy and the cost of expat assessment. Although Colgate-Palmolive's approach is probably the most accurate way to assess an individual's potential to succeed on international assignments, it comes with a substantial price tag. That approach is probably most appropriate for a multinational that needs a large cadre of global managers. For companies with lesser workforce requirements, the less costly approaches of Huntsman and LG may make more sense. In any case, the key to success is having a systematic way of assessing the cross-cultural aptitudes of people you may want to send abroad.

Finishing the Right Way

Virtually every effective company we studied took the matter of repatriation seriously. Most companies, however, do not. Consider the findings of our research: about one-third of the expats we surveyed were still filling temporary assignments three months after coming home. More than three-quarters felt that their permanent position upon returning home was a demotion from their posting abroad, and 61% said that they lacked opportunities to put their foreign experience to work. No wonder the average turnover rate of returning professionals reaches 25%. We know of one company that over a two-year period lost all the managers it sent on international assignments within a year of their return—25 people in all. It might just as well have written a check for $50 million and tossed it to the winds.

The story of a senior engineer from a European electronics company is typical. The man was sent to Saudi Arabia on a four-year assignment, at a cost to his employers of about $4 million. During those four years, he learned fluent Arabic, gained new technical skills, and made friends with important businesspeople in the Saudi community. But upon returning home, the man was shocked to find himself frequently scolded that "the way things were done in Saudi Arabia has nothing to do with the way we do things at headquarters." Worse, he was kept waiting almost nine months for a permanent assignment which, when it came, gave him less authority than he had had abroad. Not surprisingly, the engineer left to join a direct competitor a few months later and ended up using the knowledge and skills he had acquired in Saudi Arabia against his former employer.

International assignments end badly for several reasons. First, although employers give little thought to their return, expats believe that a successful overseas assignment is an achievement that deserves recognition. They want to put their new skills and knowledge to use and are often disappointed both by the blasé attitude at headquarters toward their return and by their new jobs. That disappointment can be particularly strong for senior expats who have gotten used to the independence of running a foreign operation. As one U.K. expatriate recently observed, "If you have been the orchestra conductor overseas, it is very difficult to accept a position as second fiddle back home."

Changes in and out of the office can also make homecoming difficult. The company may have reshuffled its top management, reorganized its reporting structure, or even reshaped its culture. Old mentors may have moved on, leaving the returning employee to deal with new decision makers and power brokers. Things change in people's personal lives, too. Friends may have moved away, figuratively or literally. Children may find it hard to settle back into school or relate to old playmates.

The effective companies in our research used straightforward processes to solve these problems. At Monsanto, for example, the head office starts thinking about the next assignments for returning expats three to six months before they will return. As a first step, an HR officer and a line manager who is senior to the expat—both with international experience—assess the skills that the expat has gained during her experience overseas. They also review potential job openings within Monsanto. At the same time, the expat herself writes a report that includes a self-assessment and describes career goals. The three then meet and decide which of the available jobs best fits the expat's capabilities and the organization's needs.

In the six years since it introduced the system, Monsanto has dramatically reduced the turnover rate of its returning expatriates. And because returning employees participate in the process, they feel valued and treated fairly—even if they don't get their job of first choice.

Along with finding their returning expats suitable jobs, effective companies also prepare them for changes in their personal and professional landscapes. For example, the oil and gas company Unocal offers all expats and their families a daylong debriefing program upon their return. The program focuses on common repatriation difficulties, from

communicating with colleagues who have not worked abroad to helping children fit in again with their peers. The participants watch videos
of past expats and their families discussing their experiences. That sets
the stage for a live discussion. In many cases, participants end up sharing tips for coping with repatriation, such as keeping a journal. The
journal is useful, many returning expats say, because it helps them examine the sources of their frustrations and anxieties, which in turn
helps them think about what they might do to deal with them better.

Although participants find repatriation programs useful, it is seldom
cost effective for a company to provide them in-house unless its volume of international assignments is heavy. Most companies that offer
such programs outsource them to professional training companies or
form consortiums with other companies to share the costs. Effective
companies have realized that the money they spend on these programs is a small price to pay for retaining people with global insight
and experience.

Companies that manage their expats successfully follow the three
practices that make the assignments work from beginning to end.
They focus on creating knowledge and developing global leadership
skills; they make sure that candidates have cross-cultural skills to
match their technical abilities; and they prepare people to make the
transition back to their home offices.

Given the poor record that most companies have when it comes to
managing expats, it's probably no surprise that we often encounter organizations in which none of the three practices are at work. Some
companies, however, are committed to one or two of the practices,
and so the question arises, Do you have to follow all three to see a
payback on your expat investment? The answer, our research would
suggest, is yes. The practices not only reinforce one another, they also
cover the entire expat experience, from assignment to return home.

Consider the dividends reaped by Honda of America Manufacturing,
perhaps one of the best examples of a company that implements all
three practices. Honda starts expat assignments with clear strategic objectives such as the development of a new car model or improved supplier relations. Assignees then complete a survey to identify personal
strengths and weaknesses related to the upcoming assignment. Six
months before an expat is scheduled to return home, the company
initiates an active matchmaking process to locate a suitable job for that

person; a debriefing interview is conducted upon repatriation to capture lessons learned from the assignment.

As a result of Honda's integrated approach, nearly all of its expats consistently perform at or above expectations, and the turnover rate for returning employees is less than 5%. Most important, its expats consistently attain the key strategic objectives established at the beginning of each assignment.

Companies like Honda, GE, and Nokia have learned how to reap the full value of international assignments. Their CEOs share a conviction that sustained global growth rests on the shoulders of key individuals, particularly those with international experience. As a result, those companies are poised to capture tomorrow's global market opportunities by making their international assignments—the largest single investments in executive development that they will make—financially successful today.

12
Clusters and the New Economics of Competition

Michael E. Porter

Now that companies can source capital, goods, information, and technology from around the world, often with the click of a mouse, much of the conventional wisdom about how companies and nations compete needs to be overhauled. In theory, more open global markets and faster transportation and communication should diminish the role of location in competition. After all, anything that can be efficiently sourced from a distance through global markets and corporate networks is available to any company and therefore is essentially nullified as a source of competitive advantage.

But if location matters less, why, then, is it true that the odds of finding a world-class mutual-fund company in Boston are much higher than in most any other place? Why could the same be said of textile-related companies in North Carolina and South Carolina, of high-performance auto companies in southern Germany, or of fashion shoe companies in northern Italy?

Today's economic map of the world is dominated by what I call *clusters*: critical masses—in one place—of unusual competitive success in particular fields. Clusters are a striking feature of virtually every national, regional, state, and even metropolitan economy, especially in more economically advanced nations. Silicon Valley and Hollywood may be the world's best-known clusters. Clusters are not unique,

Extensive additional discussion of clusters and cluster development can be found in Michael E. Porter's essays "Clusters and Competition" and "Competing Across Locations" in his collection titled On Competition *(Boston: Harvard Business School Press, Boston, MA: 1998).*

however; they are highly typical—and therein lies a paradox: the enduring competitive advantages in a global economy lie increasingly in local things—knowledge, relationships, motivation—that distant rivals cannot match.

Although location remains fundamental to competition, its role today differs vastly from a generation ago. In an era when competition was driven heavily by input costs, locations with some important endowment—a natural harbor, for example, or a supply of cheap labor—often enjoyed a *comparative advantage* that was both competitively decisive and persistent over time.

Competition in today's economy is far more dynamic. Companies can mitigate many input-cost disadvantages through global sourcing, rendering the old notion of comparative advantage less relevant. Instead, competitive advantage rests on making more productive use of inputs, which requires continual innovation.

Untangling the paradox of location in a global economy reveals a number of key insights about how companies continually create competitive advantage. What happens *inside* companies is important, but clusters reveal that the immediate business environment *outside* companies plays a vital role as well. This role of locations has been long overlooked, despite striking evidence that innovation and competitive success in so many fields are geographically concentrated—whether it's entertainment in Hollywood, finance on Wall Street, or consumer electronics in Japan.

Clusters affect competitiveness within countries as well as across national borders. Therefore, they lead to new agendas for all business executives—not just those who compete globally. More broadly, clusters represent a new way of thinking about location, challenging much of the conventional wisdom about how companies should be configured, how institutions such as universities can contribute to competitive success, and how governments can promote economic development and prosperity.

What Is a Cluster?

Clusters are geographic concentrations of interconnected companies and institutions in a particular field. Clusters encompass an array of linked industries and other entities important to competition. They include, for example, suppliers of specialized inputs such as components, machinery, and services, and providers of specialized infrastructure. Clusters also often extend downstream to channels and customers and laterally to manufacturers of complementary products and to companies in industries related by skills, technologies, or common inputs. Finally, many clusters include governmental and other institutions—such as universities, standards-setting agencies, think tanks, vocational training providers, and trade associations—that provide specialized training, education, information, research, and technical support.

The California wine cluster is a good example. It includes 680 commercial wineries as well as several thousand independent wine grape growers. (See Exhibit 12-1 "Anatomy of the California Wine Cluster.") An extensive complement of industries supporting both wine making and grape growing exists, including suppliers of grape stock, irrigation and harvesting equipment, barrels, and labels; specialized public relations and advertising firms; and numerous wine publications aimed at consumer and trade audiences. A host of local institutions is involved with wine, such as the world-renowned viticulture and enology program at the University of California at Davis, the Wine Institute, and special committees of the California senate and assembly. The cluster also enjoys weaker linkages to other California clusters in agriculture, food and restaurants, and wine-country tourism.

Consider also the Italian leather fashion cluster, which contains well-known shoe companies such as Ferragamo and Gucci as well as a host of specialized suppliers of footwear components, machinery, molds, design services, and tanned leather. (See Exhibit 12-2 "Mapping the Italian Leather Fashion Cluster.") It also consists of several chains of related industries, including those producing different types of leather goods (linked by common inputs and technologies) and different types of footwear (linked by overlapping channels and technologies). These industries employ common marketing media and compete with similar images in similar customer segments. A related Italian cluster in textile fashion, including clothing, scarves, and accessories, produces complementary products that often employ common channels. The extraordinary strength of the Italian leather fashion cluster can be attributed, at least in part, to the multiple linkages and synergies that participating Italian businesses enjoy.

A cluster's boundaries are defined by the linkages and complementarities across industries and institutions that are most important to competition. Although clusters often fit within political boundaries, they may cross state or even national borders. In the United

Exhibit 12-1   Anatomy of the California Wine Cluster

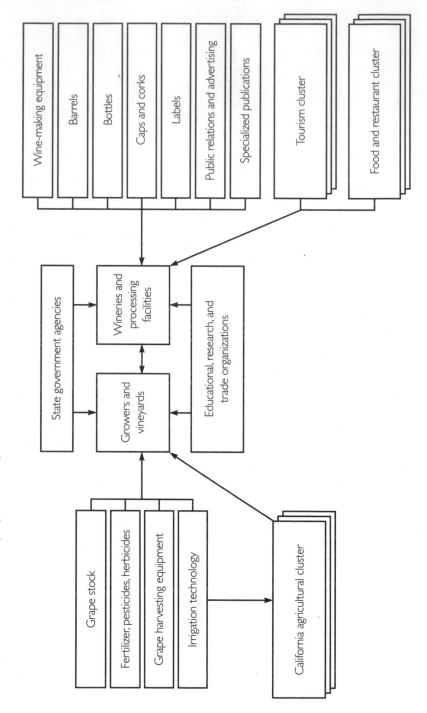

Exhibit 12-2 Mapping the Italian Leather Fashion Cluster

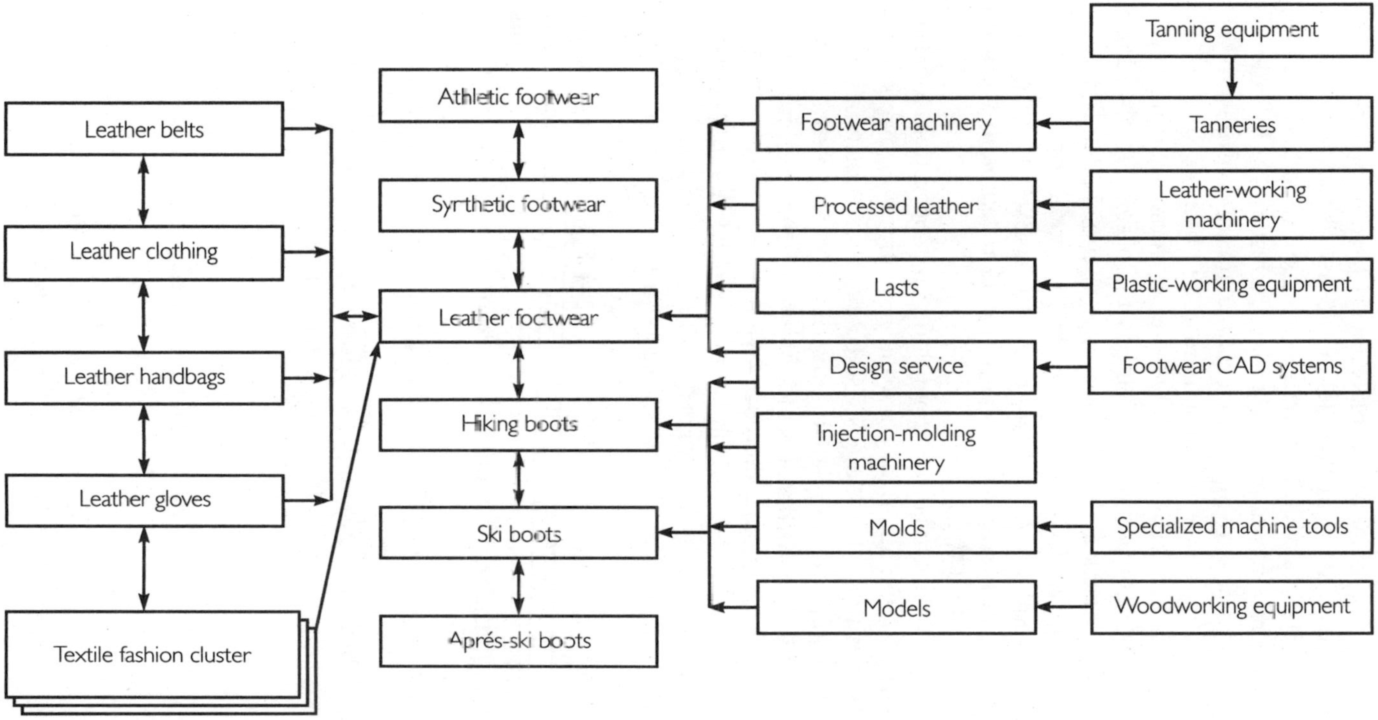

States, for example, a pharmaceuticals cluster straddles New Jersey and Pennsylvania near Philadelphia. Similarly, a chemicals cluster in Germany crosses over into German-speaking Switzerland.

Clusters rarely conform to standard industrial classification systems, which fail to capture many important actors and relationships in competition. Thus significant clusters may be obscured or even go unrecognized. In Massachusetts, for example, more than 400 companies, representing at least 39,000 high-paying jobs, are involved in medical devices in some way. The cluster long remained all but invisible, however, buried within larger and overlapping industry categories such as electronic equipment and plastic products. Executives in the medical devices cluster have only recently come together to work on issues that will benefit them all.

Clusters promote both competition and cooperation. Rivals compete intensely to win and retain customers. Without vigorous competition, a cluster will fail. Yet there is also cooperation, much of it vertical, involving companies in related industries and local institutions. Competition can coexist with cooperation because they occur on different dimensions and among different players.

Clusters represent a kind of new spatial organizational form in between arm's-length markets on the one hand and hierarchies, or vertical integration, on the other. A cluster, then, is an alternative way of organizing the value chain. Compared with market transactions among dispersed and random buyers and sellers, the proximity of companies and institutions in one location—and the repeated exchanges among them—fosters better coordination and trust. Thus clusters mitigate the problems inherent in arm's-length relationships without imposing the inflexibilities of vertical integration or the management challenges of creating and maintaining formal linkages such as networks, alliances, and partnerships. A cluster of independent and informally linked companies and institutions represents a robust organizational form that offers advantages in efficiency, effectiveness, and flexibility.

Why Clusters Are Critical to Competition

Modern competition depends on productivity, not on access to inputs or the scale of individual enterprises. Productivity rests on *how* companies compete, not on the particular fields they compete in. Companies can be highly productive in any industry—shoes, agriculture, or semiconductors—if they employ sophisticated methods, use advanced technology, and offer unique products and services. All industries can employ advanced technology; all industries can be knowledge intensive.

The sophistication with which companies compete in a particular location, however, is strongly influenced by the quality of the local business environment.[1] Companies cannot employ advanced logistical techniques, for example, without a high-quality transportation infrastructure. Nor can companies effectively compete on sophisticated service without well-educated employees. Businesses cannot operate efficiently under onerous regulatory red tape or under a court system that fails to resolve disputes quickly and fairly. Some aspects of the business environment, such as the legal system, for example, or corporate tax rates, affect all industries. In advanced economies, however, the more decisive aspects of the business environment are often cluster specific; these constitute some of the most important microeconomic foundations for competition.

Clusters affect competition in three broad ways: first, by increasing the productivity of companies based in the area; second, by driving the direction and pace of innovation, which underpins future productivity growth; and third, by stimulating the formation of new businesses, which expands and strengthens the cluster itself. A cluster allows each member to benefit *as if* it had greater scale or *as if* it had joined with others formally—without requiring it to sacrifice its flexibility.

CLUSTERS AND PRODUCTIVITY

Being part of a cluster allows companies to operate more productively in sourcing inputs; accessing information, technology, and needed institutions; coordinating with related companies; and measuring and motivating improvement.

BETTER ACCESS TO EMPLOYEES AND SUPPLIERS. Companies in vibrant clusters can tap into an existing pool of specialized and experienced employees, thereby lowering their search and transaction costs in recruiting. Because a cluster signals opportunity and reduces the risk of relocation for employees, it can also be easier to attract talented people from other locations, a decisive advantage in some industries.

A well-developed cluster also provides an efficient means of obtaining other important inputs. Such a cluster offers a deep and specialized supplier base. Sourcing locally instead of from distant suppliers lowers transaction costs. It minimizes the need for inventory, eliminates importing costs and delays, and—because local reputation is important—lowers the risk that suppliers will overprice or renege on commitments. Proximity improves communications and makes it easier for suppliers to provide ancillary or support services such as installation and debugging. Other things being equal, then, local outsourcing is a better solution than distant outsourcing, especially for advanced and specialized inputs involving embedded technology, information, and service content.

Formal alliances with distant suppliers can mitigate some of the disadvantages of distant outsourcing. But all formal alliances involve their own complex bargaining and governance problems and can inhibit a company's flexibility. The close, informal relationships possible among companies in a cluster are often a superior arrangement.

In many cases, clusters are also a better alternative to vertical integration. Compared with in-house units, outside specialists are often more cost effective and responsive, not only in component production but also in services such as training. Although extensive vertical integration may have once been the norm, a fast-changing environment can render vertical integration inefficient, ineffective, and inflexible.

Even when some inputs are best sourced from a distance, clusters offer advantages. Suppliers trying to penetrate a large, concentrated market will price more aggressively, knowing that as they do so they can realize efficiencies in marketing and in service.

Working against a cluster's advantages in assembling resources is the possibility that competition will render them more expensive and scarce. But companies do have the alternative of outsourcing many inputs from other locations, which tends to limit potential cost penalties. More important, clusters increase not only the demand for specialized inputs but also their supply.

ACCESS TO SPECIALIZED INFORMATION. Extensive market, technical, and competitive information accumulates within a cluster, and members have preferred access to it. In addition, personal relationships and community ties foster trust and facilitate the flow of information. These conditions make information more transferable.

COMPLEMENTARITIES. A host of linkages among cluster members results in a whole greater than the sum of its parts. In a typical tourism cluster, for example, the quality of a visitor's experience depends not only on the appeal of the primary attraction but also on the quality and efficiency of complementary businesses such as hotels, restaurants, shopping outlets, and transportation facilities. Because members of the cluster are mutually dependent, good performance by one can boost the success of the others.

Complementarities come in many forms. The most obvious is when products complement one another in meeting customers' needs, as the tourism example illustrates. Another form is the coordination of activities across companies to optimize their collective productivity. In wood products, for instance, the efficiency of sawmills depends on a reliable supply of high-quality timber and the ability to put all the timber to use—in furniture (highest quality), pallets and boxes (lower quality), or wood chips (lowest quality). In the early 1990s, Portuguese sawmills suffered from poor timber quality because local landowners did not invest in timber management. Hence most timber was processed for use in pallets and boxes, a lower-value use that limited the price paid to landowners. Substantial improvement in productivity was possible, but only if several parts of the cluster changed simultaneously. Logging operations, for example, had to modify cutting and sorting procedures, while sawmills had to develop the capacity to process wood in more sophisticated ways. Coordination to develop standard wood classifications and measures was an important enabling step. Geographically dispersed companies are less likely to recognize and capture such linkages.

Other complementarities arise in marketing. A cluster frequently enhances the reputation of a location in a particular field, making it more likely that buyers will turn to a vendor based there. Italy's strong reputation for fashion and design, for example, benefits companies involved in leather goods, footwear, apparel, and accessories. Beyond reputation, cluster members often profit from a variety of joint marketing mechanisms, such as company referrals, trade fairs, trade magazines, and marketing delegations.

Finally, complementarities can make buying from a cluster more attractive for customers. Visiting buyers can see many vendors in a single trip. They also may perceive their buying risk to be lower because one location provides alternative suppliers. That allows them to multisource or to switch vendors if the need arises. Hong Kong thrives as a source of fashion apparel in part for this reason.

ACCESS TO INSTITUTIONS AND PUBLIC GOODS. Investments made by government or other public institutions—such as public spending for specialized infrastructure or educational programs—can enhance a company's productivity. The ability to recruit employees trained at local programs, for example, lowers the cost of internal training. Other quasi-public goods, such as the cluster's information and technology pools and its reputation, arise as natural by-products of competition.

It is not just governments that create public goods that enhance productivity in the private sector. Investments by companies—in training programs, infrastructure, quality centers, testing laboratories, and so on—also contribute to increased productivity. Such private investments are often made collectively because cluster participants recognize the potential for collective benefits.

BETTER MOTIVATION AND MEASUREMENT. Local rivalry is highly motivating. Peer pressure amplifies competitive pressure within a cluster, even among noncompeting or indirectly competing companies. Pride and the desire to look good in the local community spur executives to attempt to outdo one another.

Clusters also often make it easier to measure and compare performances because local rivals share general circumstances—for example, labor costs and local market access—and they perform similar activities. (See Exhibit 12-3 "Mapping Selected U.S. Clusters.") Companies within clusters typically have intimate knowledge of their suppliers' costs. Managers are able to compare costs and employees' performance with other local companies. Additionally, financial institutions can accumulate knowledge about the cluster that can be used to monitor performance.

CLUSTERS AND INNOVATION

In addition to enhancing productivity, clusters play a vital role in a company's ongoing ability to innovate. Some of the same characteristics that enhance current productivity have an even more dramatic effect on innovation and productivity growth.

Because sophisticated buyers are often part of a cluster, companies inside clusters usually have a better window on the market than isolated competitors do. Computer companies based in Silicon Valley and Austin, Texas, for example, plug into customer needs and trends with a speed difficult to match by companies located elsewhere. The ongoing relationships with other entities within the cluster also help

Exhibit 12-3   Mapping Selected U.S. Clusters

Here are just some of the clusters in the United States. A few—Hollywood's entertainment cluster and High Point, North Carolina's household-furniture cluster—are well known. Others are less familiar, such as golf equipment in Carlsbad, California, and optics in Phoenix, Arizona. A relatively small number of clusters usually account for a major share of the economy within a geographic area as well as for an overwhelming share of its economic activity that is "exported" to other locations. Exporting clusters—those that export products or make investments to compete outside the local area—are the primary source of an area's economic growth and prosperity over the long run. The demand for local industries is inherently limited by the size of the local market, but exporting clusters can grow far beyond that limit.

companies to learn early about evolving technology, component and machinery availability, service and marketing concepts, and so on. Such learning is facilitated by the ease of making site visits and frequent face-to-face contact.

Clusters do more than make opportunities for innovation more visible. They also provide the capacity and the flexibility to act rapidly. A company within a cluster often can source what it needs to implement innovations more quickly. Local suppliers and partners can and do get closely involved in the innovation process, thus ensuring a better match with customers' requirements.

Companies within a cluster can experiment at lower cost and can delay large commitments until they are more assured that a given innovation will pan out. In contrast, a company relying on distant suppliers faces greater challenges in every activity it coordinates with other organizations—in contracting, for example, or securing delivery or obtaining associated technical and service support. Innovation can be even harder in vertically integrated companies, especially in those that face difficult trade-offs if the innovation erodes the value of in-house assets or if current products or processes must be maintained while new ones are developed.

Reinforcing the other advantages for innovation is the sheer pressure—competitive pressure, peer pressure, constant comparison—that occurs in a cluster. Executives vie with one another to set their companies apart. For all these reasons, clusters can remain centers of innovation for decades.

CLUSTERS AND NEW BUSINESS FORMATION

It is not surprising, then, that many new companies grow up within an existing cluster rather than at isolated locations. New suppliers, for example, proliferate within a cluster because a concentrated customer base lowers their risks and makes it easier for them to spot market opportunities. Moreover, because developed clusters comprise related industries that normally draw on common or very similar inputs, suppliers enjoy expanded opportunities.

Clusters are conducive to new business formation for a variety of reasons. Individuals working within a cluster can more easily perceive gaps in products or services around which they can build businesses. Beyond that, barriers to entry are lower than elsewhere. Needed assets, skills, inputs, and staff are often readily available at the cluster location, waiting to be assembled into a new enterprise. Local financial institutions and investors, already familiar with the cluster, may require a lower risk premium on capital. In addition, the cluster often presents a significant local market, and an entrepreneur may benefit from established relationships. All of these factors reduce the perceived risks of entry—and of exit, should the enterprise fail.

The formation of new businesses within a cluster is part of a positive feedback loop. An expanded cluster amplifies all the benefits I have described—it increases the collective pool of competitive resources, which benefits all the cluster's members. The net result is that companies in the cluster advance relative to rivals at other locations.

Birth, Evolution, and Decline

A cluster's roots can often be traced to historical circumstances. In Massachusetts, for example, several clusters had their beginnings in research done at MIT or Harvard. The Dutch transportation cluster owes much to Holland's central location within Europe, an extensive network of waterways, the efficiency of the port of Rotterdam, and the skills accumulated by the Dutch through Holland's long maritime history.

Clusters may also arise from unusual, sophisticated, or stringent local demand. Israel's cluster in irrigation equipment and other advanced agricultural technologies reflects that nation's strong desire for self-sufficiency in food together with a scarcity of water and hot, arid growing conditions. The environmental cluster in Finland emerged as a result of pollution problems created by local process industries such as metals, forestry, chemicals, and energy.

Prior existence of supplier industries, related industries, or even entire related clusters provides yet another seed for new clusters. The golf equipment cluster near San Diego, for example, has its roots in southern California's aerospace cluster. That cluster created a pool of suppliers for castings and advanced materials as well as engineers with the requisite experience in those technologies.

New clusters may also arise from one or two innovative companies that stimulate the growth of many others. Medtronic played this role in helping to create the Minneapolis medical-device cluster. Similarly,

MCI and America Online have been hubs for growing new businesses in the telecommunications cluster in the Washington, D.C., metropolitan area.

Sometimes a chance event creates some advantageous factor that, in turn, fosters cluster development—although chance rarely provides the sole explanation for a cluster's success in a location. The telemarketing cluster in Omaha, Nebraska, for example, owes much to the decision by the U.S. Air Force to locate the Strategic Air Command (SAC) there. Charged with a key role in the country's nuclear deterrence strategy, SAC was the site of the first installation of fiber-optic telecommunications cables in the United States. The local Bell operating company (now U.S. West) developed unusual capabilities through its dealings with such a demanding customer. The extraordinary telecommunications capability and infrastructure that consequently developed in Omaha, coupled with less unique attributes such as its central-time-zone location and easily understandable local accent, provided the underpinnings of the area's telemarketing cluster.

Once a cluster begins to form, a self-reinforcing cycle promotes its growth, especially when local institutions are supportive and local competition is vigorous. As the cluster expands, so does its influence with government and with public and private institutions.

A growing cluster signals opportunity, and its success stories help attract the best talent. Entrepreneurs take notice, and individuals with ideas or relevant skills migrate in from other locations. Specialized suppliers emerge; information accumulates; local institutions develop specialized training, research, and infrastructure; and the cluster's strength and visibility grow. Eventually, the cluster broadens to encompass related industries. Numerous case studies suggest that clusters require a decade or more to develop depth and real competitive advantage.[2]

Cluster development is often particularly vibrant at the intersection of clusters, where insights, skills, and technologies from various fields merge, sparking innovation and new businesses. An example from Germany illustrates this point. The country has distinct clusters in both home appliances and household furniture, each based on different technologies and inputs. At the intersection of the two, though, is a cluster of built-in kitchens and appliances, an area in which Germany commands a higher share of world exports than in either appliances or furniture.

Clusters continually evolve as new companies and industries emerge or decline and as local institutions develop and change. They can maintain vibrancy as competitive locations for centuries; most successful clusters prosper for decades at least. However, they can and do lose their competitive edge due to both external and internal forces. Technological discontinuities are perhaps the most significant of the external threats because they can neutralize many advantages simultaneously. A cluster's assets—market information, employees' skills, scientific and technical expertise, and supplier bases—may all become irrelevant. New England's loss of market share in golf equipment is a good example. The New England cluster was based on steel shafts, steel irons, and wooden-headed woods. When companies in California began making golf clubs with advanced materials, East Coast producers had difficulty competing. A number of them were acquired or went out of business.

A shift in buyers' needs, creating a divergence between local needs and needs elsewhere, constitutes another external threat. U.S. companies in a variety of clusters, for example, suffered when energy efficiency grew in importance in most parts of the world while the United States maintained low energy prices. Lacking both pressure to improve and insight into customer needs, U.S. companies were slow to innovate, and they lost ground to European and Japanese competitors.

Clusters are at least as vulnerable to internal rigidities as they are to external threats. Overconsolidation, mutual understandings, cartels, and other restraints to competition undermine local rivalry. Regulatory inflexibility or the introduction of restrictive union rules slows productivity improvement. The quality of institutions such as schools and universities can stagnate.

Groupthink among cluster participants—Detroit's attachment to gas-guzzling autos in the 1970s is one example—can be another powerful form of rigidity. If companies in a cluster are too inward looking, the whole cluster suffers from a collective inertia, making it harder for individual companies to embrace new ideas, much less perceive the need for radical innovation.

Such rigidities tend to arise when government suspends or intervenes in competition or when companies persist in old behaviors and relationships that no longer contribute to competitive advantage. Increases in the cost of doing business begin to outrun the ability to upgrade. Rigidities of this nature currently work against a variety of clusters in Switzerland and Germany.

As long as rivalry remains sufficiently vigorous, companies can partially compensate for some decline in the cluster's competitiveness by outsourcing to distant suppliers or moving part or all of production elsewhere to offset local wages that rise ahead of productivity. German companies in the 1990s, for example, have been doing just that. Technology can be licensed or sourced from other locations, and product development can be moved. Over time, however, a location will decline if it fails to build capabilities in major new technologies or needed supporting firms and institutions.

Implications for Companies

In the new economics of competition, what matters most is not inputs and scale, but productivity—and that is true in all industries. The term *high tech*, normally used to refer to fields such as information technology and biotechnology, has distorted thinking about competition, creating the misconception that only a handful of businesses compete in sophisticated ways.

In fact, there is no such thing as a low-tech industry. There are only low-tech companies—that is, companies that fail to use world-class technology and practices to enhance productivity and innovation. A vibrant cluster can help any company in any industry compete in the most sophisticated ways, using the most advanced, relevant skills and technologies. (See "Clusters, Geography, and Economic Development.")

Clusters, Geography, and Economic Development

Poor countries lack well-developed clusters; they compete in the world market with cheap labor and natural resources. To move beyond this stage, the development of well-functioning clusters is essential. Clusters become an especially controlling factor for countries moving from a middle-income to an advanced economy. Even in high-wage economies, however, the need for cluster upgrading is constant. The wealthier the economy, the more it will require innovation to support rising wages and to replace jobs eliminated by improvements in efficiency and the migration of standard production to low-cost areas.

Promoting cluster formation in developing economies means starting at the most basic level. Policymakers must first address the foundations: improving education and skill levels, building capacity in technology, opening access to capital markets, and improving institutions. Over time, additional investment in more cluster-specific assets is necessary.

Government policies in developing economies often unwittingly work against cluster formation. Restrictions on industrial location and subsidies to invest in distressed areas, for example, can disperse companies artificially. Protecting local companies from competition leads to excessive vertical integration and blunted pressure for innovation, retarding cluster development.

In the early stages of economic development, countries should expand internal trade among cities and states and trade with neighboring countries as important stepping stones to building the skills to compete globally. Such trade greatly enhances cluster development. Instead, attention is typically riveted on the large, advanced markets, an orientation that has often been reinforced by protectionist policies restricting trade with nearby markets. However, the kinds of goods developing countries can trade with advanced economies are limited to commodities and to activities sensitive to labor costs.

While it is essential that clusters form, *where* they form also matters. In developing economies, a large proportion of economic activity tends to concentrate around capital cities such as Bangkok and Bogotá. That is usually because outlying areas lack infrastructure, institutions, and suppliers. It may also reflect an intrusive role by the central government in controlling competition, leading companies to locate near the seat of power and the agencies whose approval they require to do business.

This pattern of economic geography inflicts high costs on productivity. Congestion, bottlenecks, and inflexibility lead to high administrative costs and major inefficiencies, not to mention a diminished quality of life. Companies cannot easily move out from the center, however, because neither infrastructure nor rudimentary clusters exist in the smaller cities and towns. (The building of a tourism cluster in developing economies can be a positive force in improving the outlying infrastructure and in dispersing economic activity.)

Even in advanced economies, however, economic activity may be geographically concentrated. Japan offers a particularly striking case, with nearly 50% of total manufacturing shipments located around Tokyo and Osaka. This is due less to inadequacies in infrastructure in outlying areas than to a powerful and intrusive central government, with its centralizing bias in policies and institutions. The Japanese case vividly illustrates the major inefficiencies and productivity costs resulting from such a pattern of economic geography, even for advanced nations. It is a major policy issue facing Japan.

An economic geography characterized by specialization and dispersion—that is, a number of metropolitan areas, each specializing in an array of clusters—appears to be a far more productive industrial organization than one based on one or two huge, diversified cities. In nations such as Germany, Italy, Switzerland, and the United States, this kind of internal specialization and trade—and internal competition among locations—fuels productivity growth and hones the ability of companies to compete effectively in the global arena.

Thus executives must extend their thinking beyond what goes on inside their own organizations and within their own industries. Strategy must also address what goes on outside. Extensive vertical integration may once have been appropriate, but companies today must forge close linkages with buyers, suppliers, and other institutions.

Specifically, understanding clusters adds the following four issues to the strategic agenda.

1. Choosing locations. Globalization and the ease of transportation and communication have led many companies to move some or all of their operations to locations with low wages, taxes, and utility costs. What we know about clusters suggests, first, that some of those cost advantages may well turn out to be illusory. Locations with those advantages often lack efficient infrastructure, sophisticated suppliers, and other cluster benefits that can more than offset any savings from lower input costs. Savings in wages, utilities, and taxes may be highly visible and easy to measure up front, but productivity penalties remain hidden and unanticipated.

More important to ongoing competitiveness is the role of location in innovation. Yes, companies have to spread activities globally to source inputs and gain access to markets. Failure to do so will lead to a competitive *disadvantage*. And for stable, labor-intensive activities such as assembly and software translation, low factor costs are often decisive in driving locational choices. (See Exhibit 12-4 "Mapping Portugal's Clusters.")

For a company's "home base" for each product line, however, clusters are critical. Home base activities—strategy development, core product and process R&D, a critical mass of the most sophisticated production or service provision—create and renew the company's product, processes, and services. Therefore locational decisions must be

Exhibit 12-4 Mapping Portugal's Clusters

In a middle-income economy like Portugal, exporting clusters tend to be more natural-resource or labor intensive.

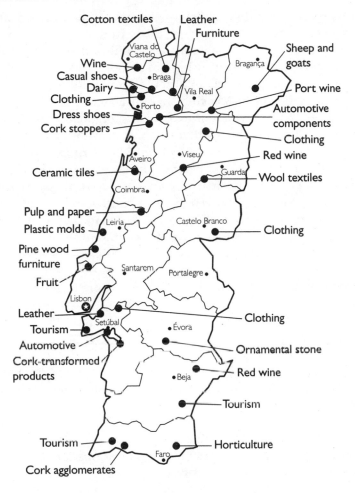

based on both total systems costs and innovation potential, not on input costs alone. Cluster thinking suggests that every product line needs a home base, and the most vibrant cluster will offer the best location. Within the United States, for example, Hewlett-Packard has chosen cluster locations for the home bases of its major product lines: California, where almost all of the world's leading personal computer and workstation businesses are located, is home to personal computers and workstations; Massachusetts, which has an extraordinary concentration of world-renowned research hospitals and leading medical instrument companies, is home to medical instruments.

As global competition nullifies traditional comparative advantages and exposes companies to the best rivals from around the world, a growing number of multinationals are shifting their home bases to more vibrant clusters—often using acquisitions as a means of establishing themselves as insiders in a new location. Nestlé, for example, after acquiring Rowntree Mackintosh, relocated its confectionary business to York, England, where Rowntree was originally based, because a vibrant food cluster thrives there. England, with its sweet-toothed consumers, sophisticated retailers, advanced advertising agencies, and highly competitive media companies, constitutes a more dynamic environment for competing in mass-market candy than Switzerland did. Similarly, Nestlé has moved its headquarters for bottled water to France, the most competitive location in that industry. Northern Telecom has relocated its home base for central office switching from Canada to the United States—drawn by the vibrancy of the U.S. telecommunications-equipment cluster.

Cluster thinking also suggests that it is better to move groups of linked activities to the same place than to spread them across numerous locations. Colocating R&D, component fabrication, assembly, marketing, customer support, and even related businesses can facilitate internal efficiencies in sourcing and in sharing technology and information. Grouping activities into campuses also allows companies to extend deeper roots into local clusters, improving their ability to capture potential benefits.

2. Engaging locally. The social glue that binds clusters together also facilitates access to important resources and information. Tapping into the competitively valuable assets within a cluster requires personal relationships, face-to-face contact, a sense of common interest, and "insider" status. The mere colocation of companies, suppliers, and institutions creates the *potential* for economic value; it does not necessarily ensure its realization.

To maximize the benefits of cluster involvement, companies must participate actively and establish a significant local presence. They must have a substantial local investment even if the parent company is headquartered elsewhere. And they must foster ongoing relationships with government bodies and local institutions such as utilities, schools, and research groups.

Companies have much to gain by engaging beyond their narrow confines as single entities. Yet managers tend to be wary, at least initially. They fear that a growing cluster will attract competition, drive up costs, or cause them to lose valued employees to rivals or spin-offs. As their understanding of the cluster concept grows, however, managers realize that many participants in the cluster do not compete directly and that the offsetting benefits, such as a greater supply of better trained people, for example, can outweigh any increase in competition.

3. Upgrading the cluster. Because the health of the local business environment is important to the health of the company, upgrading the cluster should be part of management's agenda. Companies upgrade their clusters in a variety of ways.

Consider Genzyme. Massachusetts is home to a vibrant biotechnology cluster, which draws on the region's strong universities, medical centers, and venture capital firms. Once Genzyme reached the stage in its development when it needed a manufacturing facility, CEO Henri Termeer initially considered the pharmaceuticals cluster in the New Jersey and Philadelphia area because it had what Massachusetts lacked: established expertise in drug manufacturing. Upon further reflection, however, Termeer decided to influence the process of creating a manufacturing capability in Genzyme's home base, reasoning that if his plans were successful, the company could become more competitive.

Thus Genzyme deliberately chose to work with contractors committed to the Boston area, bypassing the many specialized engineering firms located near Philadelphia. In addition, it undertook a number of initiatives, with the help of city and state government, to improve the labor force, such as offering scholarships and internships to local youth. More broadly, Genzyme has worked to build critical mass for its cluster. Termeer believes that Genzyme's success is linked to the cluster's—and that all members will benefit from a strong base of supporting functions and institutions.

4. Working collectively. The way clusters operate suggests a new agenda of collective action in the private sector. Investing in public goods is normally seen as a function of government, yet cluster thinking clearly demonstrates how companies benefit from local assets and institutions.

In the past, collective action in the private sector has focused on seeking government subsidies and special favors that often distort competition. But executives' long-term interests would be better served by working to promote a higher plane of competition. They can begin by rethinking the role of trade associations, which often do little more than lobby government, compile some statistics, and host social functions. The associations are missing an important opportunity.

Trade associations can provide a forum for the exchange of ideas and a focal point for collective action in overcoming obstacles to productivity and growth. Associations can take the lead in such activities as establishing university-based testing facilities and training or research programs; collecting cluster-related information; offering forums on common managerial problems; investigating solutions to environmental issues; organizing trade fairs and delegations; and managing purchasing consortia.

For clusters consisting of many small and midsize companies—such as tourism, apparel, and agriculture—the need is particularly great for collective bodies to assume scale-sensitive functions. In the Netherlands, for instance, grower cooperatives built the specialized auction and handling facilities that constitute one of the Dutch flower cluster's greatest competitive advantages. The Dutch Flower Council and the Association of Dutch Flower Growers Research Groups, in which most growers participate, have taken on other functions as well, such as applied research and marketing.

Most existing trade associations are too narrow; they represent industries, not clusters. In addition, because their role is defined as lobbying the federal government, their scope is national rather than local. National associations, however, are rarely sufficient to address the local issues that are most important to cluster productivity.

By revealing how business and government together create the conditions that promote growth, clusters offer a constructive way to change the nature of the dialogue between the public and private sectors. With a better understanding of what fosters true competitiveness, executives can start asking government for the right things. The example of MassMEDIC, an association formed in 1996 by the Massachusetts medical-devices cluster, illustrates this point. It recently worked successfully with the U.S. Food and Drug Administration to streamline the approval process for medical devices. Such a step clearly benefits cluster members and enhances competition at the same time.

What's Wrong with Industrial Policy

Productivity, not exports or natural resources, determines the prosperity of any state or nation. Recognizing this, governments should strive to create an environment that supports rising productivity. Sound macroeconomic policy is necessary but not sufficient. The microeconomic foundations for competition will ultimately determine productivity and competitiveness.

Governments—both national and local—have new roles to play. They must ensure the supply of high-quality inputs such as educated citizens and physical infrastructure. They must set the rules of competition—by protecting intellectual property and enforcing antitrust laws, for example—so that productivity and innovation will govern success in the economy. Finally, governments should promote cluster formation and upgrading and the buildup of public or quasi-public goods that have a significant impact on many linked businesses.

This sort of role for government is a far cry from industrial policy. In industrial policy, governments target "desirable" industries and intervene—through subsidies or restrictions on investments by foreign companies, for example—to favor local companies. In contrast, the aim of cluster policy is to reinforce the development of *all* clusters. This means that a traditional cluster such as agriculture should not be abandoned; it should be upgraded. Governments should not choose among clusters, because each one offers opportunities to improve productivity and support rising wages. Every cluster not only contributes directly to national productivity but also affects the productivity of *other* clusters. Not all clusters will succeed, of course, but market forces—not government decisions—should determine the outcomes.

Government, working with the private sector, should reinforce and build on existing and emerging clusters rather than attempt to create entirely new ones. Successful new industries and clusters often grow out of established ones. Businesses involving advanced technology succeed not in a vacuum but where there is already a base of related activities in the field. In fact, most clusters form independently of government action—and sometimes in spite of it. They form where a foundation of locational advantages exists. To justify cluster development efforts, some seeds of a cluster should have already passed a market test.

Cluster development initiatives should embrace the pursuit of competitive advantage and specialization rather than simply imitate successful clusters in other locations. This requires building on local sources of uniqueness. Finding areas of specialization normally proves more effective than head-on competition with well-established rival locations.

New Public-Private Responsibilities

Economic geography in an era of global competition, then, poses a paradox. In a global economy—which boasts rapid transportation, high-speed communication, and accessible markets—one would expect location to diminish in importance. But the opposite is true. The enduring competitive advantages in a global economy are often heavily local, arising from concentrations of highly specialized skills and knowledge, institutions, rivals, related businesses, and sophisticated customers. Geographic, cultural, and institutional proximity leads to special access, closer relationships, better information, powerful incentives, and other advantages in productivity and innovation that are difficult to tap from a distance. The more the world economy becomes complex, knowledge based, and dynamic, the more this is true.

Leaders of businesses, government, and institutions all have a stake—and a role to play—in the new economics of competition. Clusters reveal the mutual dependence and collective responsibility of all these entities for creating the conditions for productive competition. This task will require fresh thinking on the part of leaders and the willingness to abandon the traditional categories that drive our thinking about who does what in the economy. The lines between public and private investment blur. Companies, no less than governments and universities, have a stake in education. Universities have a stake in the competitiveness of local businesses. By revealing the process by which wealth is actually created in an economy, clusters open new public-private avenues for constructive action.

Notes

1. I first made this argument in *The Competitive Advantage of Nations* (New York: Free Press, 1990). I modeled the effect of the local business environment on competition in terms of four interrelated influences, graphically depicted in a diamond: factor conditions (the cost and quality of inputs); demand conditions (the sophistication of local customers); the context for firm strategy and rivalry (the nature and intensity of local competition); and related and supporting industries (the local extent and sophistication of suppliers and related industries). Diamond theory stresses how these elements combine to produce a dynamic, stimulating, and intensely competitive business environment.

   A cluster is the manifestation of the diamond at work. Proximity—the colocation of companies, customers, and suppliers—amplifies all of the pressures to innovate and upgrade.

2. Selected case studies are described in "Clusters and Competition" in my book *On Competition* (Boston: Harvard Business School Press, 1998), which also includes citations of the published output of a number of cluster initiatives. Readers can also find a full treatment of the intellectual roots of cluster thinking, along with an extensive bibliography.

13
Thriving Locally in the Global Economy

Rosabeth Moss Kanter

In the future, success will come to those companies, large and small, that can meet global standards and tap into global networks. And it will come to those cities, states, and regions that do the best job of linking the businesses that operate within them to the global economy.

Sweeping changes in the competitive landscape, including the presence of foreign competitors in domestic markets, are driving businesses to rethink their strategies and structures to reach beyond traditional boundaries. Increasing numbers of small and midsize companies are joining corporate giants in striving to exploit international growth markets or in trying to become world-class even if only to retain local customers.

At the same time, communities are under considerable pressure to understand what they need to do to enhance—and in some cases even preserve—their local vitality. Local residents and civic leaders are expressing concern about their communities' economic future, particularly in light of the impact of global forces on where businesses locate and how they operate. Some see a basic conflict between social and community interests that are largely domestic or even local, and business competitiveness issues that often are international in scope. If the class division of the industrial economy was between capital and labor, or between managers and workers, the class division of the emerging information economy could well be between cosmopolitans with global connections and locals who are stuck in one place.

To avoid a clash between global economic interests and local political interests, businesses must know how to be responsive to the needs of the communities in which they operate even as they globalize. And communities must determine how best to connect cosmopolitans and locals and how to create a civic culture that will attract and retain footloose companies. The greatest danger to the viability of communities is not globalization but a retreat into isolationism and protectionism. In the global economy, those people and organizations that are isolated and cut off are at a disadvantage. They are targets for nativists who feed on discontent by blaming outsiders, scapegoating foreigners, and urging that barriers be erected to stem the global tide. But if communities retreat into isolationism, they are unlikely to solve the very problems that led to their discontent in the first place. Ironically, the best way for communities to preserve their local control is to become more competitive globally.

This lesson began to come into sharp focus for me in 1990, when I started to explore emerging business alliances and partnerships around the world. My Harvard Business School research group and I examined more than 37 companies operating in more than 15 countries. I saw that those companies often were surpassing their peers by linking forces in international networks. But I also saw how controversial their actions were in their own countries and cities, and how irrevocably they were altering life back home. What I saw made me wonder how the rise of a global economy changes the meaning of community, which is largely rooted in place. And I started thinking about how global forces could be marshaled to support and develop communities rather than cause their demise.

Beginning in 1993, I undertook a civic-action research project in five regions of the United States that connect with the global economy in different ways: the areas surrounding Boston, Cleveland, Miami, Seattle, and Greenville and Spartanburg in South Carolina. By looking at those cities and regions through the lens of business, I was able to view local economies not as abstractions or aggregate statistics but from the point of view of those inside the organizations that struggle every day to make and sell goods or services. I could listen to what real people had to say about how they were faring. I was able to sound out business and civic leaders about their strategies for improving their constituents' economy and quality of life in light of the global changes. And I identified some ways in which the global economy can work locally by capitalizing on the availability of those resources that distinguish one place from another.

The New Criteria for Success

In the industrial economy, place mattered to companies because it gave them control over the means of production—capital, labor, and materials—and access to transportation centers that minimized the cost of moving products from one location to another. In the global information economy, however, power comes not from location per se but rather from the ability to command one of the intangible assets that make customers loyal. These assets are concepts, competence, and connections. Today a place has value if it can provide companies with at least one of these resources.

Concepts are leading-edge ideas, designs, or formulations for products or services that create value for customers. *Competence* is the ability to translate ideas into applications for customers, to execute to the highest standards. *Connections* are alliances among businesses to leverage core capabilities, create more value for customers, or simply open doors and widen horizons. Unlike tangible assets, these intangible resources are portable and fluid, and they decline rapidly in value if not constantly updated. World-class companies keep their supplies of these assets current by being more entrepreneurial, more learning oriented, and more collaborative. They continuously seek better concepts and invest in innovation. They search for ideas and experience and nurture their people's knowledge and skills. And they seek partnerships with others to extend their competencies and achieve common objectives.

Companies have several ways of deriving concepts, competence, and connections from the communities in which they are located. Regions can be superior development sites for concepts because innovators can flourish there, come into contact with new ways of thinking, and find support for turning their ideas into viable businesses. Regions also can distinguish themselves by enhancing production competence through maintaining consistently high quality standards and a highly trained workforce. And they can provide connections to global networks in which businesses find resources and partners to link them with other markets. Cities can thrive as international centers if the businesses and the people in them can learn more and develop better by being there rather than somewhere else. Places can—and do—establish linkages to world-class companies by investing and specializing in capabilities that connect their local populations to the global economy in one of three ways: as thinkers, makers, or traders.

Thinkers specialize in concepts. Such places are magnets for brainpower, which is channeled into knowledge industries. Their competitive edge comes from continuous innovation, and they set world standards in the export of both knowledge and knowledge-based products. Thinkers count on their absolute dominance in technological creativity and intellectual superiority to ensure their position on the world stage. The Boston area, for example, specializes in concepts—in creating new ideas and technologies that command a premium in world markets.

Makers are especially competent in execution. They have superior production skills and an infrastructure that supports high-value, cost-effective production. As a result, maker places are magnets for world-class manufacturing. Spartanburg and Greenville, South Carolina, are good examples of world-class makers: They have an exceptional blue-collar workforce that has attracted more than 200 companies from many countries.

Traders specialize in connections. They sit at the crossroads of cultures, managing the intersections. They help make deals or transport goods and services across borders of all types. Miami, with its Latin American and increasingly global connections, is a quintessential trader city. Organizations such as AT&T selected Miami for their Latin American headquarters because of the city's Pan-American characteristics. Miami bridges Anglo and Latino cultures in the same way that Singapore and Hong Kong traditionally have linked British and Chinese cultures.

Boston, Miami, and Spartanburg and Greenville are distinctive as models of emerging international cities because of their emphasis on one core capability. Each must develop a broader range of capabilities for its success to continue, but their stories offer lessons for businesses and cities everywhere about how to harness global forces for local advantage. For example, through a combination of local and foreign leadership and influence, the Spartanburg-Greenville area systematically upgraded its ability to meet the needs of world-class manufacturers. The history of the region's economic development is a lesson for business and community leaders seeking to understand what is required to achieve world-class status and bring local residents into the world economy.

An Unlikely Success Story

Spartanburg and Greenville, in the hill country of South Carolina, make an unlikely center for international industry. Yet these neighboring cities are the site of the highest diversified foreign investment per capita in the United States. Their success rests on the second intangible asset: competence. By achieving superiority in their ability to produce goods, these cities have derived benefits from the global economy as makers.

As in other U.S. cities, the center of activity has shifted from downtown to the shopping malls and industrial belts on the periphery. But what is found on the outskirts of Spartanburg and Greenville, and throughout the seven-county area called the Upstate, is unusual: a concentration of foreign manufacturing companies on I-85, the interstate highway that stretches from Atlanta, Georgia, to Charlotte, North Carolina. The local section of this highway is known as "the autobahn" because of the many German companies located there.

For decades, business leaders have worked with civic leaders to shape an economic development strategy that is almost a foreign policy. For the Spartanburg-Greenville region, foreign investment has been a positive force, bringing benefits to local businesses, workers, and the community beyond the infusion of capital and job creation. The presence of foreign companies has unleashed and renewed entrepreneurship and innovation, stimulated learning, heightened awareness of world standards, and connected local companies to global networks.

The cities of Spartanburg (population 46,000) and Greenville (population 58,000) and the seven surrounding counties contain almost a million people and share an airport. The region has a diversified economic base that includes textiles, high technology, metalworking, and automobiles. Unemployment stays well below the national average, and the I-85 business belt boasts the largest number of engineers per capita in the United States and the country's lowest work-stoppage rate. South Carolina's nationally recognized worker training program has upgraded the workforce and raised the average wage rate across the region.

The Upstate is now home to more than 215 companies from 18 countries, 74 of which have their U.S. headquarters there. The largest manufacturing employer is Michelin North America, a subsidiary of France's Michelin Groupe. It has three facilities in the region, a total investment of $1.5 billion, more than 9,000 employees in the state, and comparatively high factory wage rates of $15 to $16 per hour. R&D for Michelin North America also is in Greenville, and a test track and distribution center are located nearby. In 1985, the company moved its headquarters to Greenville.

The area entered the international limelight in 1992, when BMW announced it would locate its first-ever manufacturing facility outside Germany in Spartanburg County. Newspapers and magazines took note of the "boom belt" in the Southeast along I-85. The BMW facility promised to provide 2,000 jobs directly and create perhaps 10,000 more at a time when the U.S. auto industry was only beginning to emerge from recession and U.S. cities were desperate for sources of new jobs. Ecstatic locals donned T-shirts proclaiming the arrival of "Bubba Motor Works."

BMW's announcement made international headlines and created a local stir because BMW is a well-known upscale consumer product and a household name. But behind this highly visible investment stood several decades of investment by companies that were not household names but that had contributed to the worldwide reputation for competence in industrial skills that would attract BMW to the area.

The history of economic development in the Upstate represents one model for success in the global economy: a solid base of midsize entrepreneurial companies that innovate continually in basic manufacturing and employ a workforce whose skills are regularly upgraded against world standards. Four factors are critical for success:

- visionary leaders with a clear economic development strategy who work actively to recruit international companies;
- a hospitable business climate and a positive work ethic that attract innovative manufacturing companies seeking to make long-term investments;
- customized training and gradual upgrading of workers' skills; and

• collaboration within the business community and between business and government to improve quality and business performance.

Leadership with a Global Strategy

The first major businesses in a region often provide the leadership and platform for the community's growth and development. Their industrial base and character shape the prospects for those who come later and provide connections between the community and the wider economy.

In the Upstate, foreign investment began in Spartanburg, and the foundation was large textile companies. When Roger Milliken, CEO of Milliken & Company, moved the company's headquarters and his family from New York to Spartanburg in 1954, he set in motion a number of forces that eventually brought economic strength to the region as a global center. Milliken saw the need to compete with inexpensive imports by modernizing equipment and raising skill levels to improve quality and bring labor costs under control. In the late 1950s, he started urging German and Swiss manufacturers that supplied the textile industry to set up shop in Spartanburg close to their customers. For many local residents, the arrival of Milliken and other northern executives was the first "foreign" influence in the area. It highlighted the need for improvements in education and brought cosmopolitan attitudes even before the foreign companies arrived.

Richard E. Tukey, executive director of the Spartanburg Area Chamber of Commerce from 1951 until his death in 1979, was the driving force behind efforts to attract foreign investment to the Upstate. Tukey was a visionary who realized that opportunities had to be cultivated for a declining textile industry that was the area's principal economic base. People in Spartanburg were open to foreign investment because the alternatives were poor jobs in textile or poultry plants or no jobs at all. Tukey went overseas to textile machinery shows to find investors and developed a wide network of business contacts in Europe. In 1965, he helped establish the U.S. base for Menzel of Germany in just four days, including locating housing for the plant manager and finding someone to write articles of incorporation for the company. When Kurt Zimmerli, CEO of Zima, first explored moving to the area, Tukey escorted him to banks and introduced him to community leaders. Tukey sometimes was criticized for paying more attention to outside investors than to local companies, but his persistence paid off in job growth that ultimately benefited local suppliers from construction crews to retailers.

Tukey was highly regarded by many civic leaders, and his allies included South Carolina's governors and lieutenant governors. He urged them to make the Upstate more attractive to Europeans by, for example, amending alcohol laws to make it easier to import wine. Tukey helped establish a variety of institutions that gave Spartanburg an international look, and he improved its cultural and educational offerings by initiating community events such as a German-style Oktoberfest and by working with local officials to create a state educational TV capability that was top-notch.

Reinforcing the Cycle of Development

The Upstate's business climate was hospitable to long-term outside investment, and the local work ethic was attractive to innovative companies. Spartanburg was the first of the two cities to catch the foreign wave, which started in the 1960s with a set of midsize companies that established their own greenfield sites rather than acquiring U.S. companies. Those companies stayed and expanded, often because their entrepreneurs were committed to growth in Spartanburg; some expatriates eventually became U.S. citizens and community leaders.

Several aspects of foreign investment in the area are noteworthy:

Industry Diversification Based on Core Skills. The textile industry provided a customer base, but the technical capabilities of the companies that moved into the area were not confined to one industry; they could be extended to many others.

Expansion and Upgrading. The foreign companies gradually expanded the region's functions, markets, and skills. Functions tended to expand from sales and service to manufacturing. Markets tended to expand from regional to North American to overseas. A regional office often became the North American headquarters. Initially, the companies transferred technology, standards, and skills from the foreign parent; eventually, many of the U.S. units outperformed the parents and educated them. According to a 1993 Greenville Chamber of Commerce survey of 87 foreign-owned companies, 80% had expanded since their arrival in the Upstate, and about 55% were planning a capital investment project in the next three years.

Entrepreneurship and Innovation. The first foreign companies were generally midsize. They had sent over individuals who could build new ventures from scratch and had granted them considerable autonomy to do so. U.S. operations were thus highly independent rather than subordinate branches of multinational giants; and foreign managers in the United States were entrepreneurs committed to growing the local business, not expatriates on short career rotations. Survival depended on a high degree of technological innovation.

Assimilation into the Local Culture. Companies generally sent over only a few foreigners, some of whom became U.S. citizens; the large number of U.S. hires gave the companies an American flavor. The first foreign company representatives were well-educated, English-speaking, cosmopolitan Europeans who could blend easily into the local population. Switzerland, Austria, and Germany—countries not intent on maintaining language purity or separatist traditions—were most often represented. Moreover, the original companies were not household names, not particularly visible, and not of particular interest to average citizens. But the new companies had a cultural style that complemented the local culture; they tended to sink roots and assimilate. According to local leaders, it took a long time for most people to realize just how many foreign companies there were in Spartanburg.

Among the first foreign companies to locate in the region was Rieter Machine Works of Winterthur, Switzerland. Rieter, whose first U.S. chief was a friend of Roger Milliken's, located its sales and service office in Spartanburg in 1959 because the U.S. textile industry was at the time 30% to 35% of its market. (It is now 20%.) Rieter gradually expanded into manufacturing, increasing its investment in South Carolina. Although the company found numerous differences between operating in Switzerland and in the United States—from measurement to quality standards—it found that it could blend American entrepreneurial flair with Swiss technical precision to achieve outstanding results. Ueli Schmid, the current CEO of Rieter in the United States, joined Rieter in Switzerland in 1970, moved to the States in 1980, and became a U.S. citizen.

As the Upstate proved hospitable to foreign investors, expansion from sales and service offices to manufacturing began. Menzel, from Bielefeld, Germany, established its sales office in Spartanburg in 1965 but soon realized it was more practical to build machinery there. It was the first European company to do so, and its presence paved the

way for others. Menzel created an innovative material-handling system for large-roll batching used in plastics, fiberglass, rubber, and
other applications besides textiles. Now three times its original size, it
produces machinery in the United States that it does not build in
Germany and derives less than 40% of its revenue from the textile
industry.

Cosmopolitan entrepreneurs such as Hans Balmer came with the
initial German and Swiss wave. In 1972 at the age of 25, Balmer was
sent on a two-year assignment from Switzerland as Loepfe Brothers'
U.S. representative. Instead of staying just two years, he married an
American and, in 1985, founded his own business, Symtech. Now,
with nearly $50 million in sales, Symtech uses the best models of
supply-chain partnering to integrate manufacturing equipment from
multiple suppliers for its customers. Balmer also has brought other
foreign companies to Spartanburg, and he succeeded Kurt Zimmerli as
international committee chair for the Spartanburg Area Chamber of
Commerce.

An exception to the predominance of small and midsize companies
in the initial foreign surge was the German chemical giant Hoechst.
Hoechst traces its local origins to its 1967 joint venture with Hercules,
a U.S. chemical company. (In 1987, Hoechst merged with Celanese
to form Hoechst Celanese.) The company has both raw materials
and fiber plants in the area; in the chemical plant alone, equity investment totals close to half a billion dollars. A truly global organization,
Hoechst is a cosmopolitan force in Spartanburg. It gives its U.S. business relative autonomy but creates cross-cultural linkages through
employee exchanges and technology transfers between Spartanburg
and other worldwide facilities.

Besides bringing jobs to Spartanburg, Hoechst brought another
important local leader: Paul Foerster. In 1967, Foerster moved to
Spartanburg from Germany on a four-year contract to run the fibers
facility. The contract was extended until his retirement in 1990. A cultural cross-fertilizer, Foerster turned Hoechst Celanese into an important charitable contributor to the region despite the absence of a charitable tradition in Germany. Today Foerster is honorary consul for
Germany, liaison to Europe for South Carolina, past chairman of the
Spartanburg Area Chamber of Commerce, and the person responsible
for much of the international traffic through Spartanburg.

In the 1980s, attracting foreign investment became an explicit strategy for Greenville as well as for Spartanburg. Greenville has had a

successful Headquarters Recruitment Program since 1985, and in 1993, 14 foreign companies announced that they would open new regional headquarters or expand existing offices in the city. By 1994, German companies still dominated in the Upstate with 65 of the region's 215 foreign companies; British companies were second with 43, and Japanese third with 29. Although there were only 16 French companies, employment in them was almost as great as in the German companies because of Michelin's size. Foreign-owned service companies located in the region, as well. Supermarket conglomerate Ahold of the Netherlands, a member of the European Retail Alliance, employs 4,000 people in the Upstate through its Bi-Lo chain, headquartered in Greenville.

Improving Training and Education

Good attitudes are not enough; workers' skills must meet international standards. For more than 30 years, the state has led a collaborative effort to provide outstanding technical training—a crucial factor in expanding high-wage manufacturing jobs in the Greenville-Spartanburg area.

Contrary to popular belief, low wages or tax incentives were not the primary reason the first foreign companies were attracted to South Carolina's Upstate region. Indeed, recent studies by James Hines of Harvard University's John F. Kennedy School of Government have shown that state and other local tax incentives play little or no role in where foreign companies locate their businesses in the United States. Foreign investors sometimes do decide to locate in a particular place in the United States if they will get tax credits at home for state tax payments, but generally, business factors play a larger role. South Carolina's principal attraction is the competence of its workforce.

The South Carolina State Board for Technical and Comprehensive Education offers free, customized technical training of prospective workers and supervisors to companies that bring new investment to the state. The board assigns staff to prepare manuals, interview workers, and teach classes based on technical requirements established by the company. The company is not obligated to hire any worker who completes the training, nor do workers have to accept any job offer. In some cases, the state will pay to send first-time line supervisors for training elsewhere, even in a foreign country. Training benefits apply to major facility expansions as well as to new sites. A related initiative is the Buy South Carolina program, which supports just-in-time inventory systems by finding local suppliers.

A network of 16 technical colleges runs the State Tech Special Schools, including Greenville Technical College, rated by *U.S. News & World Report* as one of the best technical schools in the country. Devised as a crash program to deal with economic desperation in 1961, the State Tech Special Schools are now a national model. Since the network's inception, it has trained more than 145,000 workers for about 1,200 facilities, including more than 30,000 for the textile industry, 34,000 for metalworking, and nearly 18,000 for electrical and electronic machinery trades. In fiscal year 1992–1993, more than 6,400 people were trained for 121 companies, including U.S. companies such as Tupperware and Perdue, at a cost to the state of about $6.4 million. Companies also can draw on training from the Quality Institute of Enterprise Development, a private nonprofit venture spun off from the state's economic development board, which partners with the Upstate's technical colleges, the University of South Carolina at Spartanburg, and local chambers of commerce.

For German and Japanese companies with high technical and quality standards, such training is a major incentive. Mita South Carolina, a Japanese toner producer, used the State Tech Special Schools to build its U.S. workforce after arriving in Greenville in 1991 to manufacture for the North American market. Of its 150 current employees, only the top dozen managers are Japanese (the heads of engineering and human resources are Americans), and Japanese technicians were present only to install machinery and troubleshoot when the company started up. Some foreign managers want the workforce to meet even higher standards, and German-style apprenticeships are on the agenda.

The quality of public education also has improved because of new business investment. Foreign companies contributed by providing a sound tax base and a strong vision of what education should be by setting high standards for workers' knowledge. But, according to educators, the presence of foreign companies was an excuse for change, not a cause of it. Local interest and investment in educational reform have been consistent since the 1950s, and in the 1980s the public and private sectors collaborated on an increase in the sales tax to provide for a 30% increase in school budgets. The state saw a rise of 128 points in average SAT scores, and Richard Riley, South Carolina's governor during this decade, went on to join the Clinton cabinet as the secretary of education. Although there were widespread improvements in the entire public education system, particular innovations came in the areas of language training, world geography, and world cultures. Spartanburg's District 7 high school was one of the first in the United States to offer advanced placement courses, and it continues to receive White House Achievement Awards—the only high school in the country said to have won three times. Greenville's Southside High School is the only high school in South Carolina, and one of a handful in the United States, that awards the International Baccalaureate Diploma. This program is modeled on the curricula of European schools and enables interested students to prepare to attend European universities.

International awareness and world-class capabilities are a priority also in the Upstate's colleges and universities. Skills in mathematics, science, computers, and technology are especially important because of the region's industrial base. However, educators also are upgrading language training, exchange programs, and internships abroad. For the latter, in particular, foreign companies are a key resource connecting local residents to many parts of the world.

Raising Standards Through Collaboration

Companies new to the Upstate discover strong cross-business and cross-sector collaboration that not only enhances business performance for both domestic and foreign companies but also strengthens the area's economy. Company executives comment repeatedly about strong networking, exchange of learning among businesses, and cooperation between business and government.

Strong, active chambers of commerce are catalysts for much of the cooperation, making the connections and mounting the programs that serve as the infrastructure for collaboration. The Spartanburg Area Chamber of Commerce has 1,800 members from 13 municipalities forming seven area councils. In 1989, it joined with the Spartanburg County Foundation—a charitable organization that supports community activities—and other groups to launch the Consensus Project, a community priority-setting activity based on a set of critical indicators of Spartanburg's community "health." The project began with about 75 leaders and eventually got feedback from many citizens. It has led to adult education, programs to prevent teenage pregnancy, and Leadership Spartanburg, a program that trains community leaders.

The Spartanburg Chamber offers programs that have directly improved business performance. It has a "vice president for quality"—an unusual office signifying the Chamber's activist role in industry and one that encourages innovative companies to learn from one another. In 1981, Milliken instituted a pioneering internal quality program, leading to a string of awards: the American Malcolm Baldrige National Quality Award, the British Quality Award, Canada Awards for Business Excellence, and the European Quality Award. Milliken was the first, and in some cases the only, fabric supplier to receive quality awards from General Motors, Ford, and Chrysler. With inspiration from Milliken, the Chamber's committee on quality launched the Quality in the Workplace program in 1984, very early in the U.S. total quality movement. In addition to educating numerous local companies, including those without their own quality or training staffs, the program extended the principles of quality to nonprofits such as the United Way.

The Greenville Chamber of Commerce—the state's largest, with 3,000 members—also facilitates collaboration. Companies exchange best-practice ideas, screen employees for jobs, encourage new companies to come to the area, solve one another's problems, and sometimes even lend one another staff. A monthly Chamber-sponsored manufacturers' discussion group helps with employee relations problems—something particularly beneficial to foreign companies employing a U.S. workforce—and serves as a job-finding network by circulating résumés and lists of names. When Sara Lee opened a plant in Greenville, Fuji's plant manager helped the company implement worker teams. At a Chamber "prospect" dinner, the representative of a smaller company being enticed to the area mentioned that the company could not afford a human resources function right away. Other manufacturers present, including Mita, volunteered to build a team of their own people to serve in the interim, to screen résumés and do the hiring.

Collaboration increasingly extends beyond political jurisdictions. A joint airport helped break the barrier between the two cities, and the wooing of BMW involved still more cooperation. Encouraged by a call from the governor's office, Greenville's and Spartanburg's hospital systems wrote a joint proposal about medical services in the area for BMW. The two cities compete for business investment, and there are continuing turf battles, especially among local politicians. But there also is a great deal of cooperative and overlapping activity; Greenville relishes Spartanburg's successes and vice versa. Behind these attitudes is more than the simple desire to be friendly. Leaders of the region increasingly acknowledge their shared fate as the pressures of growth and the stress on the existing infrastructure increase the demands on local resources. Many Spartanburg businesspeople call for greater cooperation between Spartanburg and Greenville, and between business and government, and even for the merger of the cities and counties into one metropolitan area. The Upstate's record of success in addressing the challenges of becoming a world-class maker will continue to be tested as the opportunities that have resulted from achieving global competence give rise to the challenges of sustaining growth.

Localizing the Global Economy

Ask people in Spartanburg and Greenville about the influence of foreign companies on their area, and they immediately turn to culture and cuisine: the annual International Festival; the Japanese tea garden, said to be the only authentic one in the United States outside the Japanese embassy in Washington; a surprising number of international organizations per capita; and many sister-city relationships. But the real impact has to do more with opening minds than with changing eating habits. Local residents have become more cosmopolitan, with extended horizons and higher standards.

The presence of foreign companies raised the adrenaline level of the business community, providing a new perspective that increased dissatisfaction with traditional practices and motivated people to improve. It was impossible to sustain sleepy local companies in an environment in which world-class companies came looking for better technology and skills. Business leaders and the workforce are now more aware of global standards. Suppliers to foreign companies credit them with raising standards to world-class levels.

The main concern that residents have about foreign companies—a concern reluctantly but consistently voiced—is whether they will donate money or provide leadership to the community. Tensions often are framed in terms of community service, but the real problems come from local residents' suspicion that foreign companies that move capital into a community can all too easily move it out again and that locals will have no power to stop them. It takes time to educate foreign companies, many of them from countries whose social network is supported by government alone, about the United States' self-help, volunteer, and charitable traditions. But there are notable exceptions and increasing community support from foreign companies. Kurt Zimmerli, Paul Foerster, and Hans Balmer are frequently mentioned as examples of immigrants who became community leaders. Ueli Schmid secured a pool of money from Rieter to spend on discretionary local contributions. BMW makes its new facility available for community events. The self-reinforcing cycle of welcome succeeds as the Upstate's hospitable business climate creates an environment in which cosmopolitan leaders are willing to make deep commitments to the community.

Moreover, the locals' view is generally positive because foreign and outside investment has helped retain—and expand—homegrown companies in the area. For example, one of Spartanburg's oldest companies, Hersey Measurement, was saved by a joint venture between a U.S. and a German company. Hersey was founded in 1859 to manufacture rotary pumps, bolts, and general machinery, and its new owners from Atlanta decided to keep the company in Spartanburg because of the excellent workforce. They expanded operations and built a new plant that doubled the size of its local facilities. Lockwood Greene Engineers, one of the oldest engineering-services companies in the United States, was reinvigorated by a German company after the failure of a management buyout. Metromont Materials, a leader in concrete, was acquired by a British company after large U.S. companies abandoned the industry. And locals report that even for residents not working at foreign-owned facilities, jobs are better paid and of better quality as a result of foreign investment in the region as a whole.

Becoming World-Class

The story of the Spartanburg-Greenville region illustrates what it takes to acquire the mind-set of the new world class. Cities and regions must become centers of globally relevant skills to enable local businesses and people to thrive. World-class businesses need concepts, competence, and connections, and world-class places can help grow these global assets by offering capabilities in innovation, production, or trade. Cities and regions will thrive to the extent that the businesses and people in them can develop better by being there rather than somewhere else.

To create this capability, communities need both magnets and glue. They must have magnets that attract a flow of external resources—new people or companies—to expand skills, broaden horizons, and hold up a comparative mirror against world standards. The flow might involve customers, outside investors, foreign companies, students, or business travelers. Communities also need social glue—a way to bring people together to define the common good, create joint plans, and identify strategies that benefit a wide range of people and organizations. In addition to the physical infrastructure that supports daily life and work—roads, subways, sewers, electricity, and communications systems—communities need an infrastructure for collaboration to solve problems and create the future. Community leaders must mount united efforts that enhance their connections to the global economy in order to attract and retain job-creating businesses whose ties reach many places.

And business leaders must understand how strong local communities can help them become more globally competitive. Businesses benefit from investing in a region's core skills. They derive advantages not only from creating company-specific resources but from establishing linkages outside the company as well. Local collaborations with international giants operating in their area can help smaller companies raise their standards and propel them into wider, more global markets. Leaders of large companies can strengthen their own competitiveness by developing a supportive environment in the primary places where they operate to ensure the availability of the highest-quality suppliers, workforce, living standards for their employees, and opportunities for partnership with local leaders.

PART
IV
Leadership

14

Fast, Global, and Entrepreneurial: Supply Chain Management, Hong Kong Style

An Interview with Victor Fung

Joan Magretta

Supply chain management is working its way onto the strategic agendas of CEOs in an expanding list of industries, from autos to personal computers to fashion retailing. Propelling that change is the restructuring of global competition. As companies focus on their core activities and outsource the rest, their success increasingly depends on their ability to control what happens in the value chain outside their own boundaries. In the 1980s, the focus was on supplier partnerships to improve cost and quality. In today's faster-paced markets, the focus has shifted to innovation, flexibility, and speed.

Enter Li & Fung, Hong Kong's largest export trading company and an innovator in the development of supply chain management. On behalf of its customers, primarily American and European retailers, Li & Fung works with an ever expanding network of thousands of suppliers around the globe, sourcing clothing and other consumer goods ranging from toys to fashion accessories to luggage. Chairman Victor Fung sees the company as part of a new breed of professionally managed, focused enterprises that draw on Hong Kong's expertise in distribution-process technology—a host of information-intensive service functions including product development, sourcing, financing, shipping, handling, and logistics.

Founded in 1906 in southern China by Victor Fung's grandfather, Li & Fung was the first Chinese-owned export company at a time when the China trade was controlled by foreign commercial houses. In the early 1970s, Victor was teaching at the Harvard Business School, and his younger brother, William, was a newly minted Harvard M.B.A. The two young men were called home from the United States by their father to breathe new life into the company.

Since then, the brothers have led Li & Fung through a series of transformations. In this interview with *Harvard Business Review* editor-at-large Joan Magretta, Victor Fung describes how Li & Fung has made the transition from buying agent to supply chain manager, from the old economy to the new, from traditional Chinese family conglomerate to innovative public company. Victor and William Fung are creating a new kind of multinational, one that remains entrepreneurial despite its growing size and scope.

Victor Fung is also chairman of a privately held retailing arm of the company, which focuses on joint ventures with Toys "R" Us and the Circle K convenience-store chain in Hong Kong. He is also chairman of the Hong Kong Trade Development Council and of Prudential Asia.

How do you define the difference between what Li & Fung does today—supply chain management—and the trading business founded by your grandfather in 1906?

When my grandfather started the company in Canton, 90 years ago during the Ching dynasty, his "value-added" was that he spoke English. In those days, it took three months to get to China by boat from the West; a letter would take a month. No one at the Chinese factories spoke English, and the American merchants spoke no Chinese. As an interpreter, my grandfather's commission was 15%.

Continuing through my father's generation, Li & Fung was basically a broker, charging a fee to put buyers and sellers together. But as an intermediary, the company was squeezed between the growing power of the buyers and the factories. Our margins slipped to 10%, then 5%, then 3%. When I returned to Hong Kong in 1976 after teaching at Harvard Business School, my friends warned me that in ten years buying agents like Li & Fung would be extinct. "Trading is a sunset industry," they all said.

My brother and I felt we could turn the business into something different, and so we took it through several stages of development. In the first stage, we acted as what I would call a regional sourcing agent and extended our geographic reach by establishing offices in Taiwan, Korea, and Singapore. Our knowledge of the region had value for customers. Most big buyers could manage their own sourcing if they needed to deal only with Hong Kong—they'd know which ten factories to deal with and wouldn't need any help.

But dealing with the whole region was more complex. In textiles, quotas govern world trade. Knowing which quotas have been used up in Hong Kong, for example, tells you when you have to start buying from Taiwan.

Understanding products was also more complex. We knew that in Taiwan the synthetics were better, but that Hong Kong was the place to go for cottons. We could provide a package from the whole region rather than a single product from Hong Kong.

By working with a larger number of countries, we were able to assemble components; we call this "assortment packing." Say I sell a tool kit to a major discount chain. I could buy the spanners from one country and the screwdrivers from another and put together a product package. That has some value in it—not great value, but some.

In the second stage, we took the company's sourcing-agent strategy one step further and became a manager and deliverer of manufacturing programs. In the old model, the customer would say, "This is the item I want. Please go out and find the best place to buy it for me." The new model works this way. The Limited, one of our big customers, comes to us and says, "For next season, this is what we're thinking about—this type of look, these colors, these quantities. Can you come up with a production program?"

Starting with their designers' sketches, we research the market to find the right type of yarn and dye swatches to match the colors. We take product concepts and realize them in prototypes. Buyers can then look at the samples and say, "No, I don't really like that, I like this. Can you do more of this?" We then create an entire program for the season, specifying the product mix and the schedule. We contract for all the resources. We work with factories to plan and monitor production so we can ensure quality and on-time delivery.

This strategy of delivering manufacturing programs carried us through the 1980s, but that decade brought us a new challenge—and led to our third stage. As the Asian tigers emerged, Hong Kong became an increasingly expensive and uncompetitive place to manufacture. For example, we completely lost the low-end transistor-radio business to Taiwan and Korea. What saved us was that China began to open up to trade, allowing Hong Kong to fix its cost problem by moving the labor-intensive portion of production across the border into southern China.

So for transistor radios we created little kits—plastic bags filled with all the components needed to build a radio. Then we shipped the kits to China for assembly. After the labor-intensive work was completed, the finished goods came back to Hong Kong for final testing and inspection. If you missed a screw you were in trouble: the whole line stopped cold.

Breaking up the value chain as we did was a novel concept at the time. We call it "dispersed manufacturing." This method of manufacturing soon spread to other industries, giving Hong Kong a new lease on life and also transforming our economy. Between 1979 and 1997, Hong Kong's position as a trading entity moved from number 21 in the world to number 8. All our manufacturing moved into China, and Hong Kong became a huge service economy with 84% of its gross domestic product coming from services.

So dispersed manufacturing means breaking up the value chain and rationalizing where you do things?

That's right. Managing dispersed production was a real breakthrough. It forced us to get smart not only about logistics and transportation but also about dissecting the value chain.

Consider a popular children's doll—one similar to the Barbie doll. In the early 1980s, we designed the dolls in Hong Kong, and we also produced the molds because sophisticated machinery was needed to make them. We then shipped the molds to China, where they would shoot the plastic, assemble the doll, paint the figures, make the doll's clothing—all the labor-intensive work. But the doll had to come back to Hong Kong, not just for final testing and inspection but also for packaging. China at that time couldn't deliver the quality we needed for the printing on the boxes. Then we used Hong Kong's well-developed banking and transportation infrastructure to distribute the products around the world. You can see the model clearly: the labor-intensive middle portion of the value chain is still done in southern China, and Hong Kong does the front and back ends.

Managing dispersed manufacturing, where not everything is done under one roof, takes a real change of mind-set. But once we figured out how to do it, it became clear that our reach should extend beyond southern China. Our thinking was, for example, if wages are lower farther inland, let's go there. And so we began what has turned into a constant search for new and better sources of supply. Li & Fung made a quantum leap in 1995, nearly doubling our size and extending our geographic scope by acquiring Inchcape Buying Services. IBS was a large British *hong* with an established network of offices in India, Pakistan, Bangladesh, and Sri Lanka. The acquisition also brought with it a

European customer base that complemented Li & Fung's predominantly American base.

This Hong Kong model of borderless manufacturing has become a new paradigm for the region. Today Asia consists of multiple networks of dispersed manufacturing—high-cost hubs that do the sophisticated planning for regional manufacturing. Bangkok works with the Indochinese peninsula, Taiwan with the Philippines, Seoul with northern China. Dispersed manufacturing is what's behind the boom in Asia's trade and investment statistics in the 1990s—companies moving raw materials and semifinished parts around Asia. But the region is still very dependent on the ultimate sources of demand, which are in North America and Western Europe. They start the whole cycle going.

What happens when you get a typical order?

Say we get an order from a European retailer to produce 10,000 garments. It's not a simple matter of our Korean office sourcing Korean products or our Indonesian office sourcing Indonesian products. For this customer we might decide to buy yarn from a Korean producer but have it woven and dyed in Taiwan. So we pick the yarn and ship it to Taiwan. The Japanese have the best zippers and buttons, but they manufacture them mostly in China. Okay, so we go to YKK, a big Japanese zipper manufacturer, and we order the right zippers from their Chinese plants. Then we determine that, because of quotas and labor conditions, the best place to make the garments is Thailand. So we ship everything there. And because the customer needs quick delivery, we may divide the order across five factories in Thailand. Effectively, we are customizing the value chain to best meet the customer's needs.

Five weeks after we have received the order, 10,000 garments arrive on the shelves in Europe, all looking like they came from one factory, with colors, for example, perfectly matched. Just think about the logistics and the coordination.

This is a new type of value added, a truly global product that has never been seen before. The label may say "made in Thailand," but it's not a Thai product. We dissect the manufacturing process and look for the best solution at each step. We're not asking which country can do the best job overall. Instead, we're pulling apart the value chain and optimizing each step—and we're doing it globally. (See Exhibit 14-1 "Li & Fung's Global Reach.")

Exhibit 14-1   Li & Fung's Global Reach

Li & Fung produces a truly global product by pulling apart the manufacturing value chain and optimizing each step. Today it has 35 offices in 20 countries, but its global reach is expanding rapidly. In 1997, it had revenue of approximately $1.7 billion.

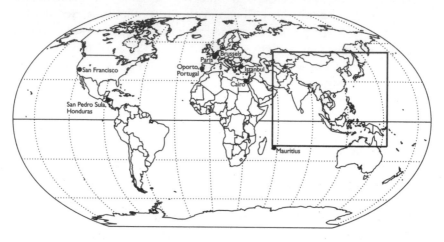

Not only do the benefits outweigh the costs of logistics and transportation, but the higher value added also lets us charge more for our services. We deliver a sophisticated product and we deliver it fast. If you talk to the big global consumer-products companies, they are all moving in this direction—toward being best on a global scale.

So the multinational is essentially its own supply-chain manager?

Yes, exactly. Large manufacturing companies are increasingly doing global supply-chain management, just as Li & Fung does for its retailing customers. That's certainly the case in the auto industry. Today assembly is the easy part. The hard part is managing your suppliers and the flow of parts. In retailing, these changes are producing a revolution. For the first time, retailers are really creating products, not just sitting in their offices with salesman after salesman showing them samples: "Do you want to buy this? Do you want to buy that?" Instead, retailers are participating in the design process. They're now

Exhibit 14-1   (continued)

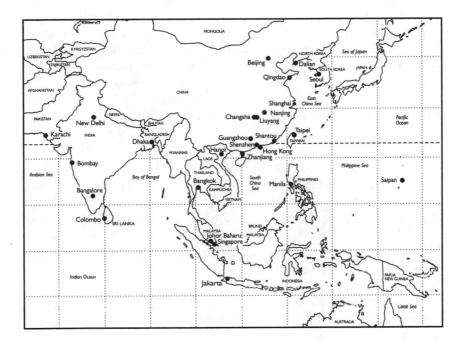

managing suppliers through us and are even reaching down to their suppliers' suppliers. Eventually that translates into much better management of inventories and lower markdowns in the stores.

Explain why that translates into lower markdowns for retailers.

Companies in consumer-driven, fast-moving markets face the problem of obsolete inventory with a vengeance. That means there is enormous value in being able to buy "closer to the market." If you can shorten your buying cycle from three months to five weeks, for example, what you are gaining is eight weeks to develop a better sense of where the market is heading. And so you will end up with substantial savings in inventory markdowns at the end of the selling season.

Good supply-chain management strips away time and cost from product delivery cycles. Our customers have become more fashion driven, working with six or seven seasons a year instead of just two or three. Once you move to shorter product cycles, the problem of obsolete inventory increases dramatically. Other businesses are facing the same kind of pressure. With customer tastes changing rapidly and markets segmenting into narrower niches, it's not just fashion products that are becoming increasingly time sensitive.

Several years ago, I had a conversation about ladies fashion garments with Stan Shih, CEO of Acer, the large Taiwan-based PC manufacturer. I jokingly said, "Stan, are you going to encroach on our territory?" He said, "No, no, but the PC business has the same basic problems you face. Things are changing so fast you don't want to wind up with inventory. You want to plan close to the market." He runs his business to cut down the delivery cycle and minimize inventory exposure by assembling PCs in local markets. So what I have to say about supply chain management for fashion products really applies to any product that's time sensitive.

Supply chain management is about buying the right things and shortening the delivery cycles. It requires "reaching into the suppliers" to ensure that certain things happen on time and at the right quality level. Fundamentally, you're not taking the suppliers as a given.

The classic supply-chain manager in retailing is Marks & Spencer. They don't own any factories, but they have a huge team that goes into the factories and works with the management. The Gap also is known for stretching into its suppliers.

Can you give me an example of how you reach into the supply chain to shorten the buying cycle?

Think about what happens when you outsource manufacturing. The easy approach is to place an order for finished goods and let the supplier worry about contracting for the raw materials like fabric and yarn. But a single factory is relatively small and doesn't have much buying power; that is, it is too small to demand faster deliveries from *its* suppliers.

We come in and look at the whole supply chain. We know the Limited is going to order 100,000 garments, but we don't know the style or the colors yet. The buyer will tell us that five weeks before delivery. The trust between us and our supply network means that we can reserve undyed yarn from the yarn supplier. I can lock up capacity at the mills for the weaving and dying with the promise that they'll get an order of a specified size; five weeks before delivery, we will let them know what colors we want. Then I say the same thing to the factories, "I don't know the product specs yet, but I have organized the colors and the fabric and the trim for you, and they'll be delivered to you on this date and you'll have three weeks to produce so many garments."

I've certainly made life harder for myself now. It would be easier to let the factories worry about securing their own fabric and trim. But then the order would take three months, not five weeks. So to shrink the delivery cycle, I go upstream to organize production. And the shorter production time lets the retailer hold off before having to commit to a fashion trend. It's all about flexibility, response time, small production runs, small minimum-order quantities, and the ability to shift direction as the trends move.

Is it also about cost?

Yes. At Li & Fung we think about supply chain management as "tackling the soft $3" in the cost structure. What do we mean by that? If a typical consumer product leaves the factory at a price of $1, it will invariably end up on retail shelves at $4. Now you can try to squeeze the cost of production down 10 cents or 20 cents per product, but today you have to be a genius to do that because everybody has been working on that for years and there's not a lot of fat left. It's better to look at the cost that is spread throughout the distribution channels—the soft $3. It offers a bigger target, and if you take 50 cents out, nobody will even know you are doing it. So it's a much easier place to effect savings for our customers.

Can you give me an example?

Sure. Shippers always want to fill a container to capacity. If you tell a manufacturer, "Don't fill up the container," he'll think you're crazy. And if all you care about is the cost of shipping, there's no question you should fill the containers. But if you think instead of the whole value chain as a system, and you're trying to lower the total cost and not just one piece of it, then it may be smarter not to fill the containers.

Let's say you want to distribute an assortment of ten products, each manufactured by a different factory, to ten distribution centers. The standard practice would be for each factory to ship full containers of its product. And so those ten containers would then have to go to a consolidator, who would unpack and repack all ten containers before shipping the assortment to the distribution centers.

Now suppose instead that you move one container from factory to factory and get each factory to fill just one-tenth of the container. Then you ship it with the assortment the customer needs directly to the distribution center. The shipping cost will be greater, and you will have to be careful about stacking the goods properly. But the total systems cost could be lower because you've eliminated the consolidator altogether. When someone is actively managing and organizing the whole supply chain, you can save costs like that.

So when you talk about organizing the value chain, what you do goes well beyond simply contracting for other people's services or inspecting their work. It sounds like the value you add extends almost to the point where you're providing management expertise to your supply network.

In a sense, we are a smokeless factory. We do design. We buy and inspect the raw materials. We have factory managers, people who set up and plan production and balance the lines. We inspect production. But we don't manage the workers, and we don't own the factories.

Think about the scope of what we do. We work with about 7,500 suppliers in more than 26 countries. If the average factory has 200 workers—that's probably a low estimate—then in effect there are more than a million workers engaged on behalf of our customers. That's why our policy is not to own any portion of the value chain that deals with running factories. Managing a million workers would be a colossal undertaking. We'd lose all flexibility; we'd lose our ability to fine-tune and coordinate. So we deliberately leave that management challenge to the individual entrepreneurs we contract with. (See Exhibit 14-2 "Supply Chain Management: How Li & Fung Adds Value.")

Our target in working with factories is to take anywhere from 30% to 70% of their production. We want to be important to them, and at 30% we're most likely their largest customer. On the other hand, we need flexibility—so we don't want the responsibility of having them completely dependent on us. And we also benefit from their exposure to their other customers.

Exhibit 14-2   Supply Chain Management: How Li & Fung Adds Value

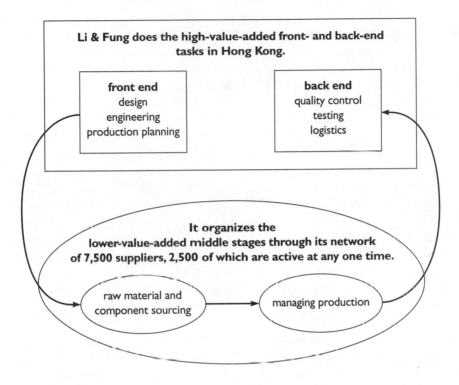

If we don't own factories, can we say we are in manufacturing? Absolutely. Because, of the 15 steps in the manufacturing value chain, we probably do 10.

The way Li & Fung is organized is unusual in the industry. Can you describe the link between your organization and your strategy?

Just about every company I know says that they are customer focused. What, in fact, does that mean? Usually it means they design key systems that fit most of their customers, they hope, most of the time. Here we say—and do—something different: We organize for the customer. Almost all the large trading companies with extensive networks of suppliers are organized geographically, with the country units as their profit centers. As a result, it is hard for them to optimize the value chain. Their country units are competing against one another for business.

Our basic operating unit is the division. Whenever possible, we will focus an entire division on serving one customer. We may serve smaller customers through a division structured around a group of customers with similar needs. We have, for example, a theme-store division serving a handful of customers such as the Warner Brothers stores and Rainforest Cafe. This structuring of the organization around customers is very important—remember that what we do is close to creating a customized value chain for every customer order.

So customer-focused divisions are the building blocks of our organization, and we keep them small and entrepreneurial. They do anywhere from $20 million to $50 million of business. Each is run by a lead entrepreneur—we sometimes call them "little John Waynes" because the image of a guy standing in the middle of the wagon train, shooting at all the bad guys, seems to fit.

Consider our Gymboree division, one of our largest. The division manager, Ada Liu, and her headquarters team have their own separate office space within the Li & Fung building in Hong Kong. When you walk through their door, every one of the 40 or so people you see is focused solely on meeting Gymboree's needs. On every desk is a computer with direct software links to Gymboree. The staff is organized into specialized teams in such areas as technical support, merchandising, raw material purchasing, quality assurance, and shipping. And Ada has dedicated sourcing teams in our branch offices in China, the Philippines, and Indonesia because Gymboree buys in volume from all those countries. In maybe 5 of our 26 countries, she has her own team, people she hired herself. When she wants to source from, say, India, the branch office helps her get the job done.

In most multinational companies, fights between the geographic side of the organization and the product or customer side are legendary—and predictable. From the product side, it's "How can I get better service for my customer? It may be small for you in Bangladesh, but it's important for my product line globally." And from the country side, it's "Look, I can't let this product group take unfair advantage of this particular factory, because it produces for three other product groups and I'm responsible for our relationships in this country overall."

Here's our solution to this classic problem: Our primary alignment is around customers and their needs. But to balance the matrix, every product-group executive also has responsibility for one country. It makes them more sensitive to the problems facing a country director and less likely to make unreasonable demands.

Can you tell us more about the role of the little John Waynes?

The idea is to create small units dedicated to taking care of one customer, and to have one person running a unit like she would her own company. In fact, we hire people whose main alternative would be to run their own business. We provide them with the financial resources and the administrative support of a big organization, but we give them a great deal of autonomy. All the merchandising decisions that go into coordinating a production program for the customer—which factories to use, whether to stop a shipment or let it go forward—are made at the division-head level. For the creative parts of the business, we want entrepreneurial behavior, so we give people considerable operating freedom. To motivate the division leaders, we rely on substantial financial incentives by tying their compensation directly to the unit's bottom line. There's no cap on bonuses: we want entrepreneurs who are motivated to move heaven and earth for the customer.

Trading companies can be run effectively only when they are small. By making small units the heart of our company, we have been able to grow rapidly without becoming bureaucratic. Today we have about 60 divisions. We think of them as a portfolio we can create and collapse, almost at will. As the market changes, our organization can adjust immediately.

What role, then, does the corporate center play?

When it comes to financial controls and operating procedures, we don't want creativity or entrepreneurial behavior. In these areas, we centralize and manage tightly. Li & Fung has a standardized, fully computerized operating system for executing and tracking orders, and everyone in the company uses the system.

We also keep very tight control of working capital. As far as I'm concerned, inventory is the root of all evil. At a minimum, it increases the complexity of managing any business. So it's a word we don't tolerate around here. All cash flow is managed centrally through Hong Kong. All letters of credit, for example, come to Hong Kong for approval and are then reissued by the central office. That means we are guaranteed payment before we execute an order. I could expand the company by another 10% to 20% by giving customers credit. But while we are very aggressive in merchandising—in finding new sources, for example—when it comes to financial management, we are very conservative.

I understand, though, that Li & Fung is involved in venture capital. Can you explain how that fits in?

We've set up a small venture-capital arm, with offices in San Francisco, London, and Brussels, whose primary purpose is corporate development. If you look at a product market grid, Li & Fung has expertise in sourcing many types of products for many types of retailers, but there are also holes in our coverage. A big piece of our corporate development is plugging those holes—the phrase we use is "filling in the mosaic"—and we use venture capital to do it.

Let's say Li & Fung is not strong in ladies fashion shoes. We'll have our venture group look for opportunities to buy into relatively young entrepreneurial companies with people who can create designs and sell them but who do not have the ability to source or to finance. That's what we bring to the deal. More important, doing the sourcing for the company lets us build presence and know-how in the segment. At the same time, we think it's a good way to enhance our returns. All venture capitalists will tell you that they bring more than money to their investments. In our case, we are able to back the companies with our sourcing network.

One of our biggest successes is a company called Cyrk. We wanted to fill a hole in our mosaic in the promotional premiums business—clothing or gift items with company logos, for example. We bought a 30% stake in Cyrk for $200,000 in 1990. We ended up doing all the M&M gum ball dispensers with them, but the real coup was a full line of promotional clothing for Philip Morris. After five years, we sold our investment for about $65 million.

We're more than happy with our investment results, but our real interest is in corporate development, in filling in the mosaic. We're not looking to grow by taking over whole companies. We know we can't manage a U.S. domestic company very well because we're so far away, and the culture is different. By backing people on a minority basis, however, we improve our sourcing strength and enhance our ability to grow existing client relationships or to win new ones. That's real synergy.

You've grown substantially both in size and in geographic scope in the last five years. Does becoming more multinational bring any fundamental changes to the company?

Since 1993, we've changed from a Hong Kong-based Chinese company that was 99.5% Chinese and probably 80% Hong Kong Chinese into a truly regional multinational with a workforce from at least 30 countries. We used to call ourselves a Chinese trading company. (The Japanese trading companies are very big, and we wanted to be a big fish in a small pond, so we defined the pond as consisting of Chinese trading companies.) As we grow, and as our workforce becomes more nationally diverse, we wonder how Koreans or Indians or Turks will feel about working for a Chinese multinational.

We're torn. We know that if we call ourselves a multinational, we're very small compared to a Nestlé or a Unilever. And we don't want to be faceless. We are proud of our cultural heritage. But we don't want it to be an impediment to growth, and we want to make people comfortable that culturally we have a very open architecture. We position ourselves today as a Hong Kong-based multinational trading company. Hong Kong itself is both Chinese and very cosmopolitan. In five years, we've come a long way in rethinking our identity.

As we grow and become more multinational, the last thing we want to do is to run the company like the big multinationals. You know—where you have a corporate policy on medical leave or housing allowances or you name it.

How do you avoid setting policies, a path that would seem inevitable for most companies?

We stick to a simple entrepreneurial principle. For the senior ranks of the company, the mobile executives, we "encash"—that is, we translate the value of benefits into dollar figures—as much as we can. Cash gives individuals the most flexibility. I cannot design a policy to fit 1,000 people, so when in doubt we give people money instead. You want a car? You think you deserve a car? We'd rather give you the cash and let you manage the car. You buy it, you service it. The usual multinational solution is to hire experts to do a study. Then they write a manual on car ownership and hire ten people to administer the manual.

If you ask yourself whether you would rather have a package of benefits or its equivalent in cash, maybe you'll say, I don't want such a nice car, but I'd prefer to spend more money on my home leave. Cash gives individuals a lot more freedom. That's our simplifying principle.

Since you operate in so many countries, do you have to index cash equivalents to local economies?

Wherever we operate, we follow local rules and best practices. We do not want uniformity for lower-level managers. If they say in Korea, "We don't want bonuses but everybody gets 16 months salary," that's the market. What we do would probably drive the HR department in a multinational crazy. But it works for us: for the top people, we figure out a cash equivalent for benefits, and for the local staff, we follow local best practices. It's fine if we do things differently from country to country. And remember, we are an incentive-driven company. We try to make the variable component of compensation as big as possible and to extend that principle as far down into the organization as possible. That's the entrepreneurial approach.

As you spread out geographically, how do you hold the organization together?

The company is managed on a day-to-day basis by the product group managers. Along with the top management, they form what we call the policy committee, which consists of about 30 people. We meet once every five to six weeks. People fly in from around the region to discuss and agree on policies. Consider, for example, the topic of compliance, or ethical sourcing. How do we make sure our suppliers are doing the right thing—by our customers' standards and our own—when it comes to issues such as child labor, environmental protection, and country-of-origin regulations?

Compliance is a very hot topic today—as well it should be. Because our inspectors are in and out of the factories all the time, we probably have a better window on the problem than most companies. If we find factories that don't comply, we won't work with them. However, because there is so much subcontracting, you can't assume that everyone is doing the right thing. That is, you have to make sure that a supplier that was operating properly last month is still doing so this month. The committee of 30 not only shapes our policies but also translates them into operating procedures we think will be effective in the field. And then they become a vehicle for implementing what we've agreed on when they return to their divisions.

There are few businesses as old as trading. Yet the essence of what you do at Li & Fung—managing information and relationships—sounds like a good description of the information economy. How do you reconcile the new economy with the old?

At one level, Li & Fung is an information node, flipping information between our 350 customers and our 7,500 suppliers. We manage all that today with a lot of phone calls and faxes and on-site visits. That's the guts of the company. Soon we will need a sophisticated information system with very open architecture to accommodate different protocols from suppliers and from customers, one robust enough to work in Hong Kong and New York—as well as in places like Bangladesh, where you can't always count on a good phone line.

I have a picture in my mind of the ideal trader for today's world. The trader is an executive wearing a pith helmet and a safari jacket. But in one hand is a machete and in the other a very high-tech personal-computer and communication device. From one side, you're getting reports from suppliers in newly emerging countries, where the quality of the information may be poor. From the other side, you might have highly accurate point-of-sale information from the United States that allows you to replenish automatically. In other words, you're maneuvering between areas that have a lot of catching up to do—you're fighting through the underbrush, so to speak—and areas that are already clearly focused on the twenty-first century.

As the sources of supply explode, managing information becomes increasingly complex. Of course, we have a lot of hard data about performance and about the work we do with each factory. But what we really want is difficult to pin down; a lot of the most valuable information resides in people's heads. What kind of attitude does the owner have? Do we work well together? How good is their internal management? That kind of organizational memory is a lot harder to retain and to share. We see the capturing of such information as the next frontier. You could look at us as a very sophisticated IT system. So that's the modern side of who we are.

What about the more traditional side?

In the information age, there is an impersonality that seems to say that all the old-world thoughts about relationships don't matter anymore. We're all taken with the notion that a bright young guy can bring his great idea to the Internet, and it's okay if no one knows him from Adam. Right?

Maybe. But at the same time, the old relationships, the old values, still matter. I think they matter in our dealings with suppliers, with customers, and with our own staff.

Right now we're so big, three of our divisions could be scheduling work with the same factory. We could be fighting ourselves for factory capacity. So I'm in the process of creating a database to track systematically all our supplier relationships. We need something that everyone in the company can use to review the performance history of all our suppliers. One of my colleagues said, "We'd better guard that with our lives, because if somebody ever got into our system, they could steal one of the company's greatest assets." I'm not so worried. Someone might steal our database, but when they call up a supplier, they don't have the long relationship with the supplier that Li & Fung has. It makes a difference to suppliers when they know that you are dedicated to the business, that you've been honoring your commitments for 90 years.

I think there is a similar traditional dimension to our customer relationships. In the old days, my father used to read every telex from customers. That made a huge difference in a business where a detail as small as the wrong zipper color could lead to disastrous delays for customers. Today William and I continue to read faxes from customers—certainly not every one, but enough to keep us in personal touch with our customers and our operations on a daily basis. Through close attention to detail, we try to maintain our heritage of customer service.

As we have transformed a family business into a modern one, we have tried to preserve the best of what my father and grandfather created. There is a family feeling in the company that's difficult to describe. We don't care much for titles and hierarchy. Family life and the company's business spill over into each other. When staff members are in Hong Kong to do business, my mother might have tea with their families. Of course, as we have grown we have had to change. My mother can't know everyone as she once did. But we hold on to our wish to preserve the intimacies that have been at the heart of our most successful relationships. If I had to capture it in one phrase, it would be this: Think like a big company, act like a small one.

Is the growing importance of information technology good or bad for your business?

Frankly, I am not unhappy that the business will be more dependent on information technology. The growing value of dispersed manufacturing makes us reach even further around the globe, and IT helps us accomplish that stretching of the company.

As Western companies work to remain competitive, supply chain management will become more important. Their need to serve smaller niche markets with more frequent changes in products is pushing us to establish new sources in less developed countries. (See "A Tradition of Innovation.")

We're forging into newly emerging centers of production, from Bangladesh to Sri Lanka to Madagascar. We're now landing in northern Africa—in Egypt, Tunisia, Morocco. We're starting down in South Africa and moving up to some of the equatorial countries. As the global supply network becomes larger and more far-flung, managing it will require scale. As a pure intermediary, our margins were squeezed. But as the number of supply chain options expands, we add value for our customers by using information and relationships to manage the network. We help companies navigate through a world of expanded choice. And the expanding power of IT helps us do that.

A Tradition of Innovation

In the company's early years, Li & Fung dealt in porcelain and other traditional Chinese products, including bamboo and rattan ware, jade and ivory handicrafts—and fireworks. Li & Fung's invention of paper-sealed firecrackers in 1907 to replace the traditional mud-sealed firecracker was a major breakthrough. At that time, the U.S. import duty on firecrackers was based on weight. The paper-sealed firecrackers not only incurred lower import duties by being lighter but also eliminated the problem of excessive dust produced by the discharge of the mud-sealed variety. Li & Fung's paper-sealed manufacturing process has become the industry's standard.

So the middle where we operate is broadening, making what we do more valuable and allowing us to deliver a better product, which translates into better prices and better margins for our customers. In fact, we think export trading is not a sunset industry but a growth business.

Was the professional management training you and William brought with you from the United States helpful in running an Asian family business?

It's an interesting question. For my first 20 years with the company, I had to put aside—unlearn, in fact—a lot of what I had learned in the West about management. It just wasn't relevant. The Li & Fung my grandfather founded was a typical patriarchal Chinese family conglomerate. Even today, most companies in Asia are built on that model. But a lot has changed in the last five years, and the current Asian financial crisis is going to transform the region even more.

Now, instead of managing a few relationships—the essence of the old model—we're managing large, complex systems. It used to be that one or two big decisions a year would determine your success. In the 1980s, for example, many of the Asian tycoons were in asset-intensive businesses like real estate and shipping. You would make a very small number of very big decisions—you would acquire a piece of land or decide to build a supertanker—and you were done. And access to the deals depended on your connections.

The Li & Fung of today is quite different from the company my grandfather founded in 1906. As it was in a lot of family companies, people had a sense over the years that the company's purpose was to serve as the family's livelihood. One of the first things William and I did was to persuade my father to separate ownership and management by taking the company public in 1973.

When our margins were squeezed during the 1980s, we felt we needed to make dramatic changes that could best be done if we went back to being a private company. So in 1988, we undertook Hong Kong's first management buyout, sold off assets, and refocused the company on its core trading business. Later we took our export trading business public again. I'm sure some of our thinking about governance structure and focus was influenced by our Western training.

But I'm more struck by the changes in the company's decision making. Right now in this building, we probably have 50 buyers making hundreds of individual transactions. We're making a large number of small decisions instead of a small number of big ones. I can't be involved in all of them. So today I depend on structure, on guiding principles, on managing a system.

Of course, I think relationships are still important, but I'm not managing a single key relationship and using it to leverage my entire enterprise. Instead, I'm running a very focused business using a systems approach. That's why I say that in the last five years, everything I learned in business school has come to matter.

Li & Fung is a good example of the new generation of companies coming out of Asia. As the currency crisis destroys the old model, stronger companies will emerge from the ashes, still bolstered by Asia's strong work ethic and high savings rates, but more narrowly focused and professionally run by what we can call the "M.B.A. sons."

What's driving Hong Kong is a large number—about 300,000—of small and midsize enterprises. About 40% of those companies are transnational; that is, they operate in two or more territories. Some may have 20 to 30 people in Hong Kong, plus a factory in mainland China with 200 or 300 people. Hong Kong runs about 50,000 factories in southern China, employing about 5 million workers. Hong Kong is producing a new breed of company. I don't think there will be many the size of General Motors or AT&T. But there will be lots of very focused companies that will break into the *Fortune* 1,000. I hope Li & Fung is one of them.

15

Growth Through Global Sustainability

An Interview with Monsanto's CEO, Robert B. Shapiro

Joan Magretta

Robert B. Shapiro, chairman and CEO of Monsanto Company, based in St. Louis, Missouri, sees the conundrum facing his company this way. On the one hand, if a business doesn't grow, it will die. And the world economy must grow to keep pace with the needs of population growth. On the other hand, how does a company face the prospect that growing and being profitable could require intolerable abuse of the natural world? In Shapiro's words, "It's the kind of question that people who choose to spend their lives working in business can't shrug off or avoid easily. And it has important implications for business strategy."

Sustainable development is the term for the dual imperative—economic growth and environmental sustainability—that has been gaining ground among business leaders since the 1992 United Nations Earth Summit in Rio de Janeiro. As Shapiro puts it, "We can't expect the rest of the world to abandon their economic aspirations just so we can continue to enjoy clean air and water. That is neither ethically correct nor likely to be permitted by the billions of people in the developing world who expect the quality of their lives to improve."

Monsanto—with its history in the chemicals industry—may seem an unlikely company to lead the way on an emerging environmental issue. But a number of resource- and energy-intensive companies criticized as environmental offenders in the 1980s have been the first to grasp the strategic implications of sustainability.

Monsanto, in fact, is seeking growth *through* sustainability, betting on a strategic discontinuity from which few businesses will be immune. To borrow Stuart L.

Hart's phrase, Monsanto is moving "beyond greening." In the following interview with *Harvard Business Review* editor-at-large Joan Magretta, the 58-year-old Shapiro discusses how Monsanto has moved from a decade of progress in pollution prevention and clean-up to spotting opportunities for revenue growth in environmentally sustainable new products and technologies.

Why is sustainability becoming an important component of your strategic thinking?

Today there are about 5.8 billion people in the world. About 1.5 billion of them live in conditions of abject poverty—a subsistence life that simply can't be romanticized as some form of simpler, preindustrial lifestyle. These people spend their days trying to get food and firewood so that they can make it to the next day. As many as 800 million people are so severely malnourished that they can neither work nor participate in family life. That's where we are today. And, as far as I know, no demographer questions that the world population will just about double by sometime around 2030.

Without radical change, the kind of world implied by those numbers is unthinkable. It's a world of mass migrations and environmental degradation on an unimaginable scale. At best, it means the preservation of a few islands of privilege and prosperity in a sea of misery and violence.

Our nation's economic system evolved in an era of cheap energy and careless waste disposal, when limits seemed irrelevant. None of us today, whether we're managing a house or running a business, is living in a sustainable way. It's not a question of good guys and bad guys. There is no point in saying, If only those bad guys would go out of business, then the world would be fine. The whole system has to change; there's a huge opportunity for reinvention.

We're entering a time of perhaps unprecedented discontinuity. Businesses grounded in the old model will become obsolete and die. At Monsanto, we're trying to invent some new businesses around the concept of environmental sustainability. We may not yet know exactly what those businesses will look like, but we're willing to place some bets because the world cannot avoid needing sustainability in the long run.

Can you explain how what you're describing is a discontinuity?

Years ago, we would approach strategic planning by considering "the environment"—that is, the economic, technological, and competitive context of the business—and we'd forecast how it would change over the planning horizon. Forecasting usually meant extrapolating recent trends. So we almost never predicted the critical discontinuities in which the real money was made and lost—the changes that really determined the future of the business. Niels Bohr was right when he said it is difficult to make predictions—especially about the future. But every consumer marketer knows that you can rely on demographics. Many market discontinuities were predictable—and future ones can still be predicted—based on observable, incontrovertible facts such as baby booms and busts, life expectancies, and immigration patterns. Sustainable development is one of those discontinuities. Far from being a soft issue grounded in emotion or ethics, sustainable development involves cold, rational business logic.

This discontinuity is occurring because we are encountering physical limits. You can see it coming arithmetically. Sustainability involves the laws of nature—physics, chemistry, and biology—and the recognition that the world is a closed system. What we thought was boundless has limits, and we're beginning to hit them. That's going to change a lot of today's fundamental economics, it's going to change prices, and it's going to change what's socially acceptable.

Is sustainability an immediate issue today in any of Monsanto's businesses?

In some businesses, it's probably less apparent why sustainability is so critical. But in our agricultural business, we can't avoid it. In the twentieth century, we have been able to feed people by bringing more acreage into production and by increasing productivity through fertilizers, pesticides, and irrigation. But current agricultural practice isn't sustainable: we've lost something on the order of 15% of our topsoil over the last 20 years or so, irrigation is increasing the salinity of soil, and the petrochemicals we rely on aren't renewable.

Most arable land is already under cultivation. Attempts to open new farmland are causing severe ecological damage. So in the best case, we have the same amount of land to work with and twice as many people to feed. It comes down to resource productivity. You have to get twice the yield from every acre of land just to maintain current levels of poverty and malnutrition.

Now, even if you wanted to do it in an unsustainable way, no technology today would let you double productivity. With current best practices applied to all the acreage in the world, you'd get about a third of the way toward feeding the whole population. The conclusion is that new technology is the only alternative to one of two disasters: not feeding people—letting the Malthusian process work its magic on the population—or ecological catastrophe.

What new technology are you talking about?

We don't have 100 years to figure that out; at best, we have decades. In that time frame, I know of only two viable candidates: biotechnology and information technology. I'm treating them as though they're separate, but biotechnology is really a subset of information technology because it is about DNA-encoded information.

Using information is one of the ways to increase productivity without abusing nature. A closed system like the earth's can't withstand a systematic increase of material things, but it can support exponential increases of information and knowledge. If economic development means using more stuff, then those who argue that growth and environmental sustainability are incompatible are right. And if we grow by using more stuff, I'm afraid we'd better start looking for a new planet.

But sustainability and development might be compatible if you could create value and satisfy people's needs by increasing the information component of what's produced and diminishing the amount of stuff.

How does biotechnology replace stuff with information in agriculture?

We can genetically code a plant, for example, to repel or destroy harmful insects. That means we don't have to spray the plant with pesticides—with stuff. Up to 90% of what's sprayed on crops today is wasted. Most of it ends up on the soil. If we put the right information in the plant, we waste less stuff and increase productivity. With biotechnology, we can accomplish that. It's not that chemicals are inherently bad. But they are less efficient than biology because you have to manufacture and distribute and apply them.

I offer a prediction: the early twenty-first century is going to see a struggle between information technology and biotechnology on the one hand and environmental degradation on the other. Information technology is going to be our most powerful tool. It will let us miniaturize things, avoid waste, and produce more value without producing and processing more stuff. The substitution of information for stuff is essential to sustainability. (See "Monsanto's Smarter Products.") Substituting services for products is another.

Monsanto's Smarter Products

Scientists at Monsanto are designing products that use information at the genetic or molecular level to increase productivity. Here are three that are on the market today.

The NewLeaf Potato. The NewLeaf potato, bioengineered to defend itself against the destructive Colorado potato beetle, is already in use on farms. Monsanto also is working on the NewLeaf Plus potato with inherent resistance to leaf virus, another common scourge. Widespread adoption of the product could eliminate the manufacture, transportation, distribution, and aerial application of millions of pounds of chemicals and residues yearly.

B.t. Cotton. In ordinary soil, microbes known as B.t. microbes occur naturally and produce a special protein that, although toxic to certain pests, are

Ordinary seed potatoes	4,000,000 pounds of raw material + energy from 1,500 barrels of oil	3,800,000 pounds of inert ingredients + 1,200,000 pounds of insecticide 2,500,000 pounds of waste	5,000,000 pounds of formulated product in 180,000 containers and packages	150,000 gallons of fuel to distribute and apply	Less than 5% of insecticide reaches target pest	Crop

harmless to other insects, wildlife, and people. If the destructive cotton budworm, for example, eats B.t. bacteria, it will die.

Some cotton farmers control budworms by applying to their cotton plants a powder containing B.t. But the powder often blows or washes away, and re-applying it is expensive. The alternative is for farmers to spray the field with a chemical insecticide as many as 10 or 12 times per season.

But Monsanto's scientists had an idea. They identified the gene that tells the B.t. bacteria to make the special protein. Then they inserted the gene in the cotton plant to enable it to produce the protein on its own while remaining unchanged in other respects. Now when budworms attack, they are either repelled or killed by the B.t.

With products like B.t. cotton, farmers avoid having to buy and apply insecticides. And the environment is spared chemicals that are persistent in the soil or that run off into the groundwater.

Roundup Herbicide and No-Till Farming. Sustainability has become an important design criterion in Monsanto's chemically based products as well as in its bioengineered products. Building the right information into molecules, for example, can render them more durable or enhance their recyclability.

Roundup herbicide is a molecule designed to address a major problem for farmers: topsoil erosion. Topsoil is necessary for root systems because of its organic matter, friability in structure, and water-holding capabilities. The subsoil underneath is incapable of supporting root systems. Historically, farmers have tilled their soil primarily for weed control and only to a minor extent for seed preparation. But plowing loosens soil structure and exposes soil to erosion.

By replacing plowing with application of herbicides like Roundup—a practice called *conservation tillage*—farmers end up with better soil quality and less topsoil erosion. When sprayed onto a field before crop planting, Roundup kills the weeds, eliminating the need for plowing. And because the Roundup molecule has been designed to kill only what is growing at the time of its initial application, the farmer can come back a few days after spraying and begin planting; the herbicide will have no effect on the emerging seeds.

The Roundup molecule has other smart features that contribute to sustainability. It is degraded by soil microbes into natural products such as nitrogen, carbon dioxide, and water. It is nontoxic to animals because its mode of action

| **NewLeaf Plus** seed potatoes | · ⟶ | **Crop** |

is specific to plants. Once sprayed, it sticks to soil particles; it doesn't move into the groundwater. Like a smart tool, it seeks out its work.

Explain what you mean by substituting services for products.

Bill McDonough, dean of the University of Virginia's School of Architecture in Charlottesville, made this come clear for me. He points out that we often buy things not because we want the things themselves but because we want what they can do. Television sets are an obvious example. No one says, "Gee, I'd love to put a cathode-ray tube and a lot of printed circuit boards in my living room." People *might* say, "I'd like to watch the ball game" or "Let's turn on the soaps." Another example: Monsanto makes nylon fiber, much of which goes into carpeting. Each year, nearly 2 million tons of old carpeting go into landfills, where they constitute about 1% of the entire U.S. municipal solid-waste load. Nobody really wants to own carpet; they just want to walk on it. What would happen if Monsanto or the carpet manufacturer owned that carpet and promised to come in and remove it when it required replacing? What would the economics of that look like? One of our customers is exploring that possibility today. It might be that if we got the carpet back, we could afford to put more cost into it in the first place in ways that would make it easier for us to recycle. Maybe then it wouldn't end up in a landfill.

We're starting to look at all our products and ask, What is it people really need to buy? Do they need the stuff or just its function? What would be the economic impact of our selling a carpet service instead of a carpet?

Can you cite other examples of how we can replace stuff with information?

Sure. Information technology, whether it's telecommunications or virtual reality—whatever that turns out to be—can eliminate the need to move people and things around. In the past, if you wanted to send a document from one place to another, it involved a lot of trains and planes and trucks. Sending a fax eliminates all that motion. Sending E-mail also eliminates the paper.

I have to add that any powerful new technology is going to create ethical problems—problems of privacy, fairness, ethics, power, or control. With any major change in the technological substrate, society has to solve those inherent issues.

You referred earlier to using information to miniaturize things. How does that work?

Miniaturization is another piece of sustainability because it reduces the amount of stuff we use. There are enormous potential savings in moving from very crude, massive designs to smaller and more elegant ones. Microelectronics is one example: the computing power you have in your PC would have required an enormous installation not many years ago.

We've designed things bigger than they need to be because it's easier and because we thought we had unlimited space and material. Now that we know we don't, there's going to be a premium on smaller, smarter design. I think of miniaturization as a way to buy time. Ultimately, we'd love to figure out how to replace chemical processing plants with fields of growing plants—literally, green plants capable of producing chemicals. We have some leads: we can already produce polymers in soybeans, for example. But I think a big commercial breakthrough is a long way off.

Today, by developing more efficient catalysts, for example, we can at least make chemical plants smaller. There will be a number of feasible alternatives if we can really learn to think differently and set design criteria other than reducing immediate capital costs. One way is to design chemical plants differently. If you looked at life-cycle costs such as energy consumption, for instance, you would design a plant so that processes needing heat were placed next to processes generating heat; you wouldn't install as many heaters and coolers that waste energy. We think that if you really dig into your costs, you can accomplish a lot by simplifying and shrinking.

Some people are talking about breakthroughs in mechanical devices comparable to what's being done with electronic devices. Maybe the next wave will come through nanotechnology, but probably in 10 or 20 years, not tomorrow.

The key to sustainability, then, lies in technology?

I am not one of those techno-utopians who just assume that technology is going to take care of everyone. But I don't see an alternative to giving it our best shot.

Business leaders tend to trust technology and markets and to be optimistic about the natural unfolding of events. But at a visceral level, people know we are headed for trouble and would love to find a way to do something about it. The market is going to want sustainable systems, and if Monsanto provides them, we will do quite well for ourselves and our shareowners. Sustainable development is going to be one of the organizing principles around which Monsanto and a lot of other institutions will probably define themselves in the years to come.

Describe how you go about infusing this way of thinking into the company.

It's not hard. You talk for three minutes, and people light up and say, "Where do we start?" And I say, "I don't know. And good luck."

Maybe some context would help. We've been grappling with sustainability issues here long before we had a term for the concept. Part of our history as a chemical company is that environmental issues have been in our face to a greater extent than they've been in many other industries.

My predecessor, Dick Mahoney, understood that the way we were doing things had to change. Dick grew up, as I did not, in the chemical industry, so he tended to look at what was coming out of our plants. The publication of our first toxic-release inventory in 1988 galvanized attention around the magnitude of plant emissions.

Dick got way out ahead of the traditional culture in Monsanto and in the rest of the chemical industry. He set incredibly aggressive quantitative targets and deadlines. The first reaction to them was, My God, he must be out of his mind. But it was an effective technique. In six years, we reduced our toxic air emissions by 90%.

Not having "grown up in the chemical industry," as you put it, do you think differently about environmental issues?

Somewhat. Dick put us on the right path. We have to reduce—and ultimately eliminate—the negative impacts we have on the world. There is no argument on that subject. But even if Monsanto reached its goal of zero impact next Tuesday, that wouldn't solve the world's problem. Several years ago, I sensed that there was something more required of us than doing no harm, but I couldn't articulate what that was.

So I did what you always do. I got some smart people together—a group of about 25 critical thinkers, some of the company's up-and-coming leaders—and sent them off to think about it. We selected a good cross-section—some business-unit leaders, a couple from the management board, and people from planning, manufacturing, policy, and safety and health. And we brought in some nontraditional outsiders to challenge our underlying assumptions about the world. My request to this group was, "Go off, think about what's happening to the world, and come back with some recommendations about what it means for Monsanto. Do we have a role to play? If so, what is it?"

That off-site meeting in 1994 led to an emerging insight that we couldn't ignore the changing global environmental conditions. The focus around sustainable development became obvious. I should have been able to come up with that in about 15 minutes. But it took a group of very good people quite a while to think it through, to determine what was real and what was just puff, to understand the data, and to convince themselves that this wasn't a fluffy issue—and that we ought to be engaged in it.

People came away from that meeting emotionally fired up. It wasn't just a matter of Okay, you threw me an interesting business problem, I have done the analysis, here is the answer, and now can I go back to work. People came away saying, "Damn it, we've got to get going on this. This is important." When some of your best people care intensely, their excitement is contagious.

So now we have a bunch of folks engaged, recognizing that we have no idea where we're going to end up. No one—not the most sophisticated thinker in the world—can describe a sustainable world with 10 billion to 12 billion people, living in conditions that aren't disgusting and morally impermissible. But we can't sit around waiting for the finished blueprint. We have to start moving in directions that make us less unsustainable.

How are you doing that?

There's a quote of Peter Drucker's—which I will mangle here—to the effect that at some point strategy has to degenerate into work. At Monsanto, there was a flurry of E-mail around the world, and in a matter of four months a group of about 80 coalesced. Some were chosen; many others just heard about the project and volunteered. They met for the first time in October 1995 and decided to organize into seven teams: three focused on developing tools to help us make better decisions, three focused externally on meeting world needs, and one focused on education and communication. (See "Monsanto's Seven Sustainability Teams.")

We realized that many of the things we were already doing were part of a sustainability strategy even if we didn't call it that. We'd been working on pollution prevention and investing in biotechnology for years before we thought about the concept of sustainability. As we made more progress in pollution prevention, it became easier for everyone to grasp how pollution—or waste—actually represents a resource that's lost. When you translate that understanding into how you run a business, it leads to cost reduction. You can ask, did we do it because it reduces our costs or because of sustainability? That would be hard to answer because optimizing resources has become part of the way we think. But having the sustainability framework has made a difference, especially in how we weigh new business opportunities.

Monsanto's Seven Sustainability Teams

Three of Monsanto's sustainability teams are working on tools and methodologies to assess, measure, and provide direction for internal management.

The Eco-efficiency Team. Because you can't manage what you don't measure, this team is mapping and measuring the ecological efficiency of Monsanto's processes. Team members must ask, In relation to the value produced, what inputs are consumed, and what outputs are generated? Managers have historically optimized raw material inputs, for example, but they have tended to take energy and water for granted because there is little financial incentive today to do otherwise. And although companies such as Monsanto have focused on toxic waste in the past, true eco-efficiency will require better measures of all waste. Carbon dioxide, for instance, may not be toxic, but it can produce negative environmental effects. Ultimately, Monsanto's goal is to pursue eco-efficiency in all its interactions with suppliers and customers.

The Full-Cost Accounting Team. This team is developing a methodology to account for the total cost of making and using a product during the product's life cycle, including the true environmental costs associated with producing, using, recycling, and disposing of it. The goal is to keep score in a way that doesn't eliminate from consideration all the environmental costs of what the company does. With better data, it will be possible to make smarter decisions today and as the underlying economics change in the future.

The Index Team. This team is developing criteria by which business units can measure whether or not they're moving toward sustainability. They are working on a set of metrics that balance economic, social, and environmental factors. Units will be able to track the sustainability of individual products and of whole businesses. These sustainability metrics will, in turn, be integrated into Monsanto's balanced-scorecard approach to the management of its businesses. The scorecard links and sets objectives for financial targets, customer satisfaction, internal processes, and organizational learning.

Three teams are looking externally to identify sustainability needs that Monsanto might address.

The New Business/New Products Team. This team is examining what will be valued in a marketplace that increasingly selects products and services that support sustainability. It is looking at areas of stress in natural systems and imagining how Monsanto's technological skills could meet human needs with new products that don't aggravate—that perhaps even repair—ecological damage.

The Water Team. The water team is looking at global water needs—a huge and growing problem. Many people don't have access to clean drinking water, and there is a worsening shortage of water for irrigation as well.

The Global Hunger Team. This team is studying how Monsanto might develop and deliver technologies to alleviate world hunger. That goal has been a core focus for the company for a number of years. For example, Monsanto had been studying how it might use its agricultural skills to meet people's nutritional needs in developing countries.

The final team develops materials and training programs.

The Communication and Education Team. This team's contribution is to develop the training to give Monsanto's 29,000 employees a common perspective. It offers a framework for understanding what sustainability means, how employees can play a role, and how they can take their knowledge to key audiences outside the company.

Can you give me some examples?

One of the seven sustainability teams is discussing how to gain a deeper understanding of global water needs and whether we at Monsanto might meet some of those needs with our existing capabilities. That is an example of a conversation that might not have occurred—or might have occurred much later—if we weren't focused on sustainability. Agricultural water is becoming scarcer, and the salination of soils is an increasing problem. In California, for example, they do a lot of irrigation, and when the water evaporates or flushes through the soil, it leaves small amounts of minerals and salts. Over time, the build-up is going to affect the soil's productivity.

Should we address the water side of the problem? Or can we approach the issue from the plant side? Can we develop plants that will thrive in salty soil? Or can we create less thirsty plants suited to a drier environment? If we had plants that could adapt, maybe semidesert areas could become productive.

Another problem is drinking water. Roughly 40% of the people on earth don't have an adequate supply of fresh water. In the United States, we have a big infrastructure for cleaning water. But in developing countries that lack the infrastructure, there might be a business opportunity for in-home water-purification systems.

I realize this is still early in the process, but how do you know that you're moving forward?

One interesting measure is that we keep drawing in more people. We started off with 80; now we have almost 140. And a lot of this response is just one person after another saying, "I want to be involved, and this is the team I want to be involved in." It's infectious. That's the way most good business processes work. To give people a script and tell them, "Your part is on page 17; just memorize it" is an archaic way to run institutions that have to regenerate and re-create themselves. It's a dead end.

Today, in most fields I know, the struggle is about creativity and innovation. There is no script. You have some ideas, some activities, some exhortations, and some invitations, and you try to align what people believe and what people care about with what they're free to do. And you hope that you can coordinate them in ways that aren't too wasteful—or, better still, that they can self-coordinate. If an institution wants to be adaptive, it has to let go of some control and trust that people will work on the right things in the right ways. That has some obvious implications for the ways you select people, train them, and support them.

Would it be accurate to say that all of your sustainability teams have been self-created and self-coordinated?

Someone asked me recently whether this was a top-down exercise or a bottom-up exercise. Those don't sound like very helpful concepts to me. This is about *us*. What do *we* want to do? Companies aren't machines anymore. We have thousands of independent agents trying to self-coordinate because it is in their interest to do so.

There is no top or bottom. That's just a metaphor and not a helpful one. People say, Here is what I think. What do you think? Does that make sense to you? Would you like to try it? I believe we must see what ideas really win people's hearts and trust that those ideas will turn out to be the most productive.

People in large numbers won't give their all for protracted periods of time—with a cost in their overall lives—for an abstraction called a corporation or an idea called profit. People can give only to people. They can give to their coworkers if they believe that they're engaged together in an enterprise of some importance. They can give to society, which is just another way of saying they can give to their children. They can give if they believe that their work is in some way integrated into a whole life.

Historically, there has been a bifurcation between who we are and the work we do, as if who we are is outside our work. That's unhealthy, and most people yearn to integrate their two sides. Because of Monsanto's history as a chemical company, we have a lot of employees—good people—with a recurrent experience like this: their kids or their neighbors' kids or somebody at a cocktail party asks them what kind of work they do and then reacts in a disapproving way because of what they *think* we are at Monsanto. And that hurts. People don't want to be made to feel ashamed of what they do.

I don't mean to disparage economic motives—they're obviously important. But working on sustainability offers a huge hope for healing the rift between our economic activity and our total human activity. Instead of seeing the two in Marxist opposition, we see them as the same thing. Economics is part of human activity.

What are the organizational implications of that?

Part of the design and structure of any successful institution is going to be giving people permission to select tasks and goals that they care about. Those tasks have to pass some kind of economic screen; but much of what people care about will pass because economic gain comes from meeting people's needs. That's what economies are based on.

The people who have been working on sustainability here have done an incredible job, not because there has been one presiding genius who has organized it all and told them what to do but because they want to get it done. They care intensely about it and they organize themselves to do it.

I don't mean to romanticize it, but, by and large, self-regulating systems are probably going to be more productive than those based primarily on control loops. There are some institutions that for a short period can succeed as a reflection of the will and ego of a single person. But they're unlikely to survive unless other people resonate with what that person represents.

We're going to have to figure out how to organize people in ways that enable them to coordinate their activities without wasteful and intrusive systems of control and without too much predefinition of what a job is. My own view is that as long as you have a concept called a job, you're asking people to behave inauthentically; you're asking people to perform to a set of expectations that someone else created. People give more if they can figure out how to control themselves, how to regulate themselves, how to contribute what they can contribute out of their own authentic abilities and beliefs, not out of somebody else's predetermination of what they're going to do all day.

How will you measure your progress toward sustainability? Do you have milestones?

For something at this early level of exploration, you probably want to rely for at least a year on a subjective sense of momentum. People usually know when they're going someplace, when they're making progress. There's a pace to it that says, yes, we're on the right track. After that, I would like to see some quantitative goals with dates and very macro budgets. As the teams begin to come to some conclusions, we will be able to ignite the next phase by setting some specific targets.

This is so big and complicated that I don't think we're going to end up with a neat and tidy document. I don't think environmental sustainability lends itself to that.

As your activities globalize, does the issue of sustainability lead you to think differently about your business strategy in different countries or regions of the world?

The developing economies can grow by brute force, by putting steel in the ground and depleting natural resources and burning a lot of hydrocarbons. But a far better way to go would be for companies like Monsanto to transfer their knowledge and help those countries avoid the mistakes of the past. If emerging economies have to relive the entire industrial revolution with all its waste, its energy use, and its pollution, I think it's all over.

Can we help the Chinese, for example, leapfrog from preindustrial to postindustrial systems without having to pass through that destructive middle? At the moment, the signs aren't encouraging. One that is, however, is China's adoption of cellular phones instead of tons of stuff: telephone poles and copper wire.

The fact that India is one of the largest software-writing countries in the world is encouraging. You'd like to see tens of millions of people in India employed in information technology rather than in making more stuff. But there's an important hurdle for companies like Monsanto to overcome. To make money through the transfer of information, we depend on intellectual property rights, which let us reconcile environmental and economic goals. As the headlines tell you, that's a little problematic in Asia. And yet it's critically important to our being able to figure out how to be helpful while making money. Knowledge transfer will happen a lot faster if people get paid for it.

Will individual companies put themselves at risk if they follow sustainable practices and their competitors don't?

I can see that somebody could get short-term advantage by cutting corners. At a matter of fact, the world economy *has* seized such an advantage—short-term in the sense of 500 years—by cutting corners on some basic laws of physics and thermodynamics. But it's like asking if you can gain an advantage by violating laws. Yes, I suppose you can—until they catch you. I don't think it is a good idea to build a business or an economy around the "until-they-catch-you principle." It can't be the right way to build something that is going to endure.

The multinational corporation is an impressive invention for dealing with the tension between the application of broadly interesting ideas on the one hand and economic and cultural differences on the other. Companies like ours have gotten pretty good at figuring out how to operate in places where we can make a living while remaining true to some fundamental rules. As more countries enter the world economy, they are accepting—with greater or lesser enthusiasm—that they are going to have to play by some rules that are new for them. My guess is that, over time, sustainability is going to be one of those rules.

Doesn't all this seem far away for managers? Far enough in the future for them to think, "It won't happen on my watch"?

The tension between the short term and the long term is one of the fundamental issues of business—and of life—and it isn't going to go away. Many chief executives have gotten where they are in part because they have a time horizon longer than next month. You don't stop caring about next month, but you also have to think further ahead. What's going to happen next in my world? If your world is soft drinks, for example, you have to ask where your clean water will come from.

How do you react to the prospect of the world population doubling over the next few decades? First you may say, Great, 5 billion more customers. That is what economic development is all about. That's part of it. Now, keep going. Think about all the physical implications of serving that many new customers. And ask yourself the hard question, How exactly are we going to do that and still live here? That's what sustainability is about.

I'm fascinated with the concept of distinctions that transform people. Once you learn certain things—once you learn to ride a bike, say—your life has changed forever. You can't unlearn it. For me, sustainability is one of those distinctions. Once you get it, it changes how you think. A lot of our people have been infected by this way of seeing the world. It's becoming automatic. It's just part of who you are.

16
Unleashing the Power of Learning
An Interview with British Petroleum's John Browne

Steven E. Prokesch

With his talk of "the shrinking half-life of ideas," "virtual team networks," and "breakthrough thinking," John Browne sounds more like a Silicon Valley CEO than the head of the giant British Petroleum Company. Then again, BP—with its flat organization, entrepreneurial business units, web of alliances, and surging profits—is starting to look and act like a vibrant Silicon Valley enterprise. Such comparisons may seem wild, but Browne thinks that all companies battling it out in the global information age face a common challenge: using knowledge more effectively than their competitors do. And he is not talking only about the knowledge that resides in one's own organization. "Any organization that thinks it does everything the best and need not learn from others is incredibly arrogant and foolish," he says.

BP is a radically different company today than a decade ago, when it was an unfocused, mediocre performer whose businesses extended to minerals, coal, animal feed, and chicks. The vast majority of its oil and gas output came from large fields in the North Sea and in Alaska's North Slope whose production was beginning to decline. BP's reserves were shrinking, and its finding and development costs were so high—three times higher than those of its major competitors—that it had difficulty making any money on new fields.

Today BP is the most profitable of the major oil companies. Its debt, which had grown as a result of acquisitions, unrestrained capital spending, and the buyback of a big block of shares from the Kuwaiti government, has been slashed to $7 billion from a 1992 peak of $16 billion. BP now has strong positions in such important oil and gas regions as the Gulf of Mexico, South America, western Africa, the Caspian Sea, the Middle East, and the Atlantic Ocean west of the Shetland Islands. BP's finding and development costs are now among the lowest in its industry. Its output is growing at about 5% per year. And even without additional discoveries, the company has the wherewithal to maintain its reserves for at least ten years.

Organizationally, BP is much smaller and simpler than it was a decade ago. It now has 53,000 employees—down from 129,000. Before, the company was mired in procedures; now it has processes that foster learning and tie people's jobs to creating value. Before, it had a multitude of baronies; now it has an abundance of teams and informal networks or communities in which people eagerly share knowledge.

Much of the credit for BP's recovery goes to David Simon, Browne's predecessor, who became CEO in June 1992, when BP's board ousted Robert Horton. Besides putting BP's financial house in order, Simon drove home two messages: performance matters, and teamwork is crucial for improving performance.

But the man who engineered the revival of BP Exploration and Production (BPX) and poised BP for growth is Browne, who headed BPX from 1989 to July 1995, when he succeeded Simon as CEO. Browne, who is 49, grew up in BP—almost literally. His father had worked for the company, and, after graduating from the University of Cambridge with a degree in physics, the younger Browne followed suit, joining as an apprentice petroleum engineer. While in his thirties, he ran BP's important Forties field in the North Sea. In 1984, he became treasurer, and in 1986, he moved to Standard Oil of Ohio, in which BP had a majority stake. Browne helped Horton rationalize the company before it fully merged with BP.

Browne is the kind of person who never accepts that something can't be done and who is always asking if there is a better way or if someone might have a better idea. Under his leadership, BP is becoming the same kind of company. One case in point: BP's unconventional idea to merge its European fuel-and-lubricant business with Mobil's. The landmark deal struck last year offers an opportunity to create one healthy first-tier player out of two second-tier players whose prospects in the mature, oversupplied market seemed bleak.

Browne discussed his ideas with Steven E. Prokesch, who conducted the interviews in London and New York while a senior editor at *Harvard Business Review.* Prokesch is now codirector of idea development at the Boston Consulting Group in Boston, Massachusetts.

Some management thinkers believe we are entering an age of globalization in which building and leveraging knowledge will be the key to success. Do you agree?

Absolutely. Knowledge, ideas, and innovative solutions are being diffused throughout the world today at a speed that would have been unimaginable 10 or 20 years ago. Companies are only now learning how to go beyond seeing that movement as a threat to seeing it as an opportunity. We see it as a tremendous opportunity.

How will the diffusion of knowledge affect the rules of competition?

Learning is at the heart of a company's ability to adapt to a rapidly changing environment. It is the key to being able both to identify opportunities that others might not see and to exploit those opportunities rapidly and fully. This means that in order to generate extraordinary value for shareholders, a company has to learn better than its competitors and apply that knowledge throughout its businesses faster and more widely than they do. The way we see it, anyone in the organization who is not directly accountable for making a profit should be involved in creating and distributing knowledge that the company can use to make a profit.

The wonderful thing about knowledge is that it is relatively inexpensive to replicate *if* you can capture it. Most activities or tasks are not onetime events. Whether it's drilling a well or conducting a transaction at a service station, we do the same things repeatedly. Our philosophy is fairly simple: Every time we do something again, we should do it better than the last time. This year, drilling will account for more than $3.8 billion in capital expenditures on exploration and production. We drill lots of wells. If we drill each well more efficiently than the last one, we can make a lot more money—which is exactly what we're trying to do.

We haven't been at it too long, but already we're reaping fantastic gains. Deepwater drilling is a good example. We have a big acreage position in the deep water of the Gulf of Mexico, where drilling is an enormous technical challenge. The water there is between 2,000 and 8,000 feet deep, and then you have to drill 7,000 to 12,000 feet below the seabed to reach hydrocarbons. Because the water is so deep, you can't affix anything to the seabed, and no human being can go down that far. So you have to use special vessels to drill. They are very expensive, and because it's fashionable to be drilling in this area, they're becoming even more expensive. In 1995, we spent 100 days on average drilling deepwater wells. We now spend 42. How did we do it? By asking every time we drilled a deepwater well, What did we learn the last time and how do we apply it the next time? And we learned not only from our own people but also from contractors and from partners such as Shell.

What kinds of learning are crucial? What are the challenges in maximizing them?

There are a variety of ways you can learn how to do something better. You can learn from your own experience. You can learn from your contractors, suppliers, partners, and customers. And you can learn from companies totally outside your business. All are crucial. No matter where the knowledge comes from, the key to reaping a big return is to leverage that knowledge by replicating it throughout the company so that each unit is not learning in isolation and reinventing the wheel again and again.

The conventional wisdom is that excelling in incremental learning is a science—a matter of installing the right processes—while excelling in breakthrough thinking is more of an art. I disagree about the latter: I think you *can* install processes that generate breakthrough thinking. We have.

Another conventional view is that it is harder to tap implicit knowledge, which is the experiential knowledge locked inside someone's head, than explicit knowledge, which can be captured in a database. But that hasn't been our experience. We have had great success in fostering the personal interactions you need to mine implicit knowledge.

Our challenge has been getting people to systematically capture the information the company needs in order to be able to use both explicit and implicit knowledge repeatedly. In the case of explicit knowledge, that means recording the actual data. In the case of implicit knowledge, it means keeping a record of the people who have the know-how to solve a problem so that others can find them when the need arises. The trouble is that both tasks are boring. So we've got to figure out how to make them exciting and enjoyable. We've made progress, but we have a long way to go. (See "Sharing Knowledge Through BP's Virtual Team Network.")

Sharing Knowledge Through BP's Virtual Team Network

At a time when *bureaucracy* is a dirty word, it's easy to forget that a bureaucracy historically served two essential purposes: it connected the leaders of a corporation to their businesses, and it allowed the businesses to exchange critical knowledge. Have times really changed? Is it possible to have it all: a flat, decentralized, global corporation that excels at learning and has leaders who are deeply engaged in helping to shape the strategy and drive the performance of the businesses? "Yes," declares John Browne, chief executive of the British Petroleum Company. "Advances in information technology now make it possible." Or so BP hopes to prove.

BP today is amazingly flat and lean for a corporation with $70 billion in revenues, 53,000 employees, and some 90 business units that span the globe. There is nobody between the general managers of the business units and the group of nine operating executives who oversee the businesses with Browne. The way Browne sees it, the people in the business units—those closest to BP's assets and customers—should run their businesses. And in his view, the value that can be derived from sharing knowledge, not geographical location, should drive the interactions among the business units, which is why he deems BP's *virtual team network* to be so important. The aim of this computer network is to allow people to work cooperatively and share knowledge quickly and easily regardless of time, distance, and organizational boundaries.

The network is a rapidly growing system of sophisticated personal computers equipped so that users can work together as if they were in the same room and can easily tap the company's rich database of information. The PCs boast videoconferencing capability, electronic blackboards, scanners, faxes, and groupware. But that's not all.

These PCs, as well as all the other 35,000-odd basic PCs in the company, are connected to an intranet that contains a rapidly growing number of home pages. Everyone at BP now has the capability and authority to create his or her own home page. The corporate philosophy: Let a thousand—or a million—home pages bloom. As of July, the intranet sites contained approximately 40,000 pages of information.

The home pages serve a number of purposes. There are sites where functional experts describe the experience they have to offer. There are sites for sharing technical data on the muds used as drilling lubricants and for sharing contacts and information about programs and processes available to reduce the amount of pipe that gets stuck in wells. There is a site where people concerned about how to get computers to handle the transition to the year 2000 can exchange ideas. Every technology discipline has its own site. The general managers of all the business units in BP Exploration and Production (BPX) have their own home pages, where they list their current projects and performance agendas.

"If it's easy for people to connect, communicate, and share knowledge, they will do it. If it isn't, they won't," says Kent A. Greenes, BP's virtual teamwork project director. To make it easier, BP is experimenting with a variety of approaches: making videos that can be seen on the network; creating electronic yellow pages that can be searched in a variety of ways; and encouraging people to list interests, expertise, and experiences that they are willing to share with anyone wishing to contact them.

During the recent development of the Andrew oil field in the North Sea, BP used the virtual team network to pass on lessons from the revolutionary project in real time. BP and its contractors and suppliers cooperated to an unprecedented degree to figure out radical ways to cut the cost and time of the project. Using the virtual team network, the project's participants briefed other BP units, partners, and contractors in places as far away as Alaska and Colombia on how they made critical decisions.

The network began in 1995 as a $12 million pilot program in BPX. About a third of the money was spent on behavioral scientists, who helped the people in the pilot programs learn how to work effectively in a virtual environment. "We realized that virtual teamwork required a new set of behaviors," says John B.W. Cross, BP's head of information technology. "It required people to be cooperative and open about what they know, and not possessive about information."

Browne felt that BP should not force the network on people. Rather, he believed that if people saw its benefits, they would ask for it. He was right. "After about six months, we suddenly found out that a lot of people in other groups were asking, 'How do we get one?' Some people were bootlegging and buying the stuff on their own," he says.

In 1996, Browne made the virtual team network available to everyone at BP under one condition: they had to pay for it out of their own budgets. "They said, 'We don't mind. It's just fantastic.' It's an example of how an organization changes itself when it sees something worthwhile," Browne says. As of July, the virtual team network had grown to 1,000 PCs, and Cross expects it to soar to 10,000 by 1999. The network links teams working in the Gulf of Mexico with teams working in the eastern Atlantic near the Shetland Islands, and the PCs are installed in refineries and chemical plants from Indonesia to Scotland.

BP also is extending membership in the virtual team network to outside organizations. For example, the company is using the network to improve the way it works with partners such as Shell in the Gulf of Mexico, and with contractors such as Brown & Root in the North Sea.

Some of the benefits of the virtual team network are easy to measure:

- A big drop in the person-hours needed to solve problems as a result of improved interactions between land-based drilling engineers and offshore rig crews.

- A decrease in the number of helicopter trips to offshore oil platforms.

- The avoidance of a refinery shutdown because technical experts at another location could examine a corrosion problem remotely.

- A reduction in rework during construction projects because designers, fabricators, construction workers, and operations people could collaborate more effectively.

BP estimates that the virtual team network produced at least $30 million in value in its first year alone. But this estimate does not take into account the harder-to-measure benefits—such as the ability to see the whites of someone's eyes in a videoconference when he or she makes a commitment.

Each member of BP's top management team and each general manager of the business units has at least one virtual team workstation. Browne has two: one in his office and one in his London home. They allow him to be in two places or more at the same time, he says, describing how he recently participated in separate management conferences in Johannesburg and Singapore from his office. "We had great discussions," he says. "We talked about BP, where it was going, the constraints, the issues that they had. Had I not had the network, what would I have done? Tried to bend my schedule to the point of absurdity? Sent a videotape?"

Browne believes that effective leadership requires personal relationships. It requires continual conversations about competitive dynamics, performance, and corporate values. "These technologies allow the center to stay engaged with the business," Cross says. "Without them, John's organizational model is not sustainable."

What's the most important rule for building an effective learning organization?

A business has to have a clear purpose. If the purpose is not crystal clear, people in the business will not understand what kind of knowledge is critical and what they have to learn in order to improve performance. A clear purpose allows a company to focus its learning efforts in order to increase its competitive advantage.

What do we mean by *purpose*? Our purpose is who we are and what makes us distinctive. It's what we as a company exist to achieve, and what we're willing and not willing to do to achieve it. We are in only four components of the energy business: oil and gas exploration and production; refining and marketing; petrochemicals; and photovoltaics, or solar. We're a public company that has to compete for capital, which means we have to deliver a competitive return to shareholders. We're in a highly competitive global industry in which cost matters. We serve a global market that offers growth opportunities, and we want to grow. But in our pursuit of exceptional performance and sustained growth, there are certain financial boundaries we will not cross and values we will not violate. The values concern ethics; health, safety, and the environment; the way we treat employees; and external relations.

Was a fuzzy purpose one of the root causes of your previous problems?

We needed to redefine exactly what we were trying to do. The world never stands still, and a company has to keep moving on. That is the only way you can maintain control of your own destiny.

Although the perceived challenge at the end of the 1980s was replacing our falling reserves, there was no framework for doing so. Our capital spending was going up, up, up. We were exploring in a lot of places—50 to 60 countries around the world. But many of those efforts were unlikely ever to deliver a competitive return on capital. For example, we were exploring in the Netherlands, the home country of Royal Dutch/Shell. The way I see it, any company that explores there had better have a solid idea of why it might stand a better chance of finding something worthwhile than Shell, which is a very good company.

In other words, many of the things we were doing were not distinctive. We were not insisting on getting value for the money we invested. You cannot live like that for long. The capital markets won't let you.

A few of us on BP's senior management team were convinced that the world had changed in some fundamental ways that offered us a chance to create a radically new future. We realized that advances in technology and opening markets were creating opportunities to find and develop big new oil and gas fields—those with 250 million barrels or more—in such places as South America, Vietnam, the Caspian Sea, and the Atlantic Ocean west of the Shetland Islands. In addition, there was demand for that oil and gas: global consumption was growing, mainly because of growth in the emerging economies.

Ultimately, we decided to focus on finding giant oil and gas fields: the cost of finding, developing, and operating them is low, they offer growth potential, and they would allow us to earn a high return on capital. We decided to focus on just 20 countries, which made us think long and hard about which were the best opportunities. And we agreed to get rid of everything else that couldn't make a material difference or offer growth potential—everything not distinctive.

Distinctive *is a word you use a lot around BP. What precisely do you mean by it?*

Things that are hard to copy, that give us a competitive edge or serve as a competitive barrier. At BP, four key elements create distinctiveness: assets and market shares, technologies, organization, and relationships.

Distinctive assets are assets that, given your culture, management, and knowledge, allow you to produce outstanding returns and achieve sustainable growth. For BPX, giant oil and gas fields are distinctive because of their low cost and because there are so few of them. For BP Oil—our refining and marketing group—large market shares, stations with high volumes, and refineries that perform in the top quartile of their markets are distinctive. Our share of the European fuel-and-lubricant market wasn't big enough to be sustainable, which is why we merged that operation with Mobil's. The partnership should deliver savings on the order of $400 million to $500 million per year, provide a platform from which to enter the new growth markets of central and eastern Europe, and give us the opportunity to learn a lot from Mobil.

We mean several things by *distinctive technologies*. The first is obvious: patented processes that give us an advantage in competing for customers and partners, and in gaining entry to new markets such as China. In our chemicals business, our patented processes for making acrylonitrile, acetic acid, and polyethylene are distinctive. Second, distinctive technologies are those that can help us increase productivity and cut costs year after year. Third, distinctive technologies are those that can help us capture and share knowledge. For example, information technology is the key to allowing people to work with others—to share knowledge and solve problems—across the boundaries of countries and companies and corporate structures.

By allowing us to stay on the leading edge, distinctive technologies of all kinds help us attract and retain the most talented people. If we aren't regarded as leading edge, why would a graduate join us instead of Microsoft or Intel? We need the most talented people in order to build a distinctive organization.

What are the qualities of a distinctive organization?

Its people are highly motivated, understand exactly what they have to do to help create great value, can see the results of their actions, and have a sense of ownership. They excel at building and using knowledge capital, which means accessing and applying knowledge that exists both inside and outside the company. They excel at forging distinctive relationships.

Why does a company need distinctive relationships?

We need to form them with partners, suppliers, customers, and the countries in which we operate so that we all can work together to maximize value. You can't expect others to share their knowledge and resources with you fully unless you have a strong relationship with them.

You can't create an enduring business by viewing relationships as a bazaar activity—in which I try to get the best of you and you of me— or in which you pass off as much risk as you can to the other guy. Rather, we must view relationships as a coming together that allows us to do something no other two parties could do—something that makes the pie bigger and is to your advantage and to my advantage.

One case in point is how Schlumberger, the oilfield-services company, developed a special device for us called a logging tool. We were drilling lots of horizontal wells, and it occurred to us that we didn't know what was going on. Was the entire horizontal well producing? Did we drill too much or too little? There was no available device that could tell us, which was surprising, because the whole industry was drilling horizontal wells. So we went to Schlumberger and said, "We have one or two rudimentary ideas on how to do this. But we'd like our scientists and your scientists to get together because we need the tool, and this could be a wonderful business opportunity for you. Recognizing that there's a little risk, we'll pay you for some of the development and we'll use some of our wells to test the tool."

And that's what we did. Some of our people went to Schlumberger's research laboratory to work with its people. Once they understood the technology, they built a prototype, which looked like a piece of pipe you put down wells. It was vast—150 feet long. Honoring our side of the agreement, we put it down one of our wells. For one horrible moment, it got stuck, which meant we'd lose not only the tool but also the well. Eventually it was okay, and we proved the concept. We asked Schlumberger to make it a bit smaller and to make it available to us first before offering it to everyone in the world. The result was that we got a tool that has taught us a lot about what we needed to do to make horizontal wells even more effective, and Schlumberger got a new business.

What does it take to build distinctive relationships?

The most important aspect of any relationship is understanding what your partners hope to get out of it and to work hard to help them achieve that goal. It is the key to transforming a contractual relationship into a genuine collaboration.

Second, you have to deliver on your promises reliably and consistently. Your promises have to be realistic, and you need to move heaven and earth to keep them.

Third, you never build a relationship between your organization and a company or a government. You build it between individuals. Our people have to have real authority. We can't cut them off at the knees. They must be people who can deliver.

Fourth, all relationships worth anything are open and flexible. In other words, you must invite people in, try to discuss the problem or opportunity, and say, "How do we solve it jointly?" If you say, "Here is my solution. I'm having a great relationship with you if you agree, and I won't have a relationship with you if you disagree," then the relationship is not to mutual advantage.

Fifth, you have to approach an opportunity—which should be the basis of every relationship—with humility. You have to recognize that others may actually know more than you do about something—that you can learn from them. For example, we know we can learn a lot from Mobil about operating refineries and marketing lubricants. Shell has taught us much about deepwater drilling, and we hope it has learned something from us.

Finally, you build relationships for the very long term. Even in tough wholesale businesses such as airplane fuel, this approach can give you an edge. How? You reject the notion that it is a commodity business. Then you try to build relationships with the airlines based on creating a long-term mutual advantage. And you strive to share long-term plans so you can service the airlines' planes effectively all over the world.

Of course, you cannot have a strong relationship with everyone. But in general, long-term relationships are the most profitable ones. Think about going into a new country. If you do just one piece of business in that country, how on earth are you going to recover the setup costs? So you have to think, What's the business after that? How do I get a sustainable position? The obvious answer is by building strong, long-term relationships.

One of the most challenging jobs in trying to create a learning organization is teaching the organization to learn. Could you talk about the steps involved?

In our case, the first was to instill the belief that competitive performance matters—that producing value is everyone's job and that to produce value you need to focus so that you don't get distracted by things that aren't central. BP is not a collection of *financial* assets. It is a combination of assets and the activities, people, and learning needed to extract maximum value from those assets. The way I see it, there are two justifications for keeping each piece of business that we own. The first is that our company has the culture and processes to manage each piece better than anybody else. The second is that the pieces inside the company learn from one another and consequently can do things better together over time.

For people to learn how to deliver performance and grow BP, we had to make them feel that, individually and collectively, they could control the destiny of our businesses. Of course, there are aspects of our business that are outside our control—oil prices, for instance. But there are many others that we can control. To drive home that message, we talk a lot about *self-help,* and we rigorously track and publicize the results that it produces.

What is self-help? It is about how we control the cost structure, get more bang for the investment buck, upgrade the quality of products and services, and improve relationships with suppliers and customers. It's about getting people to develop an intimate understanding of the structures of their businesses' margins and how they compare with those of their competitors. It is a big reason why we split the company into some 90 business units and why we now share numbers and plans much more widely. In the past five years, self-help has generated $4 billion worth of permanent improvements.

Isn't it often difficult to get people to focus on the importance of creating value and not to operate on autopilot?

Yes. In the late 1980s and early 1990s, we had a problem, which I suspect many companies—especially big ones—share. People often took an incremental or piecemeal approach to a project or an opportunity. A good example is the replacement of the pipeline in our Forties field in the North Sea. It was an old 32-inch line that was past its useful life. We decided we would build a 36-inch pipeline because we thought we could attract a lot of other business, the cost difference was very small, and we could make it last longer by using new corrosion and emission technologies.

We were going along merrily for two months when the guy running the North Sea group came to me and said, "Sign this." It was a request for $150 million to build a new platform because, as it turned out, we couldn't put the new pipeline on the old one. So I said, "I'll tell you what: we'll build it, but we'll spend only $100 million, and this is the last time something like this happens." The final cost was $110 million.

Such experiences made us realize that we had to install a disciplined planning-and-approval process to make people look at the whole: the entire project, how it fits into the strategy, and the return that must be generated in order to make the project worthwhile. If people focus from the outset on that whole, they will then devote themselves to learning what needs to be done to achieve the total goal.

What you're saying is that you had to teach people that the way to get maximum value was to excel at learning. How did you put in motion such a learning process?

By setting competitive and comparative targets and challenging people to achieve them. To get people to learn, you need to give them a challenge. Setting a target is crucial even if you don't actually know whether it's fully achievable—because in times of rapid change, you have to make decisions and get people to step outside the box.

One process that we employ to promote learning and drive performance is not that unusual. It involves understanding the critical measures of operating performance in each business, relentlessly benchmarking those measures and their related activities, setting higher and higher targets, and challenging people to achieve them.

Another, more unusual process involves breakthrough thinking. When we assess opportunities, we ask, If the usual approaches or business system cannot produce the return on capital that we need, are there others that can? Let's challenge the boundary. The development of the Andrew field, which changed the economics of developing oil and gas fields in the North Sea, demonstrates the dramatic results that that kind of thinking can produce. (See "Breakthrough Thinking: How to Develop the Undevelopable.")

Breakthrough Thinking: How to Develop the Undevelopable

Since discovering oil and gas in the Andrew field in the North Sea in 1974, the British Petroleum Company had repeatedly tried in vain to figure out how to develop it economically. In the late 1980s, the company even had considered writing down and selling its majority interest in the field. But in 1990, BP had a compelling reason to try again. The 1986 collapse of world oil prices and the discovery of giant oil fields in other parts of the world threatened the viability of the North Sea as a major oil-producing region. If BP could develop Andrew, with its estimated 112 million recoverable barrels of oil and 3.8 billion cubic meters of gas, then it also would be able to tackle profitably the mostly small fields that remained to be developed in the region. The challenge was a big one: at a time when oil prices were $14 per barrel, BP was demanding a 25% return on investment.

John Browne, then head of BP Exploration and Production (BPX), personally picked Andrew. He was one of the many senior BP executives who had had first-hand experience with its problems. As a young engineer, he had participated in an unsuccessful effort to find a profitable way to bring the field into production. In 1990, he was trying to reinvigorate BPX and turn it into a place where innovation was a way of life. He saw the challenge of developing Andrew as an opportunity to demonstrate the power of breakthrough thinking. The approach: set a seemingly unattainable target and see how close you can get to attaining it by assigning the best minds to the problem, scouring the world for the best ideas—doing whatever it takes.

Browne assembled a team of people from a wide range of disciplines and with different perspectives from both inside and outside BPX's North Sea group in the hope that the resulting dialogue would produce fresh ideas. At first, the team saw the challenge mainly as solving a petroleum-engineering problem. But by the end of 1991, the team was stuck. Even with the latest technology, it saw no way to develop the geologically complex field for less than $675 million, which was still too high a price to make the project attractive. The team's plan called for only incremental changes to the traditional cost-plus approach of paying contractors a fixed amount above the actual cost. It was not breakthrough thinking. Browne wouldn't let the team off the hook. "You've got to do what you initially promised to do," he said.

The team, which was being coached by JMW Consultants—a firm in Stamford, Connecticut, that specializes in helping teams make breakthroughs—

began to broaden its thinking and reconsider every aspect of the problem. Instead of looking only at technology for the solution, how about looking at BPX's relationship with its contractors? Instead of continuing the practice of treating contractors as adversaries and playing them off against one another, how about treating them as allies? How about giving them a financial interest in the project's success and encouraging them to work together to challenge costs, seek the best value, and innovate?

The approach turned out to be the breakthrough that BPX needed. It set an extreme target of $405 million to send the message that the project would require revolutionary new attitudes, practices, and ideas. It chose seven contractors that it deemed to be committed to pioneering a new open and collaborative approach. And it promised to let them be full-fledged partners in designing and managing the project and to let them carry it out without the heavy oversight that had been typical of BPX. Then it asked this "alliance" team to come up with a project proposal, which itself was a big departure from usual practice. Generally, BP staff would have completed all the conceptual engineering-design work and a significant amount of the detailed engineering design. Only after the project had received the go-ahead would the contractors have been brought in.

"In this case, BPX said, 'We don't have a feasible project yet. But if you help us figure out how to do it, we'll promise to give you the work,'" recalls Norman. C. Chambers, at the time a senior executive at Halliburton's Brown & Root division, the contractor responsible for management support and much of the design work and procurement.

In November 1993, the alliance submitted a detailed proposal to develop Andrew for $560 million, with oil production to begin in January 1997. Some of its innovative suggestions included employing 12 horizontal wells rather than 19 vertical wells and, instead of building the deck in modules and then assembling them offshore, building a single integrated deck that could be installed onto the offshore structure with a single lift. The plan also called for testing and certifying process equipment onshore, and reducing the total cost of equipment and materials by 30% through minimizing inspections, making direct purchases instead of going through agents, and giving suppliers the freedom to figure out the best way to meet functional specifications.

The estimate passed the 25% hurdle rate. But BP analysts, using historical cost data, gave the plan only a 38% probability of being completed within the estimate—below the 50% probability typically required for approval. But the alliance proposed an innovative risk-and-reward scheme, which persuaded BP and four other oil companies with minority stakes in the field to give it the go-ahead in February 1994. Under the arrangement, the contractors would absorb 54% of any cost overruns, with a maximum exposure of $40 million. If the project came in below $560 million, the contractors would receive more than 50% of the savings in addition to their normal pay. "We knew that unless we did something extraordinary, we would lose money, but we were willing to take the risk because of BP's commitment to doing something different," says Chambers, who is now president of Halliburton Energy Development, another Halliburton division.

The project came in at just below $444 million and was completed more than six months early. The seven contractors shared a bonus of nearly $69 million.

How did the alliance do it? By setting stretch targets and challenging every aspect of the schedule and the design, thereby slashing the cost of materials. By reducing the duplication of effort significantly. By incorporating all the skills and knowledge from the alliance's eight members into the design process, thereby ensuring that the designs could be constructed efficiently and that costly rework would be eliminated. By building a three-dimensional computer simulation of the whole project, drastically reducing the number of person-hours spent on design work. By making the contractors largely responsible for meeting quality and safety specifications. By greatly standardizing equipment, materials, and components. By working with suppliers as partners. And by breaking with convention and inviting the certifying authorities and the crew that would operate the platform to be on-site members of the team.

One dramatic result: once the three-deck platform was installed, it was producing within days rather than the usual months. "Every day, we challenged every assumption," Chambers says. "We analyzed anything that might reduce costs and speed up the development time. And we made breakthroughs practically every day."

The alliance approach is now spreading throughout BP. The company has formed similar alliances to develop its oil fields near the Shetland Islands and the Badami field in Alaska, to expand a polyethylene plant in Indonesia, and to refurbish its Grangemouth refinery in Scotland.

"One important thing about Andrew is that it is making money and producing above the design specifications," Browne says. "But it also taught us a new way of doing things by building relationships to mutual advantage with a variety of people. It was a major watershed."[1]

What is the role of a leader in institutionalizing breakthrough thinking?

The top management team must stimulate the organization, not control it. Its role is to provide strategic directives, to encourage learning, and to make sure there are mechanisms for transferring the lessons. The role of leaders at all levels is to demonstrate to people that they are capable of achieving more than they think they can achieve and that they should never be satisfied with where they are now. To change behavior and unleash new ways of thinking, a leader sometimes has to say, "Stop, you're not allowed to do it the old way," and issue a challenge.

The development of our Wytch Farm oil field near Poole, England, is a case in point. In the late 1980s, BPX was producing from onshore wells when we discovered that the field extended significantly offshore into Poole Harbor, an area of particular scientific interest and one of the most beautiful places in Europe. The question over the next few years was how to produce that oil. Because accessing the oil from land seemed technically infeasible—a horizontal well of that distance had never been drilled—the initial, knee-jerk plan was to build an artificial island in Poole Harbor and drill from that, even though it would require an act of Parliament.

Everything was going forward: a bill had been introduced, and brochures, a lobbying strategy, and a plan aimed at defusing the anticipated attacks by environmental groups had been prepared. The estimated cost was just about tolerable, but it was high, and you had to factor in what would really happen once the plan was under way: the costs would just go up and up.

Then my management team said, "Stop! We're not going to do this. We've got to figure out another way." We assembled a multidisciplinary team to tackle the challenge, borrowing the best people from wherever they resided in BPX.

The team decided that developing the offshore reserves without an artificial island was perfectly doable if we could make a breakthrough in horizontal-drilling technology and drill under the seabed from the existing onshore locations. And the team did it. It didn't try to leap mountains in one stride. Instead, it took the best available technologies and then, slowly, step by step, went beyond them. In the end, the wells were five miles long—the longest drilled in the history of the oil industry—and saved us $75 million.

This was the sort of innovation that people would come up with when we challenged them. And before too long, it became contagious. Without prodding, people began to ask themselves, Where can I innovate? Or they would realize on their own, This isn't a good idea—let's try something different. So, contrary to what some may believe, you *can* institutionalize breakthrough thinking.

How do you make sure that people do not inadvertently damage the business when they make mistakes during the learning process?

By experimenting, which is integral to learning. I think it's impossible to predict what will happen when you deploy a strategic thought inside an organization. I don't think you can predict people's behavior. Therefore, you've got to experiment. You've got to see what people actually do. You've got to see how the idea works. You've got to learn how to build something with a bit of track record, which you then can apply more widely.

We are taking that approach toward developing a chain of integrated food-and-fuel convenience retail sites in Britain with Safeway, the supermarket chain. We said to Safeway's leaders, "We think it's a terrific idea. It looks as though we could have a mutually advantageous relationship with you. We can see the strategy. We've got real estate you want. We've got a nice brand. You've got a wonderful system for delivering fresh food." The trouble is that neither of our companies really knows the other. Ideally, we'd like to do 100 sites. But first we'll conduct an experiment with 8 sites, set some targets, and measure the results. If the experiment works, we'll go full steam ahead. In that way, we'll get to know each other. We'll see whether we can have a relationship.

In all the organizational changes in which I have been involved, I've said, "Rather than take a cataclysmic approach, let's try it, see how it works, understand what we've learned, and only then apply it more widely." Then the challenge is to excel at building on that knowledge and to apply the cumulative knowledge quickly and broadly throughout the organization.

How did you design an organizational structure to promote learning?

We have built a very flat team-based organization that is designed to motivate and help people to learn. We've divided the company up into lots of business units, and there is *nothing* between them and the nine-member executive group to whom they report, which consists of the three managing directors of our business groups and their six deputies. The organization is even flatter than my description makes it sound, because each of the managing directors and his deputies work as a team in dealing with the business units.

We've worked with the managers of each business unit to create an annual performance contract that spells out exactly what they're expected to deliver, and we review their progress quarterly. In addition, we've developed all sorts of networks to encourage the sharing of knowledge throughout the organization. Finally, we've integrated our technology organization with the business units so that it is working with them both to solve the most important business problems and to exploit the most important business opportunities. Previously, the technology organization was a separate fiefdom, focused on invention. To be fair, we did get some good innovation—in gas-to-liquid technology, for example. But sometimes the technology group's inventions were pretty peripheral, such as pills for making pink flamingos pinker. Overall, we were not getting good value for our investments.

In the last five years, we've refocused our technology people on application. Now their mission is to access the best technology wherever it resides inside or outside BP and apply it quickly, cutting costs and time to market. However good a company is, it can't expect to possess more than a tiny fraction of the world's best technology. Moreover, I suspect that if a lot of companies rigorously analyzed whether their proprietary technologies really do provide a competitive edge, many would be surprised by the number that don't. For example, we had assumed that proprietary seismic technology for finding new oil fields gave us an advantage in exploration. But on closer scrutiny, we realized that it did not. For one thing, the reality is that we often have to share it either with partners or with state-owned oil companies in order to gain access to frontier areas. For another, we have found that our people's ability to combine and apply technologies—not the technologies themselves—is often what gives us an advantage.

How does your new organizational structure compare with the old one?

It's a far cry from the complicated structure we used to have, which included enormous regional organizations, matrix management, and huge staffs in the headquarters of the company and of the business groups. Excluding the people in the financial-and oil-trading organizations, the headquarters of the company and of the business groups now employ only 350 people—an incredibly small number for a company with revenues of $70 billion. In 1989, that total was about 4,000. Having lived through the days of huge staffs and complicated structures, my predecessor, David Simon, and I passionately believed that we had to push decision making out to where it could be managed most effectively—to the business units—and that we had to get rid of the clutter so that learning could flow.

We divided the company up in this fashion so that people would not feel like part of a great, big organization, so that they would not get lost, so that they would have pride of ownership. We wanted people to be able to see the impact of their actions on the business's performance. So we designed the organization in a way that let everyone see clearly how things are done and understand what each person's role is in getting it done. It's based on processes, not tasks or hierarchies. Processes linked to a purpose are powerful at changing behavior because people can see what they're aiming for.

I'm not talking just about operational processes. I mean management processes, too. When a managing director and his deputies review the past performance and future plans of every business unit quarterly with its general manager, the message is sent that performance matters. That's an assurance process. We also have a strategic process for ensuring that the units are constantly creating lots of business options for the future and are constantly sorting through them and improving them.

It sounds as though you're saying that life is complicated and we need to make it simpler.

That's right. A team of people focused on a coherent bit of a big, complex business can develop the kind of intimate knowledge of the business that's needed to maximize performance and to create the options necessary for building the future. They can work the assets harder than a large organization can, and they're much less likely to sit on those assets if they can't be made to perform or don't make sense. It's a structure that allows people to have many face-to-face interactions and to form deep personal relationships, which are critical in a learning organization.

Whether a business unit is mainly an asset, such as an oil field, or is developing downstream markets in central Europe, we make sure that it is big enough to justify putting a really great manager in charge of it. But the units are small enough that their leaders can have one-to-one interactions with people rather than town-hall-style meetings—which, in my view, are an ineffective way of communicating.

A virtue of this organizational structure is that there is a lot of transparency. Not only can the people within the business unit understand more clearly what they have to do, but I and the other senior executives can understand what they're doing. Then we can have an ongoing dialogue with them and with ourselves about how to improve performance and build the future.

A leader must not only grasp the big picture but also be able to break it down into bits that are real for individuals. Take the issue of growth. I have to remind myself constantly that the manager of our business unit in central Europe, for example, doesn't care about macro numbers—that global oil consumption is going up by 2% per year, gas consumption by 3%, and demand for the kind of chemicals we produce by 6%. She wants to know which specific growth opportunities she should pursue in, say, Poland.

To leverage learning, knowledge must flow among business units. I would think the challenge is to create links among the units to promote that flow without re-creating the organizational clutter of the past. How have you tackled that challenge?

Information technology is one solution. In addition, we have made much progress in forming what you might call learning communities. For example, each of the 40 business units that constitute BPX belongs to one of four peer groups. The members of each peer group wrestle with common problems. They have a lot to learn from one another. They share technical staff. And they all are equals.

There is no boss?

No, because if you named a boss, you'd have an organization and a hierarchy, and hierarchies—or, more specifically, the politics that accompany hierarchies—hamper the free exchange of knowledge. People are much more open with their peers: they are much more willing to share and to listen, and are much less likely to take umbrage when someone disagrees with them. Regardless of the team, if it isn't operating on a peer basis, it's not going to get the right interactions. It might sound like fantasy, but I truly consider myself only the first among equals in the top management team.

What is the basis for each peer group?

For both BP Oil—our refining and marketing group—and BP Chemicals, the basis is functional. For BPX, the basis is the life cycle of the exploration-and-production business. The members of one peer group are the business units that are finding new fields. Their concerns include getting governments to grant them permission to explore, improving seismic analysis, and minimizing the number of dry holes. The members of the second peer group are the units that develop the fields. They're the big spenders. This year, they have a capital budget of $2.2 billion, which they are free to manage on their own. Their issues range from how best to deal with corrosion problems to how to immerse a workforce in a new area in BP's health-and-safety culture. The members of the third are the units whose fields are at plateau production. They are the steady income producers—the money powerhouses. And those in the fourth are all operating old or late-life fields. Their challenges include squeezing as much as they can out of the fields, cutting costs as the fields tail off, decommissioning wells, and reducing the size of the workforce.

I think knowledge is really flowing among the units *within* each of our three main business groups: BPX, BP Oil, and BP Chemicals. Now the challenge is to get that knowledge flowing more easily *across* the groups.

Why is it important to create networks linking dissimilar businesses? Do they have much to learn from one another?

Different eyes see different things, and many of those businesses have much more in common than you might think. If you step back far enough, there isn't too much difference between operating an offshore oil platform, an ethylene plant, and a refinery. And, regardless of whether their equipment is similar, many units face common problems, including health, safety, and environmental issues, as well as how to conduct business in difficult places like Colombia and Algeria.

Given the free flow of information around the world these days, applying the same values and standards everywhere is necessary for building sustainable relationships. If we don't do that, there's a growing danger that when we try to get a new piece of business in, say, China or Venezuela, people there will say, "You do it differently in Alaska. Why aren't you doing it the same way here?"

So it is important for knowledge to flow both within and across our business groups. To that end, we're currently striving to turn BP's 350 most senior people into a team. They control assets, functional knowledge, and other resources. They are the people who really can get things done.

I have been struck by how you have been trying to create a culture that is comfortable with change and embraces continual innovation. How do you keep an organization from ossifying?

In order to be in control of your destiny, you must realize that you will stay ahead competitively only if you acknowledge that no advantage and no success is ever permanent. The winners are those who keep moving. We have tried to instill this attitude in our people.

We've tried to make it not only acceptable but also expected that people look for a better way or grab the best ideas from wherever they find them. We've benchmarked ourselves against our own industry for a long time. Now we also expect people, when they're setting targets or challenging a boundary, to look beyond the oil industry to whichever industry does something best. For example, we've learned a lot from the automobile industry about procurement, which has helped us lower the cost of building service stations. And we went to the U.S. Army to learn about capturing and sharing knowledge.

Another way to prevent ossification is to minimize the amount of organizational structure. Information technology is wonderful because it makes rich exchanges possible without formal structures.

Finally, to create an effective learning organization, you don't bolt things down. You let the organization and the ways in which it learns evolve. If you don't, organizational structures can become obstacles to the free flow of knowledge and can become disconnected from the business purpose. When I headed BPX, I set new targets every two years or so and then changed the structure and some of the people in order to deliver the targets. Why? Because I think you have to impose discontinuous change until you can see that the organization will discontinuously change itself. I think there's a limit to how much continuous improvement can achieve.

It may seem obvious, but I think many managers lose sight of the fact that the business purpose should determine the organizational structure. Many managers who have tried to transform their companies have made the mistake of reorganizing or trying to build teams *before* they had clarified and communicated the purpose. At BPX, we didn't begin to think about the kind of organization we wanted to build until we had a firm idea of where we wanted to be and of the disciplined approach to business that we wanted to take. What is the point of building anything unless you know what the business purpose is?

We're still constantly changing the organizational structure to fit our business purpose. For example, when the British gas market recently underwent deregulation, we spotted an opportunity. If we could develop the ability to respond to temporary surges in demand for gas from industrial buyers, we could make a tidy profit. But it meant that our marketing people had to be in direct contact with our people operating our production platforms. In a matter of days, we set up a gas management board composed of production and marketing people to find ways to supply that demand. We were able to move faster than any of our competitors, and that gave us an advantage.

Isn't there a danger that the learning networks you are encouraging will end up creating organizational complexity?

I don't think so. One of the beauties of the networks is that they are not organizational structures per se. Having said that, one of the virtues of BPX's peer groups is that they institute change because a business unit changes its peer group when it enters a new phase of its business's life cycle.

In general, we don't think of our business units as permanent structures. When we were setting them up, we did a lot of experimenting to get them right. We're still constantly scrutinizing them to make sure they serve their business purpose, maximize learning, and help teams perform. If they don't, we change them: we split them up or combine them.

What part does strategic planning play in a learning organization?

Our strategic planning process is designed to keep ideas flowing and to stimulate thinking. We see strategy as applying a series of frameworks that help us constantly reexamine what we are doing relative to what the world can offer and what our competitors are doing. We start with our purpose. Who are we? What sorts of businesses are we in? What are the characteristics of those businesses? What are the limits—in terms of our values and financial boundaries—to the sorts of activities that we are prepared to undertake? What makes our company distinctive?

Using those frameworks to shape our dialogues with our people, we begin to create a strategy that lives because it is always changing as competitive dynamics change or as we understand them more clearly.

You don't build a distinctive business by talking about it once a year or once every two years, and then writing a document and putting it in a drawer. You build it by having the company's leaders talk about it with the people in the business units—both formally quarter by quarter and informally even more often. Then people from the top of the company down to the business unit are thinking about it all the time and adjusting what they do every day in light of reality. It's a tremendous way to get people to grasp what is really happening in every component of the company and to help them avoid falling into the trap of thinking of strategy as something fixed or as cash flow analyses, with one answer and one answer only.

Given the uncertainty in the world, strategy cannot be about gambling on one possible outcome five or ten years down the road. Grand master plans have a habit of not being fulfilled. In my view, strategy is about buying the right options that will give us a shot at competing in the future—that will give us the right to play if we decide we want to when it becomes clearer what the game is about. To create the kind of distinctive asset base and market positions that allow one to outperform the competition and generate great returns requires a continuous process of developing strategic options, applying skills and technology to stretch their potential, and regularly winnowing them, choosing only the best.

What is the role of top management in the learning organization?

The most senior leaders in any company do only a very few things. Ultimately, they have to make decisions on the organizational architecture and the way forward. They set policies, standards, and targets, and create processes to ensure that people achieve or adhere to them. It is while those processes are being carried out that learning should take place. What determines whether it does is the questions leaders ask and the way they approach what is going on. Leadership is all about catalyzing learning as well as better performance.

Leaders have to demonstrate that they are active participants in the learning organization. You can't say "Go do it" without participating. Take the part I play in the quarterly reviews of business units' performance contracts. After the managing director of each group and his deputies have reviewed all their business units, I'll review their performance by exception. By that I mean that if something is very good or very bad, we'll focus on it to try to understand what happened and how the business units in question and other business units can learn from that exception. It's one of the ways I'd like to think I help capture and transfer learning in the company. Learning is my job, too, which, by the way, is why I recently joined Intel's board.

What do you think you can learn from Intel?

Intel is a high-tech company that has to contend day in and day out with incredibly rapid change. It really has to survive on its ideas—it has to rely on its intellectual property for the next thing it does for the customer. And it has to excel at motivating creative people who have technical skills. BP also is a high-tech company. We're trying to deal with a rapidly changing environment. And we, too, need to attract and motivate highly skilled technical people. There's plenty Intel can teach us.

I find it extraordinary that people buying personal computers actually ask whether Intel is inside. People don't ask whether BP is inside. Maybe someday they will.

Note

1. Some of the information in this insert comes from Terry Knott, *No Business As Usual* (London: British Petroleum Company, 1996), an account of the development of the Andrew field.

Executive Summaries

The End of Corporate Imperialism

C.K. Prahalad and Kenneth Lieberthal

As they search for growth, multinational corporations will have no choice but to compete in the big emerging markets of China, India, Indonesia, and Brazil. But while it is still common to question how corporations will change life in those markets, Western executives would be smart to turn the question around. The authors assert that the multinationals themselves will be transformed by their experience. In fact, they say, MNCs will have to rethink every element of their business models in order to be successful.

During the first wave of market entry in the 1980s, MNCs operated with what might be termed an imperialist mind-set. They assumed, for example, that the big emerging markets would be new markets for their old products. As a result of this mind-set, multinationals have achieved only limited success in these markets.

The authors guide readers through five questions that companies must answer to compete effectively. First and foremost, MNCs must define the emerging middle-class markets—which are significantly different from those in the West—and determine a business model that will serve their needs.

The transformation that multinationals must undergo is not cosmetic—simply developing greater cultural sensitivity will not do the trick. In order to compete in the big emerging markets, multinationals must reconfigure their resource base, rethink their cost structure, redesign their product development process, and challenge their assumptions about the cultural mix of their top-level managers. MNCs that recognize the need for such changes will likely reap the rewards of the postimperialist age.

Why Focused Strategies May Be Wrong for Emerging Markets

Tarun Khanna and Krishna Palepu

Core competencies and focus are now the mantras of corporate strategists in Western economies. But while managers in the West have dismantled many conglomerates assembled in the 1960s and 1970s, the large, diversified business group remains the dominant form of enterprise throughout many emerging markets. As those markets open up to global competition, consultants and foreign investors are increasingly pressuring groups to conform to Western practice by scaling back the scope of their business activities. Already a number of executives have decided to break up their groups in order to show that they are focusing on only a few core businesses.

There are reasons to worry about this trend, say the authors. Focus is good advice in New York or London, but something important gets lost in translation when that advice is given to groups in emerging markets. Western companies take for granted a range of institutions that support their business activities, but many of those institutions are absent in other regions of the world.

Companies must adapt their strategies to fit their *institutional context:* a country's product, capital, and labor markets; its regulatory system; and its mechanisms for enforcing contracts. In contrast to advanced economies, emerging markets suffer from weak institutions in all or most of these areas. Conglomerates can add value by imitating the functions of several institutions that are present only in advanced economies. Successful groups effectively mediate between their member companies and the rest of the economy.

Competing with Giants: Survival Strategies for Local Companies in Emerging Markets

Niraj Dawar and Tony Frost

The arrival of a multinational corporation often looks like a death sentence to local companies in an emerging market. After all, how can they compete in the face of the vast financial and technological resources, the seasoned management, and the powerful brands of, say, a Compaq or a Johnson & Johnson?

But local companies often have more options than they might think, say the authors. Those options vary, depending on the strength of globalization pressures in an industry and the nature of a company's competitive assets.

In the worst case, when globalization pressures are strong and a company has no competitive assets that it can transfer to other countries, it needs to retreat to a locally oriented link within the value chain. But if globalization pressures are weak, the company may be able to defend its market share by leveraging the advantages it enjoys in its home market.

Many companies in emerging markets have assets that can work well in other countries. Those that operate in industries where the pressures to globalize are weak may be able to extend their success to a limited number of other markets that are similar to their home base. And those operating in global markets may be able to contend head-on with multinational rivals.

By better understanding the relationship between their company's assets and the industry they operate in, executives from emerging markets can gain a clearer picture of the options they really have when multinationals come to stay.

Troubles Ahead in Emerging Markets

Jeffrey E. Garten

Throughout the 1990s, financial investors, corporate strategists, and political leaders in the United States, Western Europe, and Japan have been intensifying their focus on emerging markets. And, indeed, emerging markets are the new frontier. But like all frontiers, warns Jeffrey E. Garten, dean of the Yale School of Management, such markets present a mix of opportunity and risk. The question now is whether businesses and governments in the industrialized world are sober enough about the problems that lie ahead. There is considerable evidence to show that the tides of capitalism that rose so powerfully after the collapse of the former Soviet Union are now poised to recede. And this reversal could amount to a fundamental disruption in what has been an upward trajectory in so many countries.

What can government and business in the developed world do in the face of such likely turmoil? The industrialized nations of the OECD must ask whether they are pushing enough for growth and trade liberalization. And multinational companies can no longer leave foreign policy only to politicians and bureaucrats. They must learn to anticipate and respond to the upcoming political and economic disruptions in emerging markets. They also must remain open to opportunities for cooperation between private and public sectors in those markets. Such cooperation, advises Garten, can improve the economic environment and mitigate the risks of doing business abroad.

Managing in the Euro Zone

Introduction by Nicholas G. Carr

On January 1, 1999, 11 European nations formally adopted the euro as a common currency. What will the new monetary union mean for managers? In this Perspectives piece, senior executives from Merloni Elettrodomestici, PricewaterhouseCoopers, DaimlerChrysler, Sara Lee/DE, and ICI discuss how the euro will alter the European business landscape and change the rules of management.

The contributors suggest that the single currency will require executives to rethink many of their long-held assumptions about doing business in Europe. Because consumers will be able to easily compare prices across the Continent, for example, it will become much more difficult to have different product positioning and pricing strategies from country to country. Similarly, the need for pan-European thinking may require companies to reconsider their decentralized organizational structures, which grant autonomy to national units. And at the operational level, fragmented supply chains may turn into severe disadvantages.

There are many other changes that managers must consider with the introduction of the euro. Not only will they have to cope with confused and suspicious customers, they will also incur major up-front costs in implementing the changeover to the new currency. No two companies will take the same course in responding to the myriad challenges, but the practical insights of these five contributors will help all companies think clearly about their options.

Asia's New Competitive Game

Peter J. Williamson

These days, a Western company's toughest competition in Asia is likely to come not from familiar rivals but from lesser-known Asian companies based in countries other than Japan. These companies often use unusual tactics and strategies, and those who wish to compete with them should learn eight new rules of Asia's competitive game.

First, it is better to be always first than always right. While Western companies hesitate, Asian companies are taking risks in new markets. Second, control the bottlenecks in the supply chain. By controlling them, a company can gain power over not only its own production costs but also those of its competitors. Third, build walled cities; that is, create a dominant position in an industry. Large, emerging Asian multinationals use their dominant positions in one or more industries as a source of free-cash flow to finance international expansion.

Fourth, bring market transactions in-house. Western companies have been focusing on core activities, but in Asia, taking on noncore activities has definite benefits. Fifth, leverage your host government's goals. Because Asian governments commonly award monopoly rights and concessions to companies whose investment decisions fit in with national goals, a company that understands and aligns itself with those goals will reap the rewards.

Sixth, use a networked style of company organization. Seventh, make commercialization the equal of invention, and eighth, remember that what you don't know, you can learn.

Western companies must learn the rules of the new competitive game and then decide whether to follow them or to break them.

The Right Mind-set for Managing Information Technology

M. Bensaou and Michael Earl

Too many managers in the West are intimidated by the task of managing technology. They tiptoe around it, supposing that it needs special tools, special strategies, and a special mind-set. Well, it doesn't, the authors say. Technology should be managed—controlled, even—like any other competitive weapon in a manager's arsenal.

The authors came to this conclusion in a surprising way. Having set out to compare Western and Japanese IT-management practices, they were startled to discover that Japanese companies rarely experience the IT problems so common in the United States and Europe. In fact, their senior executives didn't even recognize the problems that the authors described. When they dug deeper into 20 leading companies that the Japanese themselves consider exemplary IT users, they found that the Japanese see IT as just one competitive lever among many. Its purpose, very simply, is to help the organization achieve its operational goals.

The authors recognize that their message is counterintuitive, to say the least. In visits to Japan, Western executives have found anything but a model to copy. But a closer look reveals that the prevailing wisdom is wrong. The authors found five principles of IT management in Japan that, they believe, are not only powerful but also universal.

M. Bensaou and Michael Earl contrast these principles against the practices commonly found in Western companies. While acknowledging that Japan has its own weaknesses with technology, particularly in white-collar office settings, they nevertheless urge senior managers in the West to consider the solid foundation on which Japanese IT management rests.

Group Versus Group: How Alliance Networks Compete

Benjamin Gomes-Casseres

Collaboration in business is no longer confined to conventional two-company alliances, such as joint ventures or marketing accords. Today groups of companies are linking together for a common purpose. Consequently, a new form of competition is spreading across global markets: group versus group. Call them networks, clusters, constellations, or virtual corporations, these groups consist of companies joined together in a larger overarching relationship. The individual companies in any group differ in size and focus, but they fulfill specific roles within their group. Furthermore, within the network or group, companies may be linked to one another through various kinds of alliances, ranging from the formality of an equity joint venture to the informality of a loose collaboration.

Are alliance groups the wave of the future or a passing fad? Have they actually helped group members compete more effectively?

Too little empirical evidence exists to answer these questions with assurance. But we do know enough, based on the experiences of the pioneers in group-based competition, such as Mips Computer Systems, to examine the questions that senior executives should be asking themselves before they organize, dive into, or decide to forgo these multialliance networks. Networks offer obvious advantages to their members, but those advantages come with costs that are not so obvious.

Making the Most of Foreign Factories

Kasra Ferdows

Many companies are not tapping the full potential of their foreign factories. They establish and manage them to benefit only from tariff and trade concessions, cheap labor, capital subsidies, and reduced logistics costs. They therefore give them a limited range of work, responsibilities, and resources. But there are companies that expect much more from their foreign factories and, as a result get much more. They use them to get closer to their customers and suppliers, to attract skilled and talented employees, and to create centers of expertise for the entire company.

The difference between the two approaches lies in the way managers have answered a seemingly simple but fundamental question: How can a factory located outside a company's home country be used as a competitive weapon not only in the markets that it serves directly but also in every market the company serves? The author has found that if managers consider manufacturing as a major source of competitive advantage, they generally expect their foreign factories to be highly productive and innovative, to achieve low costs, and to provide exemplary service throughout the world.

The author provides a framework to help managers classify the current roles their foreign factories play. The next step would be to determine the ideal future role for each factory. In order to increase manufacturing's strategic contribution, a company generally must upgrade the role of its foreign factories. And always, a company's business strategy should determine the decision to change a factory's strategic role. Superior manufacturers share one quality: they are convinced that a foreign factory can be a potent strategic asset.

Building Effective R&D Capabilities Abroad

Walter Kuemmerle

In the past, companies kept most of their research and development activities in their home country because they thought it important to have R&D close to where strategic decisions were being made. But today many companies choose to establish R&D networks in foreign countries in order to tap the knowledge there or to commercialize products for those markets at a competitive speed.

Adopting a global approach entails new, complex managerial challenges. It means linking R&D strategy to a company's overall business strategy. The first step in adopting such an approach is to build a team to lead the initiative —a team whose members are sufficiently senior to be able to mobilize resources at short notice. Second, companies must determine whether an R&D site's primary objective is to augment the expertise that the home base has to offer or to exploit that knowledge for use in the foreign country. That determination affects the choice of location and staff. For example, to augment the home base laboratory, a company would want to be near a foreign university; to exploit the home base laboratory, it would need to be near large markets and manufacturing facilities.

The best individual for managing both types of site combines the qualities of good scientist and good manager, knows how to integrate the new site with existing sites, understands technology trends, and is good at gaining access to foreign scientific communities.

As more pockets of knowledge emerge around the globe and competition in foreign markets mounts, only those companies that embrace an informed approach to global R&D will be able to meet the new challenges.

The Right Way to Manage Expats

J. Stewart Black and Hal B. Gregersen

In the global economy, having a workforce that is fluent in the ways of the world is a competitive necessity. That's why more and more companies are sending more and more professionals abroad. But international assignments don't come cheap: on average, expatriates cost a company two to three times what they would cost in equivalent positions back home.

Most companies, however, get anemic returns on their expat investments. The authors discovered that an alarming number of assignments fail in one way or another—some expats return home early, others finish but don't perform as well as expected, and many leave their companies within a year of repatriation. To find out why, the authors recently focused on the small number of companies that manage their expats successfully. They found that all those companies follow three general practices:

- When they send people abroad, the goal is not just to put out fires. Once expats have doused the flames, they are expected to generate new knowledge for the organization or to acquire skills that will help them become leaders.
- They assign overseas posts to people whose technical skills are matched or exceeded by their cross-cultural skills.
- They recognize that repatriation is a time of upheaval for most expats, and they use a variety of programs to help their people readjust.

Companies that follow these practices share a conviction that sustained growth rests on the shoulders of individuals with international experience. As a result, they are poised to capture tomorrow's global market opportunities by making their investments in international assignments successful today.

Clusters and the New Economics of Competition

Michael E. Porter

Economic geography in an era of global competition poses a paradox. In theory, location should no longer be a source of competitive advantage. Open global markets, rapid transportation, and high-speed communications should allow any company to source any thing from any place at any time. But in practice, Michael Porter demonstrates, location remains central to competition.

Today's economic map of the world is characterized by what Porter calls *clusters*: critical masses in one place of linked industries and institutions—from suppliers to universities to government agencies—that enjoy unusual competitive success in a particular field. The most famous examples are found in Silicon Valley and Hollywood, but clusters dot the world's landscape.

Porter explains how clusters affect competition in three broad ways: first, by increasing the productivity of companies based in the area; second, by driving the direction and pace of innovation; and third, by stimulating the formation of new businesses within the cluster. Geographic, cultural, and institutional proximity provides companies with special access, closer relationships, better information, powerful incentives, and other advantages that are difficult to tap from a distance. The more complex, knowledge-based, and dynamic the world economy becomes, the more this is true. Competitive advantage lies increasingly in local things—knowledge, relationships, and motivation—that distant rivals cannot replicate.

Porter challenges the conventional wisdom about how companies should be configured, how institutions such as universities can contribute to competitive success, and how governments can promote economic development and prosperity.

Thriving Locally in the Global Economy

Rosabeth Moss Kanter

In the future, success will come to those companies that can meet global standards and tap into global networks. More and more small and midsize companies are joining corporate giants in striving to exploit international growth markets. At the same time, civic leaders worry about their communities' economic future in light of the impact of global forces on the operation of business. How can communities retain local vitality yet still link the businesses located within them to the global economy?

To avoid a clash between global economic interests and local political interests, globalizing businesses must learn how to be responsive to the communities in which they operate. And communities must determine how to create a civic culture that will attract and retain footloose companies.

Rosabeth Moss Kanter surveyed five U.S. regions that connect with the global economy to determine their business and civic leaders' strategies for improving their constituents' quality of life. She has identified ways in which the global economy can work locally by capitalizing on the resources that distinguish one place from another.

Kanter argues that regions can invest in capabilities that connect their local populations to the global economy in one of three ways: as *thinkers, makers,* or *traders.* She points to the area surrounding Spartanburg and Greenville, South Carolina, as a good example of a world-class maker, with its exceptional blue-collar workforce that has attracted more than 200 companies from 18 countries. The history of the economic development of this region is a lesson for those seeking to understand how to achieve world-class status and bring local residents into the world economy.

Fast, Global, and Entrepreneurial: Supply Chain Management, Hong Kong Style
An Interview with Victor Fung

Joan Magretta

Li & Fung, Hong Kong's largest export trading company, has been an innovator in supply chain management—a topic of increasing importance to many senior executives. In this interview, chairman Victor Fung explains both the philosophy behind supply chain management and the specific practices that Li & Fung has developed to reduce costs and lead times, allowing its customers to buy "closer to the market."

Li & Fung has been a pioneer in "dispersed manufacturing." It performs the higher-value-added tasks such as design and quality control in Hong Kong, and outsources the lower-value-added tasks to the best possible locations around the world. The result is something new: a truly global product. To produce a garment, for example, the company might purchase yarn from Korea that will be woven and dyed in Taiwan, then shipped to Thailand for final assembly, where it will be matched with zippers from a Japanese company. For every order, the goal is to customize the value chain to meet the customer's specific needs.

To be run effectively, Victor Fung maintains, trading companies have to be small and entrepreneurial. He describes the organizational approaches that keep the company that way despite its growing size and geographic scope: its organization around small, customer-focused units; its incentives and compensation structure; and its use of venture capitals as a vehicle for business development.

As Asia's economic crisis continues, chairman Fung sees a new model of companies emerging—companies that are, like Li & Fung, narrowly focused and professionally managed.

Growth Through Global Sustainability: An Interview with Monsanto's CEO, Robert B. Shapiro

Joan Magretta

Robert Shapiro asks a tough question: How do we face the prospect that creating a profitable, growing company might require intolerable abuse of the natural world? Monsanto—with its history in the chemicals industry—is an unlikely candidate to be creating cutting-edge environmental solutions, but that is precisely what it is doing. The need for sustainability is transforming the company's thinking about growth.

Changes in global environmental conditions will soon create an unprecedented economic discontinuity. To invent new businesses around the concept of environmental sustainability, Shapiro begins with a simple law of physics: A closed system like the earth's cannot support an unlimited increase of material things. It can, however, withstand exponential growth in information. So Monsanto is exploring ways to substitute information for "stuff" and services for products.

In its agricultural business, the company is genetically coding plants to repel or destroy harmful insects. Putting the right information in the plant makes pesticides unnecessary. Information replaces stuff; productivity increases and waste is reduced. Monsanto also is looking at its carpet business. Today it costs too much to reuse carpets. But Monsanto realized that if the manufacturer owned the carpet and merely leased it to customers, it might be feasible to put in more cost up front and make the carpet more recyclable. Monsanto is reexamining the total life cycle of all its products and asking, What do people really need to buy? Do they need stuff or do they need a service? And what would be the economics of providing that service?

Unleashing the Power of Learning: An Interview with British Petroleum's John Browne

Steven E. Prokesch

John Browne believes that all companies battling it out in the global information age face a common challenge: using knowledge more effectively than their competitors do. And he is not talking only about the knowledge that resides in one's own company. "Any organization that thinks it does everything the best and that it need not learn from others is incredibly arrogant and foolish," he says.

British Petroleum's chief executive, who engineered the revival of BP Exploration and Production and poised BP for spectacular growth, never accepts that something can't be done and is always asking if there is a better way and if someone might have a better idea. Under his leadership, BP is doing the same. And no matter where knowledge comes from, Browne says, the key to reaping a big return is to leverage that knowledge by replicating it throughout the organization so that each unit is not learning in isolation.

To create an environment conducive to such learning, BP's leaders have taken a number of steps. They have built an extremely flat, decentralized organization: there is nobody between the general managers of the business units and the company's top management. They have installed processes to institutionalize breakthrough thinking and tie people's jobs to creating value. Finally, they have exploited advances in information technology and designed learning networks in order to encourage people to share knowledge.

About the Contributors

M. Bensaou is Associate Professor of Technology Management and Asian Business at INSEAD, and has also taught at the Harvard Business School. His research and teaching focuses on new forms of organizations, strategic alliances, joint ventures, and value-adding partnerships, as well as on the impact of information technology on markets and organizations. Professor Bensaou won the 1992 Best Doctoral Dissertation award at the International Conference on Information Systems and was a finalist for the 1993 Free Press Award. His work has been published in *Management Science* and *Information Systems Research*, and is soon to appear in *Organization Science, Strategic Management Journal, Harvard Business Review,* and *Sloan Management Review.* Professor Bensaou has been consulting for Asian, European, and U.S. corporations since 1993.

J. Stewart Black, Ph.D., is a Professor of Business Administration at the University of Michigan and the Executive Director of their Asia Pacific Human Resource Partnership. He is also the Managing Director of the Center for Global Assignments. Dr. Black has published widely on the subjects of globalization and leadership and is a frequent speaker at conferences. His most recent book, *Global Explorers,* examines the characteristics of successful global leaders and how best to develop these new capabilities.

Nicholas G. Carr is a Senior Editor at the *Harvard Business Review.* Before joining the *Review,* he was a Partner at Mercer Management Consulting, where he edited the *Mercer Management Journal.*

Niraj Dawar is Associate Professor of Marketing and the Walter A. Thompson Faculty Fellow at the Richard Ivey School of Business, University of Western Ontario. Formerly, he was Associate Professor of Marketing at INSEAD. His current research is in the area of international marketing and brand strategy. He has published numerous articles in leading journals such as the *Journal of Marketing Research,* the *Journal of Marketing,* and the *Harvard Business Review.* Professor Dawar is an active contributor to international conferences on marketing and management issues and is a consultant to multinational and local firms around the world.

Michael Earl is Professor of Information Management and Director of the Center for Information Management at London Business School, where he has also served as Deputy Dean and Acting Dean. Professor Earl's research interests involve information systems and business strategy, focusing on the formulation of IT strategies. More recently he has studied cross-cultural practices in the management of IT, the roles of the CIO and the CKO, and strategy-making in the Information Age. He has published articles in the *Harvard Business Review* and *Sloan Management Review* and has written several books, including *Management Strategies for Information Technology.* Professor Earl consults for a number of multinational companies and is a frequent speaker at conferences on both sides of the Atlantic.

Kasra Ferdows is the Heisley Family Professor of Global Manufacturing and Codirector of the Global Logistics Research Program at Georgetown University's McDonough School of Business, where he also served as acting dean from 1997 to 1998. He has taught at INSEAD, Harvard Business School, and Stanford Business School and was a principal investigator in the Global Manufacturing Futures research. His recent research focuses on the management of global factory networks.

Tony Frost is Assistant Professor of International Business and the D.G. Burgoyne Faculty Fellow at the Richard Ivey School of Business, University of Western Ontario. His research interests revolve around strategy and competition in a global context. Professor Frost's work has been published in both academic and practitioner outlets and has been presented at conferences on strategy and international business. He is the author of numerous cases on emerging markets used in classroom settings around the world.

Jeffrey E. Garten is Dean of the Yale School of Management. He was formerly Undersecretary of Commerce for International Trade in the first Clinton Administration and, before that, a Managing Director of the Blackstone Group, an investment banking firm. He writes a monthly column for *Business Week* on the global marketplace, and is the author of *A Cold Peace: America, Germany, Japan, and the Struggle for Supremacy* and *The Big Ten: The Big Emerging Markets and How They Will Change Our Lives.*

Benjamin Gomes-Casseres is a Professor at Brandeis University and previously spent ten years on the Harvard Business School faculty. As an authority on alliance strategy and management, he is a consultant to major companies and a frequent speaker at industry conferences. He is currently researching competition among multifirm constellations in Internet businesses. Professor Gomes-Casseres is the author of *The Alliance Revolution: The New Shape of Business Rivalry,* and his writings have appeared in *Sloan Management Review* and *Strategy & Business.*

Hal B. Gregersen, Ph.D., is Professor of International Strategy and Leadership at the Marriott School at Brigham Young University. He has also taught at Dartmouth College and Thunderbird, and is currently a Senior Partner at the Center for Global Assignments. As an internationally recognized authority on global leadership and international assignments, Dr. Gregersen consults widely with multinational firms on a variety of globalization challenges and is a frequent keynote speaker. He has published over 70 books and articles.

Rosabeth Moss Kanter is the Class of 1960 Professor of Business Administration at the Harvard Business School. She is the author, coauthor, or editor of 13 books, the most recent of which are *Rosabeth Moss Kanter on the Frontiers of Management* and the coedited collection *Innovation Masters.* In addition to teaching, Professor Kanter conceived of and now leads the Business Leadership in the Social Sector (BLSS) project, which involves over a hundred national leaders in dialogue about public-private partnerships. Professor Kanter has received 19 honorary doctoral degrees and over a dozen leadership awards, and has appeared on lists of the "100 Most Important Women in America" and the "50 Most Powerful Women in the World."

Tarun Khanna is an Associate Professor at the Harvard Business School. His research focuses on understanding the scope of firms' activities, particularly the corporate strategy of diversified business groups in several emerging economies of South and East Asia and Latin America. He has written several articles on these subjects and on the structuring and management of licenses and joint ventures, and has served as a consultant to firms in several industries on related issues. He is the author of *Foundations of Neural Networks.*

Walter Kuemmerle is an Assistant Professor of Business Administration and the Class of 1961 Fellow at the Harvard Business School, with a joint appointment in the technology and operations management and the entrepreneurial management areas. His research and teaching interests fall within the domain of knowledge and capital management in a global economy, specifically in foreign direct investment, venture capital, and technology strategy of multinational corporations. Professor Kuemmerle's research has appeared in academic journals, the *Harvard Business Review,* and as chapters in several books.

Kenneth Lieberthal is the William Davidson Professor of Business Administration and is also Professor of Political Science at the University of Michigan, where he has been on the faculty since 1983. Professor Lieberthal has published about a dozen books and more than five dozen articles, mostly focused on Chinese politics and economic decision making. He is currently on leave from the University of Michigan while serving in Washington, D.C. as Special Assistant to the President and Senior Director for Asia on the National Security Council.

Joan Magretta is a consultant and writer based in Cambridge, MA. A former partner at the management consulting firm of Bain & Company, she is a Contributing Editor of the *Harvard Business Review,* and winner of the 1998 McKinsey Award for the best HBR article of the year. Her latest book, *Managing in the New Economy,* is a collection of *Harvard Business Review* articles.

Krishna Palepu is the Ross Graham Walker Professor of Business Administration at the Harvard Business School and a consultant to a wide variety of businesses. His research focuses on analyzing firms' business strategies and the process through which the effectiveness of these strategies is communicated to investors. He has published numerous research papers and teaching cases on these issues and is the coauthor of *Business Analysis and Valuation: Text and Cases,* which won the American Accounting Association's Wildman Award and the Notable Contribution to Research Award. Professor Palepu is also an associate editor of several leading research journals and is on the boards of Global Trust Bank and Vision Compas, Inc.

Michael E. Porter is the C. Roland Christensen Professor of Business Administration at the Harvard Business School and a leading authority on competitive strategy. He has served as a counselor on competitive strategy to many leading U.S. and international companies and speaks widely on issues of international competitiveness to business and government audiences throughout the world. Professor Porter is the author of 14 books including *Competitive Advantage: Creating and Sustaining Superior Performance,* which won the Academy of Management's 1985 George R. Terry Book Award, as well as *The Competitive Advantage of Nations.* Actively involved in economic policy initiatives, his most recent work focuses on the development of America's inner cities.

C.K. Prahalad is the Harvey C. Fruehauf Professor of Business Administration at the University of Michigan Business School. His research focuses on the role of and the value added to top management in large, diversified, multinational corporations, and he has consulted with numerous firms worldwide. Professor Prahalad is the coauthor, with Gary Hamel, of *Competing for the Future,* named by *Business Week* as one of the year's best management books in 1994. He is also the author of many award-winning articles such as "Strategic Intent," "The Core Competence of the Corporation," and "The End of Corporate Imperialism," which won McKinsey prizes in 1989, 1990, and 1998, respectively.

Steven E. Prokesch is Director of Idea and Editorial Development at The Boston Consulting Group. Prior to joining BCG in 1997, Mr. Prokesch was a Senior Editor for the *Harvard Business Review.* He previously worked for 17 years as an editor and reporter at the *New York Times, Business Week,* and United Press International. He received the John Hancock Award for Excellence in Business Journalism for *Business Week's* 1983 special report, "New Era for Management," a first-place Associated Press award for business writing, and two *New York Times* Publisher's Awards. He was also a finalist in the 1992 competition for the Gerald Loeb Award.

Peter J. Williamson is Professor of International Management at the Euro-Asia Centre of INSEAD in France and Singapore. He holds a Ph.D. in Business Economics from Harvard University and has taught strategy and international management at both London Business School and Harvard Business School. Over the past 15 years, Professor Williamson has consulted on business strategy and international expansion to numerous companies throughout the Asia-Pacific region. His publications include work on the management of joint ventures, the emergence of the "Metanational Corporation," "Strategy as Options on the Future," strategic innovation, and effective corporate strategy in Asia following the 1997 crisis.

Note: *Information provided within the article about the contributors to "Managing in the Euro Zone" was applicable at the time of original publication.*

Index